Second Edition / College Reading Skills

Selections from the Black

Provocative
Selections
by Black Writers

Books in this Series:
The Olive Book
The Brown Book
The Purple Book

Editor: Edward Spargo

Adviser & Consultant
for this Edition
Irving P. McPhail
Morgan State University

Jamestown Publishers
Providence, Rhode Island

Selections from the Black

COLLEGE READING SKILLS SERIES

Selections from the Black
   701 - The Olive Book, ISBN 0-89061-000-2
   702 - The Brown Book, ISBN 0-89061-001-0
   703 - The Purple Book, ISBN 0-89061-002-9

Voices from the Bottom
   721 - The Olive Book, ISBN 0-89061-003-7
   722 - The Brown Book, ISBN 0-89061-004-5
   723 - The Purple Book, ISBN 0-89061-005-3

Topics for the Restless
   741 - The Olive Book, ISBN 0-89061-006-1
   742 - The Brown Book, ISBN 0-89061-007-X
   743 - The Purple Book, ISBN 0-89061-008-8

Cover and Text Design by Stephen R. Anthony
Cover Photograph by Dell Padgett

Printed in the United States

Not everyone will agree that there is need for a reading improvement text which features only selections by Black writers. Such a text, some contend, presents an unbalanced view, tends to separate and polarize Blacks and whites even more. Yet, my motive in creating the text was to effect the opposite—to offset an imbalance which already exists.

Reading improvement must begin with interesting *and* relevant material—material from the real world. To four million Black students, nothing is *more* real than their daily struggle for humanity. Until now, texts for them have been *un*balanced and *un*real.

Many feel that this text is even more necessary for the white student; for if whites tend to think in terms of the "Negro problem," consider the Black man: he has a "white problem" and it is overwhelming.

These Selections from the Black, then, speak to everyone.

I am most grateful to the many who assisted me: Helen Doolan and Norma Coleman of the Providence Public Library; Mary M. Macdonald for paste-up and art; Paul Hodges, Anthony Kasegian, Edward McLaughlin, Gerard Richard, and John Salesses for their assistance in preparing the comprehension questions; James and Livia Giroux for their invaluable editorial services; and especially my wife for all kinds of support and assistance throughout the project.

In this second edition, about one-half of the selections are new. I am indebted to Irving P. McPhail of Morgan State College for his diligence in rating and evaluating the selections, based on the experiences and opinions of his students, and for his suggestions for deleting and replacing selections. Renewed gratitude must also be expressed to James and Livia Giroux for reviewing and improving the comprehension questions and vocabulary exercises accompanying the selections retained in this edition, and for writing comprehension questions and vocabulary exercises for the new selections.

E.S.

Contents

Selections from the Black

Part One
Introductory Selection
Selections 2-10

Introductory Selection

Explains How the Text Is Organized and How to Use It to Maximum Advantage

(Before you begin reading this selection, turn to page 13 and record the hours and minutes on the line labeled *Starting Time* in the box at the bottom of the second column. If you are using this text in class and your instructor has made provisions for timing, you need not stop now; read on.)

You are using this text for two purposes: (1) to improve your reading and study skills, (2) to read what the Black man is saying now and what he has said in the past.

Our nation now realizes that the Black has a voice—and in the twenty-nine selections which follow, you will hear that voice, speaking in many ways of many things. You will read the words of slaves describing their days of oppression and struggles for survival. You will read the words of yesterday's leaders—DuBois, Washington, Garvey—to understand the background and history of today's racial situation. You will see how their thinking influenced not only the happenings of their generation, but also the happenings of yours. You will read the words of those from the near past, describing the racial climate of the 1940s and 1950s. These will help you see the situation of the Black man in its perspective.

Voices from other nations will be heard, too, especially those from Africa, speaking of the native of yesterday—our Afro-American—and the revitalized African of today.

Many master writers of fiction, too numerous to list, are included among the authors of these selections, recreating articulately and passionately the Black man's world.

Writings of those from other fields—sports, politics, journalism, business, entertainment—are included here because these Black men and women have voices, too, apart from those with which they normally speak.

Finally, this text contains the current voices of protest—both moderate and defiant—including those silenced by death and exile. Writers of both extremes, and those of the middle ground, are presented here because their words have structured and defined America's racial and social atmosphere.

The editor of this text is aware that many readers will become impatient and upset over pleas for reconciliation and cooperation with the Establishment, just as many other readers will be repelled by bitter words of violence and unrest. It cannot be helped—this is the reality *and* the dilemma.

The other purpose for using this text, that of reading and study improvement, recognizes reality, too: the reality of today. This text will help you to develop skills and techniques necessary for efficiency in our society.

Today's reader must be flexible, must choose from a repertory of skills those suitable for the reading task at hand. The skilled reader has learned that there is no one best way to read everything, that each kind of reading matter demands a corresponding kind of reading technique. As you complete the selections and exercises in this book, you will find yourself growing in technique.

USING THE TEXT

The thirty selections are designed to be read in numerical order, starting with the Introductory Selection and ending with Selection 30. Because the selections increase in difficulty as you progress through the book, the earlier ones prepare you to handle successfully the upcoming ones.

Here are the procedures to follow when reading each selection.

1. **Preview before Reading.** Previewing acquaints you with the overall content and structure of the selection before you actually read. It is like consulting a road map before taking a trip: planning the route gives you more confidence as you proceed and, perhaps, helps you avoid any unnecessary delays. Previewing should take about a minute or two and is done in this way:

a) Read the Title. Learn the writer's subject and, possibly, his point of view on it.

b) Read the Opening and Closing Paragraphs. These contain the introductory and concluding remarks. Important information is frequently presented in these key paragraphs.

c) Skim Through. Try to discover the author's approach to his subject. Does he use many examples? Is his purpose to sell you his ideas? What else can you learn now to help you when you read?

2. **Read the Selection.** Do not try to race through. Read well and carefully enough so that you can answer the comprehension questions which follow.

Keep track of your reading time by noting when you start and finish. A table on page 173 converts your reading time to a words-per-minute rate. Select the time from the table which is closest to your reading time. Record these figures in the box at the end of the selection. There is no one ideal reading speed for everything. The efficient reader varies his speed as the selection requires.

Many selections include a brief biography and perhaps a photograph of the author. Do not include this reading in your time. It is there to introduce you to the writer. Many of the selections have been reprinted from full-length books and novels. Complete information is contained in a bibliography (list of books) on page 170. If you find a particular selection interesting, you may enjoy reading the entire book.

3. **Answer Vocabulary and Comprehension Questions.** Immediately following each selection is a vocabulary exercise for you to complete. The vocabulary exercises are designed to help you improve your ability to use context (the surrounding words) as an aid to understanding words. The efficient use of context is a valuable vocabulary tool.

Each exercise contains five words from the selection, reprinted in context to help you recall how the words were used. Also given is the location of each word in the selection so that, if necessary, you can find it again and read the adjoining sentences to understand it better. The exercise asks you to select the best of the four meanings accompanying each word.

As you complete the exercises, keep in mind that the precise meaning of a word depends largely on how it is used. Because dictionaries normally list several meanings for a single word, two or three of the choices in a vocabulary exercise may be "dictionary correct," but only one is the *best* meaning for the word as used in this context.

After you complete the vocabulary exercise, turn the page to find the comprehension questions. These have been included to test your understanding of what you have read. The questions are diagnostic, too. Because the comprehension skill being measured is identified, you can detect your areas of weakness.

Read each question carefully and, without looking back, select one of the four choices given which answers that question most accurately or most completely. Frequently all four choices, or options, given for a question are *correct*, but one is the *best* answer. For this reason the comprehension questions are highly challenging and require you to be highly discriminating. You may, from time to time, disagree with the choice given in the Answer Key. When this happens, you have an opportunity to sharpen your powers of discrimination. Study the question again and seek to discover why the listed answer may be best. When you disagree with the text, you are thinking; when you objectively analyze and recognize your errors, you are learning.

The Answer Key begins on page 165. Find the answers for your selection and correct your comprehension and vocabulary work. When you discover a wrong answer, circle it and check the correct one.

The box following each selection contains space for your comprehension and vocabulary scores. Each correct vocabulary item is worth twenty points and each correct comprehension answer is credited with ten points.

Pages 174 and 175 contain graphs to be used for plotting your scores and tallying your incorrect responses. On page 174 record your comprehension score at the appropriate intersection of lines, using an *X*. Use a circle, or some other mark, on the same graph to record your vocabulary results. Some students prefer to use different color inks, or pencil and ink, to distinguish between comprehension and vocabulary plottings.

On page 175 fill in the squares to indicate the comprehension questions you have failed. By referring to the Skills Profile as you progress through the text, you and your instructor will be able to tell which kinds of questions give you the most trouble. As soon as you detect a specific weakness in comprehension, consult with your instructor to see what supplementary materials he can provide or suggest.

A profitable habit for you to acquire is the practice of analyzing the questions you have answered incorrectly. If time permits, return to the selection to find and underline the passages containing the correct answers. This helps you to see what you missed the first time. Some interpretive and generalization type questions are not answered specifically in the text. In these cases bracket that part of the selection which alludes to the correct answer. Your instructor may recommend that you complete this step outside of class as homework.

4. **Complete the Accompanying Exercises.** The page preceding the comprehension questions contains exercises designed to improve your word analysis and word meaning skills. The important

areas of phonics, spelling and syllabication, dictionary skills, contextual aids, prefixes, suffixes and roots, and expectancy clues are all covered.

Each exercise contains the directions you need and many of them provide sample items to help you get started. The same answer key you have been using gives the correct responses for these exercises.

If class time is at a premium, your instructor may prefer that you complete these exercises outside of class.

The following selections in this text are structured just like this introductory one. Having completed this selection and its exercises, you will then be prepared to proceed to Selection 2.

Starting Time: _____	Finishing Time: _____
Reading Time: _____	Reading Rate: _____
Comprehension: _____	Vocabulary: _____

VOCABULARY: The following words have been taken from the selection you have just read. Put an *X* in the box before the best meaning or synonym for the word as used in the selection.

1. **articulately**, page 11, column 1, paragraph 5
   "...recreating articulately and passionately the Black man's world."
   ☐ a. clearly
   ☐ b. painfully
   ☐ c. expressively
   ☐ d. argumentatively

2. **dilemma**, page 11, column 2, paragraph 1
   "...this is the reality *and* the dilemma."
   ☐ a. assumption
   ☐ b. alternative
   ☐ c. predicament
   ☐ d. solution

3. **repertory**, page 11, column 2, paragraph 3
   "...must chose from a repertory of skills..."
   ☐ a. stock
   ☐ b. reputation
   ☐ c. theater
   ☐ d. cast

4. **corresponding**, page 11, column 2, paragraph 3
   "...demands a corresponding kind of reading technique."
   ☐ a. written
   ☐ b. matching
   ☐ c. different
   ☐ d. reporting

5. **efficient**, page 12, column 1, paragraph 5
   "The efficient use of context is a valuable vocabulary tool."
   ☐ a. economical
   ☐ b. active
   ☐ c. knowledgeable
   ☐ d. effective

EXPECTANCY CLUES

The most important aids to word recognition and, therefore, fluency in reading are meaning clues. Good readers use such clues effectively and automatically. Meaning clues permit the reader to anticipate words before actually reading them.

Expectancy clues are one type of meaning clue. These refer to the sorts of words and concepts one might expect to encounter in a given subject. For example, in a story about big city life the reader should expect to meet words like *subway, traffic congestion, urban renewal, ghetto, high-rise apartments,* and so on. Anticipating or expecting these words enables the reader to move along the printed lines rapidly with understanding.

Here are two exercises to help you develop your skill in using expectancy clues.

The following words, except two, all appeared in a story about school. Think first about the kinds of words you would find in such a story and then examine the words below. Underline the two words you would *not* expect to find in this story.

1. bell	6. book	11. ruler
2. teacher	7. principal	12. blackboard
3. pupil	8. cafeteria	13. dismissal
4. shovel	9. counselor	14. examination
5. desk	10. tree	15. detention

Which of the following phrases would you expect to read in a newspaper story about a fire? Put an *X* in the box before them.

☐ 1. leap onto the truck quickly

☐ 2. overcome by smoke

☐ 3. plant the tree

☐ 4. spread open the net

☐ 5. of suspicious origin

☐ 6. in an upstairs window

☐ 7. change to a different channel

☐ 8. huge crowd gathered

☐ 9. filled with blue ink

☐ 10. sirens blaring in the night

☐ 11. homeless and without shelter

☐ 12. climb up the ladder

☐ 13. man the hoses

☐ 14. splashing in the pool

☐ 15. responding to a false alarm

☐ 16. work of an arsonist

☐ 17. carried to safety

☐ 18. a piece of pie with coffee

☐ 19. spreading to a nearby house

☐ 20. hook and ladder truck

VISION AND READING

Reading is the process of obtaining information from the printed page. It is a skill, and like any skill it can be acquired, developed through practice, and refined. The purpose of this book is to help you develop your reading skill.

Perhaps it would be more accurate to speak of skills, rather than skill, because reading is not just one activity — it is several activities performed in unison for a specific objective, comprehension.

The activities of reading involve two levels, physical and mental.

The first physical step in reading is seeing the words. This involves vision or eyesight. It goes without saying that faulty vision (not corrected by glasses) can interfere with one's reading. It's possible to compensate for visual deficiencies but at the cost of efficiency and ease. For the reader who is unaware of vision problems, there are certain symptoms which indicate that an eye examination is in order:

1. Holding the book too close to the eyes may be a symptom. A distance of fourteen inches is considered normal.

2. Tearing, itching, or redness of the eyes while reading are indications of possible eye strain.

3. Blinking or squinting are reactions of the eyes in an uncomfortable reading situation. Check the lighting; sit so that illumination comes over the shoulder rather than from the front.

4. Excessive fatigue may be symptomatic. You should not become tired after brief periods of reading. A student should be able to read for two or three hours before becoming tired. Poor posture frequently causes early fatigue, so check your posture—be comfortable, not cramped or bent.

5. Headaches during or following reading are a common and reliable symptom of eye disability.

COMPREHENSION: For each of the following statements and questions, select the option containing the most complete or most accurate answer.

1. Reading skills
(f)
   - ☐ a. improve with age and maturity.
   - ☐ b. can be improved through instruction and practice.
   - ☐ c. require a detailed understanding of phonics.
   - ☐ d. are dependent on native intelligence and opportunity.

2. The introductory selection
(g)
   - ☐ a. eliminates the need for oral instruction.
   - ☐ b. explains in detail the proper use of the text.
   - ☐ c. permits the student to learn by doing.
   - ☐ d. allows for variety and interest.

3. *Selections from the Black* is based on which
(e) of the following premises?
   - ☐ a. A text of all-Black writings is needed.
   - ☐ b. Black students learn best from Black writers.
   - ☐ c. The writings of Black authors should provoke student interest.
   - ☐ d. Traditional reading improvement texts are racist.

4. The introductory selection suggests that
(h)
   - ☐ a. most readers are not flexible.
   - ☐ b. students will discover their own best way to read.
   - ☐ c. students today read better than students of the past.
   - ☐ d. thirty selections is an ideal number for a reading improvement text.

5. The author considers previewing
(g)
   - ☐ a. essential for efficient reading.
   - ☐ b. more useful for nonfiction than fiction.
   - ☐ c. a student rather than an adult reading technique.
   - ☐ d. important and useful.

6. The editor explains that he expects some of
(c) the given answers will
   - ☐ a. appease racists.
   - ☐ b. provoke discussion.
   - ☐ c. offend whites.
   - ☐ d. challenge history.

7. The selection stresses the modern reader's
(b) need for
   - ☐ a. a repertory of skills.
   - ☐ b. rapid reading skills.
   - ☐ c. an extensive reading background.
   - ☐ d. comprehension skills.

8. How does he writer feel about reading speed
(f) (rate)?
   - ☐ a. It is a minimal aspect of the total reading situation.
   - ☐ b. It ranks second (following comprehension) in the priority of skills.
   - ☐ c. It is interrelated with comprehension.
   - ☐ d. It should be developed at an early age.

9. How much time should be devoted to pre-
(b) viewing a selection?
   - ☐ a. Time will vary with each selection.
   - ☐ b. About one minute.
   - ☐ c. No specified time is suggested.
   - ☐ d. None; the instructor times the selection.

10. The way the vocabulary exercises are con-
(c) structed suggests that
   - ☐ a. the meaning of a word depends on how it is used.
   - ☐ b. the final authority for word meaning is the dictionary.
   - ☐ c. words have precise and permanent meanings.
   - ☐ d. certain words will be difficult to understand.

Comprehension Skills: a—isolating details; b—recalling specific facts; c—retaining concepts; d—organizing facts; e—understanding the main idea; f—drawing a conclusion; g—making a judgment; h—making an inference; i—recognizing tone; j—understanding characters; k—appreciation of literary forms.

How to Win at Basketball: Cheat

"Maybe we weren't cool. But we were protected from that hot-water pipe."

Bill Cosby

When I played basketball in the slums of Philadelphia—outdoors on concrete courts—there was never a referee. You had to call your own fouls. So the biggest argument was always about whether you called the foul *before* the shot went in, or whether you had waited to see if the ball went in. See, if you yelled "foul," you didn't get the basket. You just got the ball out-of-bounds.

Sometimes you called a *light* foul. Like you have a guy driving in on you and you punch him in the eye a little. That's a light foul in the playgrounds.

Another light foul is submarining a guy who's driving in on you. He comes down on the concrete, and you visit him every two weeks in the hospital. Of course, there is always a pole sitting in the middle of the court. Something has to hold up the basket. So you let a guy drive in, and you just kind of screen him a little bit, right into the pole. This is where you visit him three times a week in the hospital.

There's always a big argument, too, about whether you stepped out-of-bounds or not. That's a four-hour argument. So usually you take one shot — 20-minute argument. Another shot — 20-minute argument. Out-of-bounds — four-hour argument. So this one game—the winner is the first team to score 20 points—can go maybe two weeks. The most important thing is to remember the score from day to day. Sometimes you argue four hours about *that.*

To play on any team outdoors, you have to have a pair of old jeans that you cut off and shred a little bit above the knees so they look like beachcomber pants. You get an old sweat shirt of some university—mine was Temple—and you go outside to the playground, and play basketball all day, until dark, and your mother has to come get you.

Let me say something about mothers. When I was a kid, mothers were never really interested in sports. Even if you became a fantastic star, your mother was probably the last person to know. She was more concerned with you being on time for dinner.

My mother was a fantastic color changer. Whatever color my uniform was, my mother would always put it into the washing machine with different-colored stuff—the red bedspread, the green curtains, the yellow tablecloth, or the purple bathroom rug. And when the uniform came out, instead of being white it would be avocado.

I've worn a pink uniform, and I've worn a running yellow-and-blue uniform—which of course startled my teammates quite a bit. One time, I had to learn how to use karate in order to answer for a pale-lavender uniform.

Later, I graduated from playground basketball to indoor basketball. I played for a place called the Wissahickon Boys' Club along with a very famous defensive back by the name of Herb Adderley.

Well, very few teams could whip the Wissahickon Boys' Club on our own court, mainly because our court was different. First of all, the floor hadn't been varnished and the out-of-bounds lines hadn't been painted since the day the gym was built, about two weeks after Dr. Naismith invented basketball. We didn't have to see them. We could feel where they were. Our sneakers had soles as thick as a piece of paper. But it was hell on the other team.

So was the ball. We used a leather ball that had been played with outside—in the dark of night, in the rain, in the snow. It was about as heavy as a medicine ball, and just as lively. There were stones and pieces of glass stuck into it, and it never had enough air, because the valve leaked. You could wear yourself out just trying to dribble it.

Now about the basket. The rim was loose, and hanging, and shaking. And all you had to do was kind of lay that heavy ball up softly. The rim acted like a trampoline. It lifted the ball up and threw it through the center of the hoop and you always had two points.

Another thing about playing at the Wissahickon Boys' Club. We would get ol' Weird Harold, who was six feet nine and weighed about 90 pounds, to mark black X's all over the backboard. Now, only our team knew what each X stood for. See, we aimed maybe two inches under a mark, and, zap, two points. If you followed our mark, you'd miss the rim. We always had something going for ourselves.

16

The ceiling in the gym was only fifteen feet high. For those who may not know that much about basketball, that means our ceiling was only five feet above the rim of the basket itself. When other teams came to play us, they weren't aware right away that the ceiling was low. So when they shot the ball, they hit the ceiling—which was out-of-bounds. And we would get the ball. Meanwhile, we had practiced shooting our jump shots and set shots on a direct line drive. No arch, no nothing—just straight ahead into the basket. Sort of Woody Sauldsberry style.

We also had a hot-water pipe that ran around the wall, and the wall of the gym was out-of-bounds. So whenever a guy on the other team would go up for a rebound or a jump shot, or drive into the basket, we would kind of screen him into the hot-water pipe.

At the Wissahickon Boys' Club, we had graduated to the point where we had referees for the games. We had them because they were honest and fair and impartial. Which is what they teach at boys' clubs. Also because we were playing teams from other neighborhoods and had to finish the games in one day. The referees cut down on the long arguments.

We had two steady refs whom we named Mr. Magoo and The Bat. You might say they did not have Superman vision. They more or less had to make their calls on what they could hear. Like if they heard a slap, and thought they saw the ball fly out of a guy's hands, they cried "foul" for hacking. So whenever a guy would go up for a rebound or something, all we had to do was just give him a little nudge, and boom! He'd wind up against the wall and probably that hot-water pipe. His screams would tell The Bat and Mr. Magoo he was out-of-bounds.

When new teams came down to play us and saw our uniforms, which consisted of heavy old long-sleeved flannel pajama tops over below-the-knee corduroy knickers, they'd call us "turkeys" and all kinds of chicken names. Maybe we weren't cool. But we were protected from that hot-water pipe.

One time, Cryin' Charlie's mother had his PJ tops in the washing machine at game time, and we had to make him non-playing coach that day so he wouldn't cry.

In the middle of the court, we had five boards that happened to be about the loosest boards that you ever stepped on in your life. So that while dribbling downcourt on a fast break, if you hit one of those five boards, the ball would not come back to you. Many times, a guy on the other team would dribble downcourt on the fast break, and all of a sudden he'd be running, and his arm would be pumping, but there was no ball coming back up to

him. All we had to do was just stand around at the loose boards, and without even stickin' the guy, let him go ahead and do his Lamont Cranston dribble, and we could pick up the ball, dead and waiting, right there. Whenever *we* went on a fast break, we dribbled *around* those loose boards.

One team I remember we lost to was the Nicetown Club for Boys & Girls. We played in their gym. They had a balcony that extended out over one side of the court about ten feet. It was almost exactly the same height as the rim of the basket. So if you went up for a jumper, the balcony would block your shot. The defense of the Nicetown Club was to force the flow of your offense to the side of the court with the balcony. When we tried to shoot from there, the Bill Russell balcony would block the shot, and the ball would bounce back and hit our man in the eye. Whenever *they* came downcourt, they would play on the free side of the floor away from the balcony.

I would say, on a home-and-home basis, the Wissahickon Boys' Club and the Nicetown Club were even.

In high school, I had one of the greatest jump shots—from two feet out—anybody ever saw. The only man who stopped me was Wilt Chamberlain.

We played Wilt's high school, Overbrook, and they had a guy on the team by the name of Ira Davis, who was a great track man. He ran the 100 in like nine-point-something, and a few years later was in the Olympic Games. Ira was great on the fast break. So Chamberlain would stand under our basket and growl at us. And when he growled, guys would just throw the ball at him—to try and hit him with it. And he would catch it and throw it downcourt to Ira Davis, who would score 200 points on the fast break. We lost to them something like 800 to 14.

My best shot was where I would dribble in quickly, stop, fake the man playing me into the air, and then go up for my two-foot jump shot. Well, I was very surprised when I found Mr. Chamberlain waiting under the basket for me; I faked, and faked and faked and faked and faked, and then I threw the ball at him and tried to hit him. But he caught it and threw it downcourt to Ira Davis: 802 to 14.

So then we tried to razzle-dazzle him. But for some reason, he could always follow the ball with that one eye of his in the middle of his forehead. And of course, the only thing we could do was just throw the ball at him.

We had one play we used on Wilt that had some success. We had one kid that was completely crazy.

He wasn't afraid of anything in the world. Not even the Big Dipper. He was about as big as Mickey Rooney, and we had him run out on the court and punch Chamberlain right in the kneecap. And when Chamberlain bent over to grab our guy, we shot our jumpers. That foul alone was worth our 14 points.

Now that I'm a celebrity making a million dollars a year, we have Celebrity Basketball. I play with guys like James Garner, Jim Brown, Don Adams, Sidney Poitier, Mike Connors, Mickey Rooney, and Jack Lemmon.

In Celebrity Basketball, you pull up to the fabulous Forum in your Rolls-Royce, and your chauffeur puts you in a beach chair and wheels you out on the court. And after each shot, you have a catered affair.

And the ball. The pros wish they could find a ball this great. It's gold covered and has a little transistor motor inside, with radar and a homing device, and it dribbles and shoots itself.

A sixty-piece orchestra plays background music while you're down on the court, and starlet cheerleaders are jumping up and down. After every basket, we all stop and give the guy who scored it a standing ovation.

Another thing about when I used to play basketball in the playgrounds. If you went to a strange playground, you didn't introduce yourself. You had to prove yourself first. No names.

"Over here, my man."

"Yeah, nice play, my man."

Later on, if you earned it, you'd be given a name: Gunner, My Man, or Herman or Shorty or something.

Now, when we play the Celebrity games, they come out on the court and they say, "Hi, my name is such and such. I'm from so forth and so on," and the whole thing. And I say, "Oh, very nice to meet you."

But later, during the game, I forget the cat's name anyway and I just go right back to "Over here, my man. I'm free in the corner, my man." And I'm back in the old neighborhood.

Starting Time: _____	Finishing Time: _____
Reading Time: _____	Reading Rate: _____
Comprehension: _____	Vocabulary: _____

VOCABULARY: The following words have been taken from the selection you have just read. Put an X in the box before the best meaning or synonym for the word as used in the selection.

1. **impartial**, page 17, column 1, paragraph 3
"...they were honest and fair and impartial."
☐ a. biased
☐ b. particular
☐ c. just
☐ d. unequal

2. **celebrity**, page 18, column 1, paragraph 2
"Now that I'm a celebrity..."
☐ a. star player
☐ b. famous person
☐ c. party goer
☐ d. distinguished athlete

3. **ovation**, page 18, column 1, last paragraph
"...and give the guy who scored it a standing ovation."
☐ a. reception
☐ b. celebration
☐ c. applause
☐ d. victory

4. **strange**, page 18, column 2, paragraph 1
"If you went to a strange playground,"
☐ a. unusual
☐ b. distant
☐ c. abnormal
☐ d. unfamiliar

5. **earned**, page 18, column 2, paragraph 4
"Later on, if you earned it,"
☐ a. gained
☐ b. procured
☐ c. acquired
☐ d. merited

SELECTIONS FROM THE BLACK

SYLLABICATION

Syllabication (frequently written *syllabification*) refers to the process of dividing a word into its parts or syllables.

A syllable is a word or part of a word spoken with just one sound. A word produced with one sound is a one-syllable word; a word produced with two sounds is a two-syllable word, and so on.

Knowing how to reduce words to their syllables aids both reading and spelling. Frequently a long word can be recognized and understood if pronounced by syllables. And in spelling, of course, knowledge of syllables contributes to accuracy.

There are rules or generalizations which we can follow when dividing words.

When one consonant comes between two vowels in a word, the word is divided before the consonant. In the word **climate**, the consonant **m** comes between the vowels **i** and **a**; therefore, we divide the word into **cli** and **mate**, before the **m**.

In the following sentences divide the words in bold print according to this rule. Write the word on the line following the sentence, inserting hyphens (-) between the syllables. The first one has been done for you.

1. The organization launched a **crusade** for equal representation.

    _____*cru-sade*_____

2. The recipe calls for **equal** parts of vanilla and lemon flavorings.

    _____

3. The **flavor** comes from those delicious ingredients.

    _____

4. His group considered him a **hero** for his defiant stand.

    _____

5. Always read the **label** before taking any medicine.

    _____

6. Unemployment is a **local** and chronic problem.

    _____

7. The **lunar** module landed safely on the surface of the moon.

    _____

8. A **major** problem concerns disposal of industrial wastes.

    _____

9. Check the **meter** at least twice during the season.

    _____

10. **Notice** the fine coloring and soft texture.

    _____

11. **Return** all books to the library.

    _____

MECHANICS OF READING

There are three activities which the eyes must perform in the act of reading.

1. **Fixations.** The fixations are the stops which the eyes make along the printed line. It is necessary for your eyes to stop, or fixate, because these are the only periods of clear vision. The eyes cannot see clearly enough when moving; they must stop to read, and then move on to the next point of fixation. Good readers are able to see several words during each fixation, making their reading rapid and efficient. Poor readers, on the other hand, fixate at each word—they are word-by-word readers.

2. **Regressions.** All readers make regressions. These are backward movements of the eyes on a line of print, taking another look at something already read. Frequent regressions indicate faulty comprehension—something is blocking or interfering with the reader's understanding and he wants another look. As you would suspect, good readers make fewer regressions, whereas the eye movements of poor readers are characterized by many regressions.

3. **Return Sweep.** At the end of each line your eyes must sweep back to the beginning of the next line. In small or fine print, like newspapers, you may find yourself skipping a line on the return sweep. This is natural and happens occasionally to everyone. To help young readers develop accurate return sweep movements, the lines of print are well-spaced in beginners' books.

Studies have shown that eye movements reflect comprehension, or the lack of it. To eliminate problems of excessive fixations, frequent regressions, and inaccurate return sweep, the reader must practice reading on very easy materials—stories so easy that the mind can race along, fostering rapid and efficient eye movements.

COMPREHENSION: For each of the following statements and questions, select the option containing the most complete or most accurate answer.

1. Cosby's philosophy could be expressed by
(e) which of the following?
   - ☐ a. He who laughs last, laughs best.
   - ☐ b. If you can't beat 'em, join 'em.
   - ☐ c. The bigger they are, the harder they fall.
   - ☐ d. There are certain advantages to being disadvantaged.

2. Bill Cosby's humor depends largely upon
(i)
   - ☐ a. circumstances.
   - ☐ b. exaggeration.
   - ☐ c. inference.
   - ☐ d. local color.

3. Refereeing on concrete courts was a matter of
(c)
   - ☐ a. intimidation.
   - ☐ b. size and stamina.
   - ☐ c. yelling.
   - ☐ d. touch-and-go.

4. Bill Cosby would probably be the first to
(h) admit that his mother was
   - ☐ a. a sports fan.
   - ☐ b. a good cook.
   - ☐ c. color blind.
   - ☐ d. his best fan.

5. For the Wissahickon team, second-rate facili-
(h) ties sometimes proved to be
   - ☐ a. advantageous.
   - ☐ b. maddening.
   - ☐ c. discouraging.
   - ☐ d. dangerous.

6. An outstanding characteristic of the Wissa-
(j) hickon team was its
   - ☐ a. brutality.
   - ☐ b. humor.
   - ☐ c. inventiveness.
   - ☐ d. solidarity.

7. A Lamont Cranston dribble is
(h)
   - ☐ a. a guaranteed basket.
   - ☐ b. hitting the air.
   - ☐ c. a Bill Cosby specialty.
   - ☐ d. an illegal procedure.

8. The crazy kid punched Chamberlain in the
(f) knee. To Cosby and his teammates this was just another example of
   - ☐ a. poor sportsmanship.
   - ☐ b. the end justifying the means.
   - ☐ c. incompetent refereeing.
   - ☐ d. erratic behavior.

9. In retrospect, millionaire Cosby remembers
(h) the concrete courts with
   - ☐ a. resentment.
   - ☐ b. nostalgia.
   - ☐ c. sadness.
   - ☐ d. shame.

10. Which of the following best expresses Cosby's
(e) feelings about Celebrity Basketball?
   - ☐ a. As riches grow, cares follow.
   - ☐ b. It is better to live rich, than to die rich.
   - ☐ c. Eat with the rich, but play with the poor, who are capable of joy.
   - ☐ d. Simple pleasures, remembered with fondness, have no counterpart that money can buy.

Comprehension Skills: a—isolating details; b—recalling specific facts; c—retaining concepts; d—organizing facts; e—understanding the main idea; f—drawing a conclusion; g—making a judgment; h—making an inference; i—recognizing tone; j—understanding characters; k—appreciation of literary forms.

SELECTIONS FROM THE BLACK

Not Your Singing, Dancing Spade

He wouldn't be caught dead singing or dancing off the stage.

Julia Fields

It was ridiculous to have an issue of such an insipidly written magazine in the apartment, he knew. Nevertheless, he picked it up again and began to read the article written about himself. The audacity of it, and the incredible and insane arrogance it suggested, made him feel helpless against the terrible tide of consciousness so established and so knowledgeable to him and to his people. His brains were sealed, signed for, and delivered, just as his body would have been in the previous century.

He focused his eyes and finished the article, his black hands and black eyes drooping wearily over the side of the plush gold sofa. Then he lay down upon it, keeping his shoes on. It was not very comforting at all.

The article stated clearly that his childhood dream had been to pursue and to possess a "blonde goddess," that he could never be happy without her. It made fun of a black entertainer he had dated. It said he paid her to give him his "freedom." There was no picture of her. But there was a listing and pictures of national and international ladies with fair hair to whom he had been linked romantically at one time or another.

There was a picture of him with his wife—his wife bright and grinning, and his teeth matching her fairness kilometer for kilometer. His hair was falling into his eyes. It always seemed to be falling into his eyes, whenever he was playing golf, or driving, or dancing, or singing. And he always had to toss his head, give his neck a quick snappy jerk in order to keep his tumbling hair neat. It always got into his eyes. He bent over to light a cigarette. The hair fell into his eyes. He used his free hand to brush it back, knowing that it would tumble into his eyes again.

His wife entered the room. She was very, very white. He had asked her to stay out of the sun. And the black maid entered with a tray of beverages. The children liked the maid and his wife liked the maid. He hated her. She was almost as black as himself, and her hair was short. He always felt like singing an old down-home blues whenever he saw her. . . . "I don't want no woman if her hair ain't no longer'n mine; she ain't nothing but trouble and keep you worried all the time." But no matter how much hatred he showed towards her, the woman was always kind and serene; yet, there was the very faintest hint of laughter and incredible mockery in her eyes when she looked at him. He knew the look. He himself had given it to others many times.

The article in the magazine shouldn't have bothered him so much, he told himself. It wasn't the first time, nor would it be the last. He had to pay the price. They were requiring it of him, and he had to make it. He had to keep making it. It was too late to stop. Where would he go? There was no place elsewhere but down. Down to scorn. Back, slowly, but certainly, to a world which had become alien, black, strange and nameless. The wolves would chew him black.

Back to black indeed. Never. What did it matter? The whites had begun their assaults late; the blacks had berated him all his life. "Black bastard. Black bastard. Bad hair." "Boy, get a brush." And comparisons: "Almost Bunky's color." "No, not quite as black as Bunky." "Child, I couldn't see nuthin' but eyes and teeth." "I like him, sure, but my daddy would kill me if I married a man that black." "Child, I wouldn't want to mess up my children with that color." He was recalling the words of parents, relatives and lovers. His yellow mother. His jet-black father who was his mother's footstool. His mother's freckles. Her rituals with Black and White ointment. Her "straight" nose. All of his pictures were in profile. Except the one in the magazine. In that one, all of his black faults were on view. In that picture, the heat had turned the expensive pomade on his hair to plain and simple shining grease. Ah, chicken-eaters of the world, unite. You have nothing to lose except your shame.

He began to dress, immaculately as always, for there was, his agent had said, a chance to make another million. Melanin and millions. Millions and melanin.

Numbly, he moved about the dressing room, larger than his parents' living room had been.

Mutely, he dressed. Dejectedly, he faced himself in the mirror. Silently, the green gall of self-revulsion passed through his psyche and soul. Swiftly, he recalled the chance to make a million and the wife who would spend it on furs, jewels, fun, cosmetics, and servants. And the whole world would see what black bastards with millions and melanin could do. Yes, they would.

The agent's smooth voice, on the phone, reassured him about the million. There was nothing to reassure him about himself. Nothing. Nothing.

Down the stairs, voices were shrill suddenly. His little girl was sobbing. He heard the maid say, "Be quiet. You'll wake up your mama."

"But Cathy said my daddy's a nigger monkey."

"What do you care what Cathy says?"

"And Daddy puts gasoline in his hair to make it nice like her daddy's hair. Isn't Daddy's hair nice?"

"Of course it's nice. That little sickly Cathy with those strings hanging 'round her face. Don't pay her no attention. She's just jealous because your daddy's got the original beauty."

"The what?"

"The first, best beauty in the world. Black. Your daddy's a pretty man. That's why everybody likes him. Where've you seen Cathy's daddy's pictures? Not nearly many places as your daddy. Your daddy is a beautiful man."

"Is he?"

"Yes. Of course he don't know how pretty he is. Anyhow, it's easy to be pale. Like milk. It ain't got nothing in it. Like vanilla ice cream. See? Now take any other flavor. Take chocolate. Milk with cocoa. You love chocolate malt, don't you?"

"Yes."

"Take strawberry. Any ice cream. It's nothing as just plain milk. What goes in makes it beautiful. It can be decorated, but by itself, it lacks a lot. Your daddy was born decorated. Born a pretty king. Born beautiful. Don't believe Cathy. She's dumb."

"Born beautiful. Daddy was born beautiful. That silly Cathy. She's a dumb one. My daddy is pretty. I always thought so."

"Yes, I always thought so, too."

Numbly, he stood there. He had to listen. The annihilated searching, seeking to be. Terror. Who had first given assumption and such supreme arrogance to the captives? He knew she had read the article that had denied her existence. A black female. The race and sex which, according to them, could never move him to love, to cherish, to desire. *Caldonia, Caldonia, what makes your big head so hard?*

He remembered his boyhood. And all the lyrics that laughed at and lamented black womanhood. Blackness. Black manhood. Black childhood. Black.

They had made the world for him, had set all the traps. He had been born to it. The horror of blackness. They had outdone themselves. They had outdone him. And it was not meant that he should ever be saved. He must believe. And they could assume postures and lies. And they could believe in his self-hatred. And they could rest comfortably, believing that he believed, and continue their believing.

They were so arrogant, so stupefied by history and circumstances that they could accept any incredible thing they said about him. Terror. Who was the bondsman? Who was the freed man? He knew.

Life began to flow again. His blood sang vital and red. Freedom. Power, even. Yes, I *am* beautiful. Born black. Born with no lack. Decorated. Born decorated.

At the foot of the stairs, he could hear the maid again angrily muttering. With dancer's feet, he moved nearer. Nearer to hear, nearer to self, to recovery.

"Lies, lies, lies. Sometimes we have to lie to make it. Even to live. We got to lie to ourselves, to our friends and to our enemies. To those we love and to those we hates. If they so smart they ain't got to b'lieve us."

He saw her throw the movie magazine clear down his long, sumptuous living room. And he heard his little daughter laughing as she went to get the magazine.

"Here. Put it in the trash can."

"But it's got Daddy's picture. Daddy's picture's in it."

"Your daddy's picture's everywhere. Besides, that's not a good picture of him. Some fool took it. Here." The child obeyed.

"Arrogant, uppity folks'll believe anything. Let 'em pay. And pay. White bastards."

"What? What?" the child questioned.

"Nothing. Go on to the playroom until I call you for lunch. I got to vacuum up this room."

Then he was there standing in the beautiful, luxurious room facing the black woman with the short hair.

"Humph," he heard her say as she turned to push a low, red, incredulously plush and ridiculously expensive chair aside for her vacuuming.

"Here, let me be of service," he said.

"Never mind."

"Let me!" he said again, and gently pushed her aside.

SELECTIONS FROM THE BLACK

"Humph," she said again. But he got a glimpse of her face, which had years of anger and defiance and hope written in chicken-scratch wrinkles and crows' feet. And there was the mockery he always saw there. And yet, a kindness, a laughter which was very sweet and strong. And the barest hint of tears in the eyes, tears like monuments to despair.

When he replaced the chairs and kissed his wife and child, he said his goodbye to the black woman and sang a snatch of his latest recording as he walked to the elevator. He felt light—weightless and yet strong and pretty. "I feel pretty," he thought. Well, not that kind of pretty, he mocked himself. But it was surprising that he sang, for he had promised himself that he was only an entertainer, that he wasn't your singing, dancing spade, that he, a professional only, wouldn't be caught dead, drunk or straitlaced, singing off the stage or away from the T.V. cameras, or dancing like some hamhocking jigaboo.

Nevertheless, his chauffeur smiled happily when he cut a step from his latest musical sensation as he entered the limousine with the sacrilegious words, "I feel pretty," floating, cakewalking from his lips.

Starting Time: _____	Finishing Time: _____
Reading Time: _____	Reading Rate: _____
Comprehension: _____	Vocabulary: _____

VOCABULARY: The following words have been taken from the selection you have just read. Put an X in the box before the best meaning or synonym for the word as used in the selection.

1. **insipidly**, page 21, column 1, paragraph 1
"It was ridiculous to have an issue of such an insipidly written magazine..."
☐ a. tastelessly
☐ b. insolently
☐ c. badly
☐ d. inconsistently

2. **berated**, page 21, column 2, paragraph 3
"...the blacks had berated him all his life."
☐ a. liberated
☐ b. abused
☐ c. befriended
☐ d. rejected

3. **arrogance**, page 22, column 1, next to last paragraph
"Who had first given assumption and such supreme arrogance to the captives?"
☐ a. self-confidence
☐ b. humility
☐ c. insolence
☐ d. superiority

4. **postures**, page 22, column 2, paragraph 1
"And they could assume postures and lies."
☐ a. positions
☐ b. moods
☐ c. poses
☐ d. powers

5. **incredulously**, page 22, column 2, 6 lines from bottom
"...incredulously plush and ridiculously expensive chair..."
☐ a. unbelievably
☐ b. apparently
☐ c. immeasurably
☐ d. inappropriately

CONTEXTUAL AIDS: COMPARISON AND CONTRAST

Studies of good readers show that they are aware of the context of what they are reading. This means that they are anticipating what is coming next by what has gone before.

Context refers to the words surrounding those you are reading. These surrounding words create the total situation from which we get meaning. Using the context as an aid to rapid understanding is a valuable tool to the reader.

The many ways in which context functions to help the reader recognize words are called contextual aids.

Contextual Aid 5. Words can be understood when they are compared or contrasted with known words. Similarly an unknown word in a phrase or clause can be understood when compared or contrasted with a word in another phrase or clause.

In the expression, **a question of life or _____** , the reader can easily fill in the correct word, **death,** the word in contrast to **life.**

In the following sentences, examples of this type of contextual aid have been used to compare with or contrast to nonsense words. Underline the nonsense word and write the correct word on the line following each sentence. The first one has been done for you.

1. Once I worked alone; now I have a granbelk.

   _____ *partner* _____

2. If you don't ride, you'll have to pund.

   _____

3. I know they're people but they act like fracdons.

   _____

4. In mythology the sun god was greater than the pend god.

   _____

5. Is the exhibition public or bander?

   _____

6. Will it be on radio or laltenap?

   _____

7. Did you buy that at retail or mhrasdon?

   _____

8. If it isn't round, then it must be prule.

   _____

9. Are you a seller or a durper?

   _____

10. Once they are connected, they're impossible to donevent.

    _____

11. The examination will reveal whether you resp or fail.

    _____

COMPREHENSION AND READING

Reading is both a visual and a mental skill. The visual aspects involve seeing the words and moving the eyes. The mental activities call for recognizing the words and understanding the thought. This mental activity is generally referred to as comprehension. The first skills needed for thorough comprehension are word recognition skills.

Once the word has been seen, it must be recognized if it is to be understood. We recognize words by remembering them, pronouncing them or analyzing them. The words we remember are those in our sight vocabulary. These are words we have seen often enough to recognize on sight. You may recall memorizing lists of "sight words" in the early grades in school. Good readers are sight readers—they have developed a large vocabulary of words which they recognize immediately when reading. Such readers slow down to sound out or pronounce only when they come to a new and unfamiliar word. Frequently in reading clinics and reading improvement courses, projectors are used to flash sight words on the screen for split-second durations. This training is designed to develop and reinforce the reader's stock of sight words.

The second way we recognize words is by pronouncing them. We do this for words which are not part of our sight vocabulary but which are in our listening vocabulary. These are words we recognize when we hear. Our knowledge of phonics helps us to pronounce unfamiliar words—this is why phonics skills are valuable.

The third technique we use in word recognition is analysis, which means breaking a word into recognizable parts. Our knowledge of syllabication and word parts helps us to do this.

Reading programs which feature only one method of attacking new words shortchange the student. To become competent readers, we need to use all the word recognition skills.

COMPREHENSION: For each of the following statements and questions, select the option containing the most complete or most accurate answer.

1. The theme of the selection can best be ex-
(e) pressed by which of the following?

   ☐ a. Search for identity
   ☐ b. Demand for excellence
   ☐ c. Preoccupation with money
   ☐ d. Guided by ambition

2. The selection begins on a note of
(i)
   ☐ a. contentment.
   ☐ b. annoyance.
   ☐ c. aggressiveness.
   ☐ d. grief.

3. The narrator can be described as
(j)
   ☐ a. misunderstood.
   ☐ b. a distraught husband.
   ☐ c. a social climber.
   ☐ d. untalented.

4. The narrator's preoccupation with hair repre-
(h) sents his

   ☐ a. satisfaction with being Black.
   ☐ b. desire to be white.
   ☐ c. concern for his image.
   ☐ d. scorn for the maid.

5. The narrator was offended by the magazine
(f) article because

   ☐ a. it confused his daughter.
   ☐ b. it questioned his talent.
   ☐ c. it misrepresented his past.
   ☐ d. it struck a sensitive chord.

6. Bunky is the
(b) ☐ a. daughter.
   ☐ b. maid.
   ☐ c. narrator.
   ☐ d. family pet.

7. The concept "Black is beautiful" is best ex-
(g) pressed by

   ☐ a. the maid.
   ☐ b. Cathy.
   ☐ c. the narrator.
   ☐ d. Caldonia.

8. The daughter's reaction to Cathy's remarks
(g) and to the maid's use of the expression "white bastards" represents

   ☐ a. a racist attitude.
   ☐ b. a racial awakening.
   ☐ c. a prejudiced mind.
   ☐ d. an educated attitude.

9. The maid could be thought of as
(j)
   ☐ a. a mother.
   ☐ b. a cook.
   ☐ c. a friend.
   ☐ d. a teacher.

10. The reader knows the narrator has been "con-
(f) verted" when

   ☐ a. he sings "I Feel Pretty."
   ☐ b. he offers to help the maid.
   ☐ c. he remembers his boyhood.
   ☐ d. he cuts a step from his latest musical sensation.

Comprehension Skills: a—isolating details; b—recalling specific facts; c—retaining concepts; d—organizing facts; e—understanding the main idea; f—drawing a conclusion; g—making a judgment; h—making an inference; i—recognizing tone; j—understanding characters; k—appreciation of literary forms.

Soledad Brother

"...I live an hour at a time, right in the present, looking...for the trouble I know is coming."

George Jackson

May, 1970

Angela,

I am certain that they plan to hold me incommunicado. All of my letters except for a few to my immediate family have come back to me with silly comments on my choice of terms. The incoming mail is also sent back to the outside sender. The mail which I do receive is sometimes one or two weeks old. So, my sweet sister, when I reach you, it will be in this manner.

. . . I'm going to write on both sides of this paper, and when I make a mistake I'll just scratch over it and continue on. That is my style, completely informal.

Was that your sister with you in court? If so, she favored you. Both very beautiful people. You should have introduced me.

They are going to take your job, I know they are—anything else would be expecting too much. They can't, however, stop you from teaching in public institutions, can they?

They hate us, don't they? I like it that way, that is the way it's supposed to be. If they didn't hate me I would be doing something very wrong, and then I would have to hate myself. I prefer it this way. I get little hate notes in the folds of my newspaper almost every day now. You know, the racist stuff, traditional "Dear nigger" stuff, and how dead I am going to be one day. They think they're mad at me now, but it's nothing compared to how it will be when I really get mad myself. . . .

Pigs are punks, Angela. We've made a terrible mistake in overestimating these people. It reflects on us badly that we have allowed them to do the things they have done to us. Since they are idiots, what does that make us. I just read Bobby Seale's account of that scene in Chicago (*Ramparts,* June '70). It started in San Francisco with that flight to evade charge. One of the pigs commented that "this was so easy." But it shouldn't have been. Brothers like that are the best of us. It shouldn't have gone down like that. We should never make it easy for them—by relaxing—at this stage of the educational process. Examples are crucially important. Well that's the name of the game right now.

I think of you all the time. I've been thinking about women a lot lately. Is there anything sentimental or otherwise wrong with that? There couldn't be. It's never bothered me too much before, the sex thing. I would do my exercise and the hundreds of katas, stay busy with something . . . this ten years really has gone pretty quickly. It has destroyed me as a person, a human being that is, but it was sudden, it was a sudden death, it seems like ten days rather than ten years.

Would you like to know a subhuman. I certainly hope you have time. I'm not a very nice person. I'll confess out front, I've been forced to adopt a set of responses, reflexes, attitudes that have made me more kin to the cat than anything else, the big black one. For all of that I am not a selfish person. I don't think so anyway, but I do have myself in mind when I talk about us relating. You would be the generous one, I the recipient of that generosity.

They're killing niggers again down the tier, all day, every day. They are killing niggers and "them protesters" with small workings of mouth. One of them told a pig today that he was going to be awful disappointed with the pig if the pig didn't shoot some niggers or protesters this evening when he got off work. The pig found it very amusing. They went off on a twenty-minute political discussion, pig and his convict supporter. There is something very primitive about these people. Something very fearful. In all the time I've been down here on Maximum Row, no brother has ever spoken to one of these people. We never speak about them, you know, across the cells. Every brother down here is under the influence of the party line, and racist terms like "honky" have never been uttered. All of these are beautiful brothers, ones who have stepped across the line into the position from which there can be no retreat. All are fully committed. They are the most desperate and dauntless of our kind. I love them. They are men and they do not fight with their mouths. They've brought them here from prisons all over the state to be warehoused or murdered. Whichever is more expedient. That Brother Edwards who was murdered in that week in January told his lawyer that he would never get out of prison alive. He was at the time of that statement on Maximum Row, Death Row, Soledad, California. He was twenty-one years old. We have made it a point to never exchange words with these people. But they never relent. Angela, there are some people who will never learn new responses. They will carry what they incorporated into their characters at early youth to the grave. Some can never be educated. As an historian you know how long and how fervently we've appealed to these people to take some of the murder out of their system, their economics, their propaganda. And as an intelligent observer you must see how our appeals were received. We've wasted many generations and oceans of blood trying to civilize these elements over here. It cannot be done in the manner we have attempted it in the past. Dialectics, understanding, love, passive resistance, they won't work on an activistic, maniacal, gory pig. It's going to grow much worse for the black male than it already is, much, much worse. We are going to have to be the vanguard, the catalyst, in any meaningful change.

When generalizing about black women I could never include *you* in any of it that is not complimentary. But my mother at one time tried to make a coward of me, she did the same with Jon. She is changing fast under crisis situation and apocalyptic circumstance. John and Fleeta's mothers did the same to them, or I should say tried. And so did every brother's mother I've ever drawn out. I am reasonably certain that I can draw from every black male in this country some comments to substantiate that his mother, the black female, attempted to aid his survival by discouraging his violence or by turning it inward. The blacks of slave society, U.S.A., have always been a matriarchal subsociety. The implication is clear, black mama is going to have to put a sword in that brother's hand and stop that "Be a good boy" shit. Channel his spirit instead of break it, or help to break it I should say. Do you understand? *All* of the sisters I've ever known personally and through other brothers' accounts begged and bullied us to look for *jobs* instead of being satisfied with the candy-stick take. The strongest impetus a man will ever have, in an individual sense, will come from a woman he admires.

When "Soul" did that feature on you, I discussed you with some of the comrades. One of them asked me what my response would be if it were my job to guard your body (for the party) from the attack of ten armed pigs. I told them my response would be to charge. There would be eleven people hurting but you wouldn't be one of them. Everyone agreed it was the correct response.

As an individual, I am grateful for you. As the black male, I hope that since your inclination is to teach you will give serious consideration to redeeming this very next generation of black males by reaching for today's black female. I am not too certain about my generation. There are a few, and with these few we will keep something. But we have altogether too many pimps and punks, and black capitalists (who want a piece of the putrescent pie). There's no way to predict. Sometimes people change fast. I've seen it happen to brothers overnight. But then they have to learn a whole new set of responses and attack reflexes which can't be learned overnight. So cats like me who have no tomorrows have to provide examples. I have an ideal regarding tomorrow, but I live an hour at a time, right in the present, looking right over my nose for the trouble I know is coming.

There is so much that could be done, right now. . . . But I won't talk about those things right here. I will say that it should never be easy for them to destroy us. If you start with Malcolm X and count *all* of the brothers who have died or been captured since, you will find that not even one of them was really *prepared* for a fight. No imagination or fighting style was evident in any one of the incidents. But each one that died professed to know the nature of our enemies. It should never be so easy for them. Do you understand what I'm saying? Edward V. Hanrahan, Illinois State Attorney General, sent fifteen pigs to raid the Panther headquarters and murder Hampton and Clark. Do you have any idea what would have happened to those fifteen pigs if they had run into as many Viet Cong as there were Panthers in that building. The VC are all little people with less general education than we have. The argument that they have been doing it longer has no validity at all, because they were doing it just as well when they started as they are now. It's very contradictory for a man to teach about the murder in corporate capitalism, to isolate and expose the murderers behind it, to instruct that these madmen are completely without stops, are licentious—totally depraved—and then not make adequate preparations to defend himself from the madman's attack. Either they don't really believe their own spiel or they harbor some sort of subconscious death wish.

None of this should have happened as it did. I don't know if we'll learn in time or not. I am not well here. I pretend that all is well for the benefit of my family's peace of mind. But I'm going to cry to you, so you can let the people of Fiftieth Street know not to let this happen to them, and that they must resist that cat with *all* of their strength when he starts that jail talk.

When the menu reads steak we get a piece of rotten steer (I hope) the size of a quarter. When it reads cake we get something like cornbread. Those are the best things served. When two guys fight, the darker guy will get shot. To supplement their incomes the pigs will bring anything into the prison and sell it to the convict who smuggles money in from his visits. Now black people don't visit their kin in the joint much and those that do can't afford to give up any money. So we have less of everything that could make life more comfortable—and safe (weapons are brought in too). Pigs are fascist right out front, the white prisoner who is con-wise joins the Hitlerian party right here in the joint. He doesn't have to worry about the rules, he stays high. When he decides to attack us, he has the best of weapons (seldom will a pig give a con a gun, though. It has happened, however, in San Quentin three times to my knowledge. But they will provide cutlery and zip guns). The old convict code died years ago. These cons work right with the police against us. The only reason that I am still alive is because I take everything to the extreme, and they know it. I never let any of them get within arm's reach, and their hands must be in full view. When on the yard I would stay close to something to get under. Nothing, absolutely nothing comes as a surprise to me.

Starting Time: _____   Finishing Time: _____

Reading Time: _____   Reading Rate: _____

Comprehension: _____   Vocabulary: _____

VOCABULARY: The following words have been taken from the selection you have just read. Put an X in the box before the best meaning or synonym for the word as used in the selection.

1. **dauntless**, page 26, column 2, paragraph 3
"They are the most desperate and dauntless of our kind."
☐ a. fearful
☐ b. daring
☐ c. haunting
☐ d. careless

2. **vanguard**, page 27, column 1, paragraph 1
"We are going to have to be the vanguard, the catalyst, in any meaningful change."
☐ a. hope
☐ b. leaders
☐ c. prisoners
☐ d. army

3. **substantiate**, page 27, column 1, paragraph 2
"...some comments to substantiate that his mother,"
☐ a. illustrate
☐ b. deny
☐ c. focus
☐ d. confirm

4. **impetus**, page 27, column 1, paragraph 2
"The strongest impetus a man will ever have,"
☐ a. stimulus
☐ b. initiative
☐ c. restraint
☐ d. desire

5. **professed**, page 27, column 2, paragraph 2
"But each one that died professed to know the nature of our enemies."
☐ a. hoped
☐ b. pretended
☐ c. pledged
☐ d. claimed

PREFIXES

Many English words consist of a base or root word to which prefixes (beginnings) and suffixes (endings) have been added. To the root word **agree** (a verb) we can add both a prefix and a suffix to get **disagreeable** (an adjective) which has an opposite meaning.

A prefix is added to the beginning of a word and causes a change in the meaning of that word. We have just seen how the prefix **dis** reverses the meaning of **agree**.

Two Prefixes

1. post- is a Latin prefix which means **after, following** or **later.** A **postscript** is written after the rest of the letter.

2. con- is also from Latin and means **together** or **with.** When people **congregate**, they meet together.

In the following sentences, the words in bold print need prefixes. Add one of these two prefixes to each word and write your word on the line following the sentence.

1. **Graduate** courses are taken after graduation.

   _____

2. He agreed with me; his thinking **firms** mine.

   _____

3. A **mortem** examination revealed how death had occured.

   _____

4. The choir and orchestra performed in **cert.**

   _____

5. After surgery is done, the **operative** period is most critical.

   _____

6. The **fluence** of the rivers is the place where they flow together.

   _____

7. No one's here right now; let's **pone** the meeting.

   _____

8. We should merge and **solidate** our position in the market.

   _____

9. P.M. (afternoon) is the abbreviation for **meridian.**

   _____

10. An alliance or league is called a **federation.**

    _____

11. Traffic gets **gested** where the roads meet.

    _____

COMPREHENSION AND READING

Following word recognition in reading comes the other aspects of comprehension. These are generally grouped into the areas of retention, organization, interpretation, and appreciation.

In retention, the reader is called upon to isolate details, recall specifics and retain concepts. These all have to do with remembering facts which were read.

The reader is also expected to organize as he reads. He does this in the following ways.

1. Classifying. As he reads, the reader arranges facts into groups for easier understanding. Thus the facts contributing to comprehension of a single concept are seen as a unit, separate from those dealing with other concepts.

2. Establishing a Sequence. For real understanding of the author's ideas the reader must be aware of the order in which events occur; understanding the facts as a related series, each following the previous one and contributing to the next.

3. Following Directions. An extremely important aspect of comprehension, too many readers fall short when called upon to follow directions. An organization skill, following directions requires the reader to arrange the facts and to understand the sequence of events required of him. Too often readers fail to follow directions because of inability to classify facts properly and to establish a correct sequence.

4. Seeing Relationships. An author presents his ideas in an organized fashion, presenting first the concepts needed to understand other, more complex concepts which follow. The reader must understand this relationship for true comprehension.

5. Generalizing. This requires the reader to infer principles from the particulars which the author has formulated.

COMPREHENSION: For each of the following statements and questions, select the option containing the most complete or most accurate answer.

1. George Jackson measures his effectiveness in
(c) terms of

☐ a. special privileges.
☐ b. prison guards.
☐ c. Angela Davis.
☐ d. white hatred.

2. "Pigs are punks, Angela." Jackson's advice is
(b) that they should never be

☐ a. challenged.
☐ b. feared.
☐ c. underestimated.
☐ d. overestimated.

3. George Jackson considers successful Black
(c) resistance to white oppression

☐ a. educational.
☐ b. unsafe.
☐ c. untimely.
☐ d. expensive.

4. The prisoner survived the dangers and the de-
(c) humanizing prison conditions by

☐ a. sleeping long hours.
☐ b. developing keen, sensory awareness.
☐ c. corresponding with friends.
☐ d. organizing a brotherhood of prisoners.

5. Historically, Black efforts to educate white
(b) extremists have been

☐ a. wasted.
☐ b. well-received.
☐ c. half-hearted.
☐ d. deficient.

6. Fully committed Black brothers react to abu-
(f) sive, racist language with

☐ a. indifference.
☐ b. violence.
☐ c. silence.
☐ d. insult.

7. Jackson traces the subservience and apathy of
(h) some Black males to

☐ a. the merchants and capitalists who exploit the poor.
☐ b. the law enforcement officials who allow police brutality.
☐ c. the absence of a strong, virile, family influence.
☐ d. the large concentration of Black people in cities.

8. To some extent, the future of "the blacks in
(f) slave society, U.S.A." depends on

☐ a. the schools.
☐ b. the Black female.
☐ c. the Black capitalists.
☐ d. the white liberals.

9. Which of the following expresses the recurring
(e) message in George Jackson's letter?

☐ a. "To know your enemy is to prepare for him."
☐ b. "We've wasted many generations and oceans of blood."
☐ c. "They're killing niggers again down the tier, all day, every night."
☐ d. "Mine is an abject level of slavery."

10. Jackson sees little difference between
(g)
☐ a. the Black man's lot in or out of prison.
☐ b. Maximum Row and Death Row.
☐ c. Black sisters and Black capitalists.
☐ d. thinking and executing thoughts of violence.

Comprehension Skills: a—isolating details; b—recalling specific facts; c—retaining concepts; d—organizing facts; e—understanding the main idea; f—drawing a conclusion; g—making a judgment; h—making an inference; i—recognizing tone; j—understanding characters; k—appreciation of literary forms.

Jubilee

The Authentic Story of the Author's Great-Grandmother

Margaret Walker

"There's a star in the East
on Christmas morn"

Christmas time on the plantation was always the happiest time of the year. Harvest time was over. The molasses had been made. Marster's corn was in his crib and the slaves' new corn meal had been ground. Lye hominy and sauerkraut were packed away in big jars and stone or clay crocks. Elderberry, blackberry, poke weed and dandelion, black cherry and scuppernong, muscatine and wild plum, crab apple and persimmon, all had been picked and made into jars of jelly, jam, preserves, and kegs of wine. There were persimmon beer and home-made corn likker, and a fermented home brew for future use. Despite Big Missy's clever vigilance with her ipecac, some of those jars of jelly and preserves and peach brandy had inevitably gone out of the pantry window into the waiting fingers of black hands. What the slaves could not conveniently steal, they begged and made for themselves. Many of the delicacies that they loved were free for the taking in the woods. Who did not know how to mix the dark brown sugar or black cane molasses or sorghum with various fruits and berries to make the good wine and brew the beer and whiskey from the corn or rye that every clever finger learned early how to snatch and hide? When the frost turned the leaves and the wind blew them from the trees, it was time to go into the woods and gather nuts, hickory nuts and black walnuts, and chinkapinks. There were always more pecans on the place than could be eaten and the hogs rooted out the rotting ones. If Marster had not given them a goober patch, they had patches of goober peas around their cabins anyway. Sometimes there were whole fields of these wonderful peanuts. Like the industrious squirrels around them they scrupulously gathered the wild harvest and wrapped them in rags, laying-by their knick-knacks for the long winter nights. When the autumn haze ended and the chilling winter winds descended upon them it was time to hunt the possum and to catch a coon. No feast during the Christmas holidays would be good without a possum and a coon. Of course, Vyry said, "You got to know how to cook it, or it

ain't no good. You got to boil that wild taste out with red-hot pepper and strong vinegar made out of sour apple peelings and plenty salt. You got to boil it in one water and then take it out and boil it in another water, and you got to soak the blood out first overnight and clean it real good so you gits all the blood out and you got to scrape all the hair left from the least bit of hide and then you got to roast it a long, slow time until you poured all that fat grease off and roast sweet potatoes soft and sugary, and if that stuff don't make you hit your mama till she holler and make you slobber all over yourself, they's something wrong with you and the almighty God didn't make you at the right time of the year. Marster, he like foxes, but what good is a fox when you can't eat him? Make sense to catch varmints stealing chickens, foxes and wolves, for that matter, and it's good to catch an old black bear, or a ferocity vicious bobcat, and nasty old varmint like a weasel when he come sneaking around, but when you hunting for meat and you wants fresh meat, kill the rabbit and the coon, kill the squirrel and the possum and I'll sho-nuff be satisfied."

If the slave did not kill his meat, he wasn't likely to eat fresh meat, although at hog-killing time they were given the tubs of chitterlings, the liver and the lights, and sometimes even the feet. After a very good harvest Marster might let them have a young shoat to barbecue, especially at Christmas time. Marse John was generous to a fault and always gave plenty of cheap rum and gallons of cheap whiskey to wash the special Christmas goodies down.

Big Missy had a taste for wild game too, but it was quail and pheasant, wild turkey and wild ducks, and occasionally the big fat bucks that came out of their own woods for wonderful roasts of venison. The Negroes were not allowed to kill these and if they made a mistake and accidentally killed birds or deer they had better not be caught eating it. Vyry had learned from Aunt Sally how to lard quail with salt fat pork and how to cook potted pheasant in cream, to roast and stuff turkey and geese and ducks, but she knew also the penalty for even tasting such morsels if Big Missy found out about it. Sometimes, however, half a turkey or

goose was stolen from the springhouse, after some expert had carefully picked the lock. Most of the time, however, they did not worry about Big Missy's game as long as they could get enough of what they could put into their hands while foraging through the woods. By some uncanny and unknown reason real white flour came from somewhere for Christmas, and eggs were hoarded from a stray nest for egg bread instead of plain corn pone, but real butter cake and meat and fruit pies were seldom found in a slave cabin. Sometimes on Christmas they tasted snacks of real goodies such as these as part of their Christmas. On Christmas morning all the field hands stood outside the Big House shouting, "Christmas gift, Christmas gift, Marster." Then, and only then, did they taste fresh citrus fruit. Every slave child on the place received an orange, hard Christmas candy, and sometimes ginger cake. There were snuff and chewing tobacco for the women, whiskey and rum for the men. Sometimes there were new clothes, but generally the shoes were given out in November before Thanksgiving.

On Christmas morning there was always a warm and congenial relationship between the Big House and the slave Quarters. If it was cold, and very often it was not, the slaves huddled in rags and shawls around their heads and shoulders, and Marse John would open his front door and come out on the veranda. His guests and family and poor white kin, who were always welcomed in the house at Christmas time, came out with him and gathered round to hear his annual Christmas speech to the slaves. He thanked them for such a good crop and working so hard and faithfully, said it was good to

have them all together, and good to enjoy Christmas together when they all had been so good. He talked about the meaning of Christmas — "When I was a boy on this very place at Christmas time, seems only yesterday..." He got sentimental about his father and mother, and he told a "darkey" joke or two, and then he wished them a merry Christmas, ordered whiskey and rum for everyone, handed out their gifts of candy and oranges and snuff and tobacco, and asked them to sing a song, please, for him and his family and all their guests. Then they sang their own moving Christmas carols, "Wasn't that a mighty day when Jesus Christ was born" and "Go tell it on the Mountain that Jesus Christ is born" and the especially haunting melody that everybody loved:

> There's a star in the East
> on Christmas morn,
> Rise up shepherds and foller,
> It'll lead to the place where
> the Savior's born,
> Rise up shepherds and foller.

Then Marse John and all his white family and their friends would wipe their weeping eyes and blow their running noses and go inside to the good Christmas breakfast of fried chicken and waffles and steaming black coffee with fresh clotted cream. And the slaves, happy with the rest that came with the season, went back to their cabins, certain that for one day of the year at least they would have enough to eat. They could hardly wait for night and the banjo parties to begin. On Marse John's plantation, Christmas was always an occasion and all during the holidays there were dancing parties and dinners with lots of wonderful food and plenty of the finest liquor. Marse John and Big Missy became celebrated for their fine turkeys and English fruit cakes and puddings, duffs full of sherry and brandy, excellent sillabub and eggnog, all prepared by their well-trained servants, who cooked and served their Master's fare with a flourish.

Starting Time: _____	Finishing Time: _____
Reading Time: _____	Reading Rate: _____
Comprehension: _____	Vocabulary: _____

SELECTIONS FROM THE BLACK

Photo: Dell Padgett

VOCABULARY: The following words have been taken from the selection you have just read. Put an *X* in the box before the best meaning or synonym for the word as used in the selection.

1. **vigilance**, page 31, column 1, line 13
"Despite Big Missy's clever vigilance..."
☐ a. watchfulness
☐ b. vehemence
☐ c. precautions
☐ d. inspection

2. **scrupulously**, page 31, column 1, 9 lines from bottom
"...they scrupulously gathered the wild harvest..."
☐ a. excitedly
☐ b. carefully
☐ c. carelessly
☐ d. secretly

3. **uncanny**, page 32, column 1, paragraph 1
"By some uncanny and unknown reason..."
☐ a. uncertain
☐ b. extraordinary
☐ c. improper
☐ d. natural

4. **congenial**, page 32, column 1, paragraph 2
"On Christmas morning there was always a warm and congenial relationship..."
☐ a. compatible
☐ b. agreeable
☐ c. congenital
☐ d. gentlemanly

5. **haunting**, page 32, column 2, paragraph 1
"...and the especially haunting melody that everybody loved:"
☐ a. mysterious
☐ b. frightening
☐ c. unforgettable
☐ d. emotional

ROOTS

Many English words consist of a base or root word to which prefixes (beginnings) and suffixes (endings) have been added. To the root word **agree** (a verb) we can add both a prefix and a suffix to get **disagreeable** (an adjective) which has an opposite meaning.

Roots are Latin and Greek stems on which our English words are based. For example **bio** (life) is a Greek root on which our word **biology** (the study of plant and animal life) is built.

Two Roots

1. **graph** is a Greek root which means **to draw** or **write**. We write our names when we sign our **autographs**.

2. **poly** is also a Greek root and it means **many**. A **polygamist** has many wives.

In the following sentences these two roots have been left out. Space has been left indicating where the root belongs. Add one of these two roots and write your word on the line following the sentence.

1. A paper written on a particular subject is called a **mono—**.

   _____

2. Music that has been recorded is played back on a **phono—**.

   _____

3. **—syllabic** words have many syllables.

   _____

4. A person skilled in writing shorthand is called a **steno—er**.

   _____

5. The **—graph**, an instrument which records several body reactions, is used as a lie detector.

   _____

6. **—ology**, the study of handwriting, is believed by some to reveal character traits.

   _____

7. In geometry we studied **—gons**, many-sided figures.

   _____

8. The soft, black carbon used for lead in pencils is called **—ite**.

   _____

9. A piano is a **—phonic** instrument.

   _____

10. A **—technic** school offers instruction in many technical subjects.

    _____

11. A **photo—er** records events with a camera.

    _____

COMPREHENSION AND READING

Retention and organization are two aspects of comprehension expected of the reader. The other two are interpretation and appreciation.

The most critical kind of comprehension required of the reader is interpretation. The interpretation skills are these.

1. **Understanding the Main Idea.** As you would expect, proper interpretation of the author's presentation is based on understanding his main idea. Very often this is not stated but must be gathered or interpreted by the reader.

2. **Drawing Conclusions.** Based on the ideas presented, the reader must make the one judgment or form the one opinion allowed by the facts. There should be no doubt about which conclusion the author expects you to reach.

3. **Making Inferences.** Unlike a conclusion, an inference is a reasonable conclusion or judgment based on the facts. The idea you infer may not be the only one suggested, but it is clearly the one the author intended. The most critical kinds of comprehension demanded of the reader are those of making inferences.

4. **Predicting Outcomes.** The author uses his ideas to lead the reader to certain ends or objectives. He may not tell you outright the outcome but he has laid the groundwork of facts you need to predict the intended result.

5. **Making a Judgment.** Sometimes the author expects his readers to make a judgment suggested by the facts and arguments.

6. **Recognizing Tone.** Finally, we are expected to demonstrate a sensitive awareness of the author's work. We do this by recognizing tone—reacting to the joy or sadness of the article, by understanding characters—visualizing a realness the author has strived to create, and by seeing humor when that has been the author's goal.

COMPREHENSION: For each of the following statements and questions, select the option containing the most complete or most accurate answer.

1. At Christmas time on the plantation the at-
(i) mosphere was one of

☐ a. equal sharing.
☐ b. forced jollity.
☐ c. warm contentment.
☐ d. suppressed resentment.

2. The slaves managed to get special food and
(b) drink

☐ a. by stealth.
☐ b. from the larder.
☐ c. from Big Missy.
☐ d. from neighbors.

3. The slaves made wine from
(b)
☐ a. corn, fruit and rye.
☐ b. goobers and sour apple peelings.
☐ c. sugar or molasses and fruits and berries.
☐ d. aged vinegar and berries.

4. The highlight of the slaves' Christmas feast
(b) was

☐ a. goobers.
☐ b. possum and coon.
☐ c. venison.
☐ d. quail and pheasant.

5. Vyry learned how to cook wild game from
(a) ☐ a. Marse John.
☐ b. Big Missy.
☐ c. Little Louise.
☐ d. Aunt Sally.

6. Marse John is represented as
(j) ☐ a. indifferent.
☐ b. generous.
☐ c. frugal.
☐ d. reliable.

7. On Christmas morning the slaves were ex-
(c) pected to

☐ a. work.
☐ b. perform.
☐ c. help.
☐ d. pray.

8. The reader's reaction to the traditional Christ-
(g) mas morning gathering on Marse John's veranda could produce feelings of

☐ a. disgust.
☐ b. contentment.
☐ c. annoyance.
☐ d. hope.

9. The life of the plantation owner is described as
(h) ☐ a. sentimental and religious.
☐ b. comfortable and secure.
☐ c. kind and gentle.
☐ d. virtuous and rewarding.

10. The slave's life on the plantation is described
(h) as

☐ a. poor and difficult.
☐ b. miserable and unhappy.
☐ c. comfortable and secure.
☐ d. poor but light-hearted.

Comprehension Skills: a—isolating details; b—recalling specific facts; c—retaining concepts; d—organizing facts; e—understanding the main idea; f—drawing a conclusion; g—making a judgment; h—making an inference; i—recognizing tone; j—understanding characters; k—appreciation of literary forms.

Freedom – When?

"When we catch that nigger Farmer, we're gonna kill him."

James Farmer

I was waiting at the Plymouth Rock Church. I watched the Negroes come running back, those who could run, bleeding, hysterical, faint, some of the stronger ones carrying the injured. The nurse started to bandage the wounds and the rest of us began to sing "We Shall Overcome"; but the troopers rode roaring through the streets right up to the door of the church. The Freedom Rock Church, we call it now. They dismounted and broke into the church, yelling and hurling tear gas bombs in front of them—bomb after bomb, poisoning the air. The gas masks protecting the troopers' faces transformed them into monsters as they stood and watched our people growing more and more frantic, screaming with pain and terror, trampling on one another in their frenzied efforts to escape through the back door to the parsonage behind the church. When the people had finally escaped, the troopers set about destroying the empty church. They knocked out the windows, overturned the benches, laid waste everything they could reach, and flooded the gutted building with high-pressure hoses until Bibles and hymnals floated in the aisles.

Then they attacked the parsonage to which we had fled. They sent tear gas bombs smashing through the windows, until all the windows were shattered and almost everyone inside was blinded and choking. The screaming as unbearable. I caught sight of Ronnie Moore administering mouth-to-mouth resuscitation to a young woman. People writhed on the floor, seeking oxygen. A few managed to push through the rear door into the parsonage yard, but the troopers, anticipating them, had ridden around to the back with more bombs to force them in again. And then bombs thrown into the parsonage forced them back out into the yard. All these men and women, who just that morning had resolutely banded together to reach out for freedom and dignity, were reduced now to running from torment to torment, helpless victims of a bitter game.

We tried to telephone for help, but the operators were not putting through any outgoing calls from the Negro section. Within the community, though, there was telephone service, and several calls got through to us in the parsonage. What had appeared to be random and mindless brutality proved to have had a mad purpose after all. It was a manhunt. Troopers were in the streets, kicking open doors, searching every house in the Negro community, overturning chairs and tables, looking under beds and in closets, yelling, "Come on out, Farmer, we know you're in there. Come on out, Farmer! We're going to get you." We could hear the screaming in the streets as the troopers on horseback resumed their sport with the cattle prods and billy clubs. "Get up, nigger! Run, nigger, run!" Holding their victims down with the cattle prod, they were saying, "We'll let you up, nigger, if you tell us where Farmer is." Two of our girls, hiding beneath the church, overheard one trooper saying to another, "When we catch that nigger Farmer, we're gonna kill him."

Spiver Gordon, CORE field secretary in Plaquemine, who, people say, looks like me, told me later that he wandered out of the church into the street at this time. Sighting him, state troopers ran up shouting, "Here he is, boys. We got Farmer." A trooper beckoned to a crowd of hoodlums who were watching nearby, many holding chains, ropes, clubs. "What post we gonna hang him from?" said one. After Spiver convinced them he wasn't me, he took a good lacing for looking like me. An officer said, "He ain't Farmer. You've beat him enough. Put him in the car and arrest him."

There seemed no prospect of aid from any quarter. We were all suffering intensely from the tear gas, and the troopers kept us running with the bombs. In desperation I sent two people creeping through the grass from the parsonage to a funeral hall half a block away to ask for refuge. The owners of the hall agreed to shelter us (although I doubt that they knew what they were taking on). So we crawled on our bellies through the grass, in twos, threes, fours, making use of guerrilla tactics that some remembered from the war but none of us had ever learned as a technique of non-violent demonstration, until we reached our new sanctuary. Night had fallen by the time all three hundred of us were safely inside, jammed together like straws in a broom into two rooms and a hallway.

The sound of screaming still echoed in the streets as the troopers beat down another Negro ("Run, nigger, run!") or invaded another house. The telephones were still useless.

Very shortly the troopers figured out where we were. One of them—a huge, raging, red-faced man—kicked open the back door of the funeral home and screamed, "Come on out, Farmer. We know you're in there. We're gonna get you." I was in the front room. I could look down the hallway, over all the heads, right into his face: it was flushed and dripping with sweat; his hair hung over his eyes, his mouth was twisted. Another trooper burst through the door to stand beside him. "Farmer! Come out!"

I had to give myself up. I felt like a modern Oedipus who, unaware, brought down a plague upon the city. In this hall, their lives endangered by my presence, were three hundred people, many of whom had never even seen me before that day. I began to make my way into the hall, thinking that I would ask to see the warrant for my arrest and demand to know the charges against me. But before I could take three steps the men around me grabbed me silently and pulled me back into the front room, whispering fiercely, "We're not going to let you go out there tonight. That's a lynch mob. You go out there tonight, you won't be alive tomorrow morning."

The trooper, meanwhile, had discovered a large Negro in the back room. He shouted triumphantly: "Here he is, we got that nigger Farmer! Come on in, boys. We got him here."

"I'm not Farmer," the man said. A third trooper came in.

"That ain't Farmer," he said. "I know that nigger." They went through his identification papers. He wasn't Farmer.

Suddenly, to everyone's astonishment, a woman pushed her way through the crowd to the back room and confronted the troopers. It was the owner of the funeral home, a "Nervous Nellie," as they say, who had previously held herself apart from the movement. I can never know—she herself probably does not know—what inner revolution or what mysterious force generated in that crowded room plucked her from her caul of fear and thrust her forth to assert with such a dramatic and improbable gesture her new birth of freedom. A funeral hall is as good a place as any for a person to come to life, I suppose, and her action sparked a sympathetic impulse in everyone who watched as she planted herself in front of the first trooper and shook a finger in his face: "Do you have a search warrant to come into my place of business?"

The trooper stared down at her, confounded, and backed away. "No," he said.

"You're not coming into my place of business without a search warrant. I'm a taxpayer and a law-abiding citizen. I have a wake going on here."

I prayed inwardly that her valiant subterfuge would not prove to be a prophecy.

"This ain't no wake," the trooper said, looking around at the throng of angry, frightened people crushed together before him. "These people ain't at no wake."

"Well, you're not coming into my place of business without a search warrant." The accusing finger pushed him back to the door, where he muttered for a moment to his men outside, then turned and yelled, "All right. We got all the tear gas and all the guns. You ain't got nothin'. We'll give you just five minutes to get Farmer out here. Just five minutes, that's all." He slammed the door.

The door clanged in my ears like the door of a cell in death row. "I'll go out and face them," I said, but once again I was restrained. They would stick by me, these strangers insisted, even if they all had to die, but they would not let me out to be lynched. Someone standing near me pulled out a gun. "Mr. Farmer," he said, "if a trooper comes through that door, he'll be dead."

"If a trooper comes through that door, he may be dead," I conceded. "But what about the trooper behind him and all the ones behind that one? You'll only provoke them into shooting and we won't have a chance." Very reluctantly he allowed me to take the gun from him. It is hard for people to practice non-violence when they are looking death in the face. I wondered how many others were armed.

Then my own private thoughts engulfed me. Reverend Davis was leading a group in the Lord's Prayer; another group was singing "We Shall Overcome." I was certain I was going to die. What kind of death would it be? Would they mutilate me first? What does it feel like to die? Then I grew panicky about the insurance. Had I paid the last installment? How much was it? I couldn't remember. I couldn't remember anything about it. My wife and little girls—how would it be for them? Abbey was only two then—too young to remember; but Tami was four and a half, and very close to me—she would remember. Well, damn it, if I had to die, at least let the organization wring some use out of my death. I hoped the newspapers were out there. Plenty of them. With plenty of cameras.

I was terrified. The five minutes passed. Six. Seven. Eight. A knock at the front door. My lawyers from New Orleans, Lolis Elie and Robert

Collins, identified themselves and squeezed in, breathless. New Orleans radio had broadcast the news that a manhunt was in progress in Plaquemine, and they had driven over immediately. The community, they said, was in a state of siege. Everywhere one looked one saw troopers, like an invading army. The two lawyers had crawled through the high grass to seek refuge in the graveyard, but when they got there the place came alive: there was a Negro behind every tombstone ("All find safety in the tomb," sang Yeats, in another context). Apparently everyone had counted on the dead to be more hospitable than the living. Apparently, also, everyone knew where I was, but no one was telling the white men. The troopers, it seemed, had been bluffing; they could not be wholly sure I was in the funeral home. It occurred to me that my physical safety, in some elusive way that had very little to do with me, had

become a kind of transcendant symbol to all these people of the possibilities of freedom and personal dignity that existed for them. By protecting me, they were preserving their dreams. But did they understand, I wondered, that through their acts of courage during this desperate night they had taken the first great steps toward realizing these possibilities? Did they sense that they had gained at least some of that freedom for which they longed here, and now?

Starting Time: _____   Finishing Time: _____

Reading Time: _____   Reading Rate: _____

Comprehension: _____   Vocabulary: _____

VOCABULARY: The following words have been taken from the selection you have just read. Put an *X* in the box before the best meaning or synonym for the word as used in the selection.

1. **sanctuary**, page 36, column 2, last paragraph
"...until we reached our new sanctuary."
☐ a. church
☐ b. refuge
☐ c. mortuary
☐ d. cemetery

2. **generated**, page 37, column 1, paragraph 7
"—what inner revolution or what mysterious force generated in that crowded room..."
☐ a. stifled
☐ b. germinated
☐ c. distributed
☐ d. produced

3. **improbable**, page 37, column 1, paragraph 7
"...to assert with such a dramatic and improbable gesture..."
☐ a. improper
☐ b. impossible
☐ c. futile
☐ d. unlikely

4. **confounded**, page 37, column 1, last paragraph
"The trooper stared down at her, confounded,"
☐ a. confused
☐ b. distracted
☐ c. surprised
☐ d. contradicted

5. **subterfuge**, page 37, column 2, paragraph 2
"I prayed inwardly that her valiant subterfuge would not prove to be a prophecy."
☐ a. attempt
☐ b. deception
☐ c. subtlety
☐ d. heroism

SYLLABICATION

Knowing how to reduce words to their syllables aids both reading and spelling. Frequently a long word can be recognized and understood if pronounced by syllables. And in spelling, of course, knowledge of syllables contributes to accuracy.

There are rules or generalizations which we can follow when dividing words. One such rule tells us that when two consonants come between two vowels, the word is divided between the consonants. For example, the word **window** is divided into **win** and **dow** because the two consonants, **n** and **d**, come between the two vowels, **i** and **o**.

In the following sentences divide the words in bold print according to this rule. Write the word on the blank line following each sentence, inserting hyphens between the syllables. The first one has been done for you.

1. I've been wanting to meet his **sister** for some time now.

   _____ *sis-ter* _____

2. The composition course stressed **essay** writing.

   _____

3. He **blundered** badly during the first few days on his new job.

   _____

4. Following the speeches, there will be time for **comment**.

   _____

5. Make every effort to **conduct** the investigation quietly.

   _____

6. It's only natural that we would **differ** in that regard.

   _____

7. With no alternatives, what could you **expect** him to do?

   _____

8. His **fellow** students became discouraged and dropped out.

   _____

9. He had an obligation to **fulfill** to those who had helped him.

   _____

10. Toy autos are propelled by **friction** motors.

    _____

11. The **funny** stories made us laugh.

    _____

12. Her smile attracts like a **magnet**.

    _____

13. **Turkey** is the popular food at Thanksgiving.

    _____

PREVIEWING

Students frequently ask, "What can I do to improve my reading?" Believe it or not, there is a one-word answer to this question: preview.

The single most important technique which you can acquire in any reading course is the habit of previewing.

Most students (and everyone else, too) jump in with the first word and meet the author's words and ideas head-on. This is a poor approach because it is inefficient.

What do athletic coaches do before upcoming games? They scout the opponents. Why? To see how they play and to form a game plan for the team to follow.

To be efficient in reading you must do this same thing—scout the author to see how he writes and to discover the best way to read him.

What do you do before assembling a jig-saw puzzle? You study the picture to see what the puzzle looks like when the pieces are all in the right places.

Do this too in reading: see the whole picture before you begin putting the words and ideas together. See where the author is going, what he plans to do or say, what concepts or examples he uses to present his ideas. If you can discover the author's main point and his arguments supporting it, you can begin to organize and interpret his ideas right from the start—you can read intelligently—and see how everything fits.

Don't read at a disadvantage. Preview first to get the picture. There are no educational guarantees in life but this is as close as you can come to ensuring better reading and comprehension in less time.

Pregame warm-ups improve performance on the field. Preview to improve your performance on the page.

On the following pages you will learn how to preview and the steps to follow when previewing a selection.

COMPREHENSION: For each of the following statements and questions, select the option containing the most complete or most accurate answer.

1. The police were aroused by
(c)
   - a. the marching demonstrators.
   - b. the presence of Farmer.
   - c. the people's reaction.
   - d. the red-faced trooper.

2. Throughout the selection the author skillfully
(i) elicits the reader's
   - a. fear and anxiety.
   - b. approval and satisfaction.
   - c. interest and hope.
   - d. sympathy and anger.

3. James Farmer was being sought by the police
(h) for
   - a. his association with known criminals.
   - b. his involvement with CORE.
   - c. a crime committed in Louisiana.
   - d. his rabble-rousing activities in the town of Plaquemine.

4. The Black citizens of Plaquemine were
(h)
   - a. aggressive.
   - b. victimized.
   - c. cowardly.
   - d. organized.

5. Hope for freedom and dignity motivated
(g) the people to march; actually, they were treated like
   - a. cowards.
   - b. animals.
   - c. traitors.
   - d. oppressors.

6. The beseiged were seriously hampered by the
(c) lack of
   - a. weapons.
   - b. leadership.
   - c. communications.
   - d. refuge.

7. The treatment of the Blacks by the troopers
(h) was
   - a. foolhardy.
   - b. justified.
   - c. vicious.
   - d. legal.

8. Farmer disarmed the man with the gun be-
(h) cause
   - a. he wanted to assert his authority.
   - b. he wanted to "buy time" for himself.
   - c. he feared for the man's safety.
   - d. he feared an increase in the level of violence.

9. "Nervous Nellie's" change from uncommitted
(f) to committed was triggered by her
   - a. status as a taxpayer.
   - b. trust in the law.
   - c. fear of property damage.
   - d. "feelings for humanity."

10. When he considered the possibility of his
(b) death, Farmer thought about
   - a. the angry mob.
   - b. his church and his minister.
   - c. an escape plan.
   - d. his family and the public.

> Comprehension Skills: a—isolating details; b—recalling specific facts; c—retaining concepts; d—organizing facts; e—understanding the main idea; f—drawing a conclusion; g—making a judgment; h—making an inference; i—recognizing tone; j—understanding characters; k—appreciation of literary forms.

SELECTIONS FROM THE BLACK

A Raisin in the Sun

"You just can't force people to change their hearts, son."

Lorraine Hansberry

(Beneatha goes to the door and opens it as Walter and Ruth go on with the clowning. Beneatha is somewhat surprised to see a quiet-looking middle-aged white man in a business suit holding his hat and a briefcase in his hand and consulting a small piece of paper)

Man: Uh—how do you do, miss. I am looking for a Mrs.—*(He looks at the slip of paper)* Mrs. Lena Younger?

Beneatha (Smoothing her hair with slight embarrassment): Oh—yes, that's my mother. Excuse me. *(She closes the door and turns to quiet the other two)* Ruth! Brother! Somebody's here.

(Then she opens the door. The man casts a curious quick glance at all of them) Uh—come in, please.

Man (Coming in): Thank you.

Beneatha: My mother isn't here just now. Is it business?

Man: Yes. . .well, of a sort.

Walter (Freely, the Man of the House): Have a seat. I'm Mrs. Younger's son. I look after most of her business matters.

(Ruth and Beneatha exchange amused glances)

Man (Regarding Walter, and sitting): Well — My name is Karl Lindner. . .

Walter (Stretching out his hand): Walter Younger. This is my wife—*(Ruth nods politely)*—and my sister.

Lindner: How do you do.

Walter (Amiably, as he sits himself easily on a chair, leaning with interest forward on his knees and looking expectantly into the newcomer's face): What can we do for you, Mr. Lindner?

Lindner (Some minor shuffling of the hat and briefcase on his knees): Well—I am a representative of the Clybourne Park Improvement Association—

Walter (Pointing): Why don't you sit your things on the floor?

Lindner: Oh—yes. Thank you. *(He slides the briefcase and hat under the chair)* And as I was saying—I am from the Clybourne Park Improvement Association and we have had it brought to our attention at the last meeting that you people—or at least your mother—has bought a piece of residential property at—*(He digs for the slip of paper again)*—four o six Clybourne Street. . .

Walter: That's right. Care for something to drink? Ruth, get Mr. Lindner a beer.

Lindner (Upset for some reason): Oh—no, really. I mean thank you very much, but no thank you.

Ruth (Innocently): Some coffee?

Lindner: Thank you, nothing at all.
  (Beneatha is watching the man carefully)

Lindner: Well, I don't know how much you folks know about our organization. *(He's a gentle man; thoughtful and somewhat labored in his manner)* It is one of these community organizations set up to look after—oh, you know, things like block upkeep and special projects and we also have what we call our New Neighbors Orientation Committee. . .

Beneatha (Drily): Yes—and what do they do?

Lindner (Turning a little to her and then returning the main force to Walter): Well—it's what you might call a sort of welcoming committee, I guess. I mean they, we, I'm the chairman of the committee—go around and see the new people who move into the neighborhood and sort of give them the lowdown on the way we do things out in Clybourne Park.

Beneatha (With appreciation of the two meanings, which escape Ruth and Walter): Un-huh.

Lindner: And we also have the category of what the association calls—*(He looks elsewhere)*—uh—special community problems. . .

Beneatha: Yes—and what are some of those?

Walter: Girl, let the man talk.

Lindner (With understated relief): Thank you. I would sort of like to explain this thing in my own way. I mean I want to explain to you in a certain way.

Walter: Go ahead.

Lindner: Yes. Well. I'm going to try to get right to the point. I'm sure we'll all appreciate that in the long run.

Beneatha: Yes.

Walter: Be still now!

Lindner: Well—

Ruth (Still innocently): Would you like another chair—you don't look comfortable.

Lindner (More frustrated than annoyed): No, thank you very much. Please. Well—to get right to the point I—*(A great breath, and he is off at last)* I am sure you people must be aware of some of the incidents which have happened in various parts of the city when colored people have moved into certain areas—*(Beneatha exhales heavily and starts tossing a piece of fruit up and down in the air)* Well—because we have what I think is going to be a unique type of organization in American community life—not only do we deplore that kind of thing—but we are trying to do something about it *(Beneatha stops tossing and turns with new and quizzical interest to the man)* We feel— *(gaining confidence in his mission because of the interest in the faces of the people he is talking to)* —we feel that most of the trouble in this world, when you come right down to it— *(He hits his knee for emphasis)* —most of the trouble exists because people just don't sit down and talk to each other.

Ruth (Nodding as she might in church, pleased with the remark): You can say that again, mister.

Lindner (More encouraged by such affirmation): That we don't try hard enough in this world to understand the other fellow's problem. The other guy's point of view.

Ruth: Now that's right.
(Beneatha and Walter merely watch and listen with genuine interest)

Lindner: Yes—that's the way we feel out in Clybourne Park. And that's why I was elected to come here this afternoon and talk to you people. Friendly like, you know, the way people should talk to each other and see if we couldn't find some way to work this thing out. As I say, the whole business is a matter of *caring* about the other fellow. Anybody can see that you are a nice family of folks, hard working and honest I'm sure. *(Beneatha frowns slightly, quizzically, her head tilted regarding him)* Today everybody knows what it means to be on the outside of *something.* And of course, there is always somebody who is out to take the advantage of people who don't always understand.

Walter: What do you mean?

Lindner: Well—you see, our community is made up of people who've worked hard as the dickens for years to build up that little community. They're not rich and fancy people; just hard-working, honest people who don't really have much but those little homes and a dream of the kind of community they want to raise their children in. Now, I don't say we are perfect and there is a lot wrong in some of the things they want. But you've got to admit that a man, right or wrong, has the right to want to have the neighborhood he lives in a certain kind of way. And at the moment the overwhelming majority of our people out there feel that people get along better, take more of a common interest in the life of the community, when they share a common background. I want you to believe me when I tell you that race prejudice simply doesn't enter into it. It is a matter of the people of Clybourne Park believing, rightly or wrongly, as I say, that for the happiness of all concerned that our Negro families are happier when they live in their *own* communities.

Beneatha (With a grand and bitter gesture): This, friends, is the Welcoming Committee!

Walter (Dumfounded, looking at Lindner): Is this what you came marching all the way over here to tell us?

Lindner: Well, now we've been having a fine conversation. I hope you'll hear me all the way through.

Walter (Tightly): Go ahead, man.

Lindner: You see—in the face of all things I have said, we are prepared to make your family a very generous offer. . .

Beneatha: Thirty pieces and not a coin less!

Walter: Yeah?

Lindner (Putting on his glasses and drawing a form out of the briefcase): Our association is prepared, through the collective effort of our people, to buy the house from you at a financial gain to your family.

Ruth: Lord have mercy, ain't this the living gall!

Walter: All right, you through?

Lindner: Well, I want to give you the exact terms of the financial arrangement—

Walter: We don't want to hear no exact terms of no arrangements. I want to know if you got any more to tell us 'bout getting together?

Lindner (Taking off his glasses): Well—I don't suppose that you feel. . .

Walter: Never mind how I feel—you got any more to say 'bout how people ought to sit down and talk to each other? . . . Get out of my house, man.
  (He turns his back and walks to the door)

Lindner (Looking around at the hostile faces and reaching and assembling his hat and briefcase): Well—I don't understand why you people are reacting this way. What do you think you are going to gain by moving into a neighborhood where you just aren't wanted and where some elements—well—people can get awful worked up when they feel that their whole way of life and everything they've ever worked for is threatened.

Walter: Get out.

Lindner (At the door, holding a small card): Well—I'm sorry it went like this.

Walter: Get out.

Lindner (Almost sadly regarding Walter): You just can't force people to change their hearts, son.
  (He turns and puts his card on a table and exits. Walter pushes the door to with stinging hatred, and stands looking at it. Ruth just sits and Beneatha just stands. They say nothing. Mama and Travis enter)

Starting Time: _____   Finishing Time: _____

Reading Time: _____   Reading Rate: _____

Comprehension: _____   Vocabulary: _____

VOCABULARY: The following words have been taken from the selection you have just read. Put an *X* in the box before the best meaning or synonym for the word as used in the selection.

1. **Amiably,** page 41, column 1, line 31
  "(Amiably, as he sits himself easily on a chair,"
  ☐ a. amusedly
  ☐ b. anxiously
  ☐ c. sociably
  ☐ d. rudely

2. **labored,** page 41, column 2, line 18
  "(He's a gentle man; thoughtful and somewhat labored in his manner)"
  ☐ a. unnatural
  ☐ b. plain
  ☐ c. overworked
  ☐ d. antagonistic

3. **deplore,** page 42, column 1, line 24
  "—not only do we deplore that kind of thing—"
  ☐ a. discourage
  ☐ b. regret strongly
  ☐ c. feel deeply
  ☐ d. condemn

4. **quizzical,** page 42, column 1, line 27
  "(Beneatha stops tossing and turns with new and quizzical interest to the man)"
  ☐ a. inquisitive
  ☐ b. puzzled
  ☐ c. comical
  ☐ d. fanciful

5. **Dumfounded,** page 42, column 2, line 32
  "(Dumfounded, looking at Lindner)"
  ☐ a. irritated
  ☐ b. infuriated
  ☐ c. embarrassed
  ☐ d. amazed

SUFFIXES

Many English words consist of a base or root word to which prefixes (beginnings) and suffixes (endings) have been added. To the root word **agree** (a verb) we can add both a prefix and a suffix to get **disagreeable** (an adjective) which has an opposite meaning.

A suffix is added to the end of a word and changes the part of speech of that word. We have just seen how the suffix **able** changes **agree** from a verb to an adjective.

Two Suffixes

1. **-less** (without) is an Old English adjective suffix. The noun **motion** becomes an adjective, **motionless**.

2. **-ship** is an Old English noun suffix. It can be added to words which are already nouns, like **companion**, and the new word, **companionship**, is still a noun.

In the following sentences, root words have been set in bold print. Add one of these suffixes to each root and write the new word on the line following the sentence. As you add suffixes to words, you may have to drop or change letters.

1. **Sleep** nights left him weak and inactive.

   _____

2. The hall rang out with sounds of **fellow**.

   _____

3. **Care** work like this is unacceptable.

   _____

4. His **leader** qualities can be developed and used to advantage.

   _____

5. He was **mind** of danger as he rushed headlong into the fight.

   _____

6. If you value our **friend**, don't let me down.

   _____

7. His surprise at the testimonial dinner, given in his honor, left him **speech**.

   _____

8. Failure to attend meetings will result in loss of **member**.

   _____

9. The shattered gem was **value**.

   _____

10. The **workman** of these vases is of the highest quality.

    _____

HOW TO PREVIEW, I

Previewing is known by many names. It is called surveying and prereading too.

1. Read the Title. You would do this anyway before reading a selection, but in previewing we want you to be aware of what you can *learn* from the title. Not only can you learn the author's subject, you can also frequently learn how he *feels* toward his subject. Lester David once wrote an article entitled *The Natural Inferiority of Women.* From the title you can tell the author's feeling on the subject, and you would expect to find in the article arguments supporting his position and illustrations demonstrating his case. With just this little bit of information, the reader can approach this selection intelligently, knowing what to expect.

Another article by Mark Clifton was entitled *The Dread Tomato Addiction.* You would expect to find humor or satire in the author's account.

Headlines and titles are considered quite influential by authors and editors. Many magazines survive on the appeal or shock value of the titles of their articles.

2. Read the Subhead. In textbooks especially, and in many popular magazines as well, subheads are used following the title to give the reader even more information on the subject. In textbooks this is frequently a one-line digest of the chapter—"Here's what we are going to cover." In magazines teaser-type statements follow the title to further spark the reader's curiosity. Look for a subhead when previewing.

3. Read the Illustration. If a picture or illustration accompanies the article, don't just look at it, *read* it. Interpret it to learn what you can about the content of the article. The Chinese have said that a picture is worth ten thousand words. Good illustrations are much more than pretty pictures. See what you can learn visually before reading.

SELECTIONS FROM THE BLACK

COMPREHENSION: For each of the following statements and questions, select the option containing the most complete or most accurate answer.

1. Karl Lindner is portrayed as
(j)
   - ☐ a. crude but honest.
   - ☐ b. a thinly-disguised snob.
   - ☐ c. shameless and thoughtless.
   - ☐ d. a gentle and troubled man.

2. Beneatha's suspicions are aroused when
(f)
   - ☐ a. she opens the door.
   - ☐ b. Lindner refuses all offers of hospitality.
   - ☐ c. mention is made of the neighborhood council.
   - ☐ d. Lindner leaves his calling card.

3. Walter tries to give the impression that he is
(j)
   - ☐ a. a shrewd businessman.
   - ☐ b. biding his time.
   - ☐ c. interested in a better offer.
   - ☐ d. unaware of Lindner's purpose.

4. For the Younger family, the expression "Welcoming Committee" is
(i)
   - ☐ a. exaggerated.
   - ☐ b. appropriate.
   - ☐ c. ironic.
   - ☐ d. inconsiderate.

5. The residents of Clybourne Park are
(h)
   - ☐ a. considerate.
   - ☐ b. hospitable.
   - ☐ c. generous.
   - ☐ d. conservative.

6. The theme of this scene is best expressed by which of the following?
(e)
   - ☐ a. "... the whole business is a matter of *caring* about the other fellow."
   - ☐ b. "... Negro families are happier when they live in their *own* communities."
   - ☐ c. "Thirty pieces and not a coin less!"
   - ☐ d. "You just can't force people to change their hearts, son."

7. "Thirty pieces and not a coin less!" is an allusion to
(h)
   - ☐ a. the title of a Broadway musical.
   - ☐ b. the betrayal of Christ by Judas.
   - ☐ c. a private family joke.
   - ☐ d. the price paid to the Indians for Manhattan.

8. Walter refuses to sell the Clybourne property at a profit because
(j)
   - ☐ a. he is stubborn.
   - ☐ b. he lacks business sense.
   - ☐ c. he is pressured by his family.
   - ☐ d. he is a man of principle.

9. "You just can't force people to change their hearts, son," reveals
(h)
   - ☐ a. Lindner's true feelings.
   - ☐ b. the stubbornness of the Younger family.
   - ☐ c. the emotional basis of white racism.
   - ☐ d. Walter's true feelings.

10. Two races are represented in this scene. One is portrayed as straightforward; the other as
(g)
   - ☐ a. dignified.
   - ☐ b. insinuating.
   - ☐ c. reserved.
   - ☐ d. hesitant.

> Comprehension Skills: a—isolating details; b—recalling specific facts; c—retaining concepts; d—organizing facts; e—understanding the main idea; f—drawing a conclusion; g—making a judgment; h—making an inference; i—recognizing tone; j—understanding characters; k—appreciation of literary forms.

Letters to a Black Boy

N.B.C. Newscaster Teague Addresses His Infant Son, Adam, in Language Common to Fathers Everywhere

Robert L. Teague

Dear Adam,

Having explained that your daddy is not in the front lines of the Black Revolution, I think a word may be in order about the private little wars I fight with Mister Charlie every day. Today I fought a major battle. The weapon of the enemies was familiar, but extremely powerful in this terrain—the office where I work. Ah, but they reckoned without your daddy's derring-do.

Without explanation I was summoned to the fifty-second floor. That's where the power structure of my company holds its councils of war. Never before had I reconnoitered that sanctified stronghold.

When I arrived, still wondering what kind of operation this might be, I found a dozen Mister Charlies waiting in ambush. More than that, they were clearly ready to annihilate the self I think I am; they were smiling.

The battle was joined with handshakes all around. There wasn't a man in the trenches, including your daddy, earning less than forty thousand dollars a year. We were not quite equals, however.

Then they told me. I had been chosen—I supposed by a vote—to represent our company at a job-opportunity conference in Jersey City. There was a lot of unrest over there, they said in a stuttering, roundabout way.

"Our company is very pleased to be participating in a conference like this," one of my adversaries said. "We think there should be more conferences like this in a lot of places where they are needed. Now. Where do you fit in? Well, you'll be stationed at a booth with visual exhibits and equipment that show what our company is all about. There'll be a lot of young fellows circulating among the various booths set up by a dozen corporations. A lot of young fellows from the minority groups, I might add. They'll be coming around to ask questions that you should have no trouble answering."

There was a long, embarrassing cease-fire. One dozen Charlies were waiting for my response. I couldn't help the silence; I was too choked with rage to talk.

Finally, I felt controlled enough to try a probing counterattack. Without four-letter words.

"Well, gentlemen," I said slowly, carefully, but a bit too fiercely. "If you're *telling* me I have to go to this job-opportunity conference, I'll go. Frankly, I need this job I've got. But if you're *asking* me about going, then I say I want nothing to do with it."

There was another ominous silence over the foxholes. I looked at my bosses around the perimeter. Twelve good men and true. Their smiles had been replaced by reddening masks of astonishment. There was nothing about this situation in the field manual.

As for me—I was just plain angry and scared. They could wipe me out right there.

Dimly, in some barely accessible region of my mind, I realized that I should have softened my answer. Not my position, but my answer. I should have given them some indication of my deep involvement with my job in their company, my sense of allegiance and belonging, my appreciation for their giving me a rare opportunity for self-expression and self-fulfillment. It was also true that since joining the company, I had never had a feeling—until that job-conference summons—that I was being misused or exploited in any way. Not for a moment.

These men had met me on my own terms. I had not been hired to be a Negro reporter. As a matter of fact, I had been hired before they knew the color of my skin. One of them had admired some of my by-line writing in *The New York Times,* and called to offer me a job as a radio news writer. Furthermore, once I accepted the job, they treated me no differently from white writers hired about the same time.

All of us fledglings had been dumped into "the pool." Which meant writing half a dozen news scripts a day, or night, for other people to read on the air. It was the lowest rung in the business. We were told, in effect, that with luck, hard work, devotion to duty and to deadlines, we could work our way up to writing for television. After that, they said, with more luck, et cetera, we might work our way up to street reporter for radio or TV. And after that, with more et cetera, we might wind up

SELECTIONS FROM THE BLACK

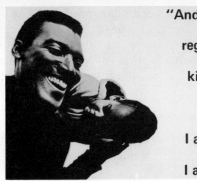

"And I resent being regarded as some kind of freak all of a sudden. I am not a freak. I am a man."

Bob Teague was so popular as a football player at the University of Wisconsin that when he returned to his native Milwaukee he was urged to run for the City Council. He chose journalism instead, going from *The Milwaukee Journal* to *The New York Times* and then into television broadcasting. He lives in New York with his wife, Matt Turney, who is a star performer with the Martha Graham Dance Company, and their son, Adam Fitz-James Teague.

With warmth, with humor, with pride, with a human touch that transcends all differences of race and belief, Bob Teague, whose nightly news broadcasts on N.B.C. are seen by over two million, addresses his infant son, Adam Fitz-James Teague, in language common to all fathers everywhere. The Adam-Smasher, as he is known in the Teague household, was ten months old when this book was begun for him. He is now two. It will be a few years before he can read these letters. In the meantime, they are for all black boys and white boys and their fathers and, yes, their mothers.

as broadcasters! Hallelujah! With maybe a five-minute news show of our own.

They had seemed to be in no hurry at all to advance me or anyone else in the pool. Which was frustrating at times. But I did have the feeling that my black skin, a handicap most of my life, might now work to my advantage. It would be poetic justice.

That is not how it worked out.

It took me the better part of a year to make the grade in radio writing, and advance to writing for television. There was a great deal I had to learn about editing film and video tape, mixing sound, mixing film and tape, interlocking film with separate sound tracks, projecting two reels of films at the same time, and much more. I learned by asking questions about the things I didn't understand. And by reading books about film and video tape and what makes television work.

Even with concentrated effort, however, it took about a year and a half to qualify as a full-time street reporter. Now I had to learn how to direct the shooting of film at the scene of news events, how to compete with other bird dogs in the street in mass interviews, and much more.

After two years and nine months, I got a nightly fifteen-minute newscast, having filled in occasionally on five-minute TV news shows beforehand. Now I had to learn how to speak all over again. That meant elocution lessons, breathing exercises, memory exercises and, again, much more. It was hard work. The hardest phase perhaps was learning to put together a compact yet comprehensive, understandable and entertaining news package. And supervising writers, production assistants, film editors and video-tape editors working with me.

Then, after four and a half years with the company, I was promoted to half-hour newscasts. The hard work continued, and I found still more to learn.

In all that climb, I was never anything less than a general-assignment working stiff, never anything less than my colleagues. I was not fenced in or fenced out of news assignments, whether the subject was politics, murder, civil rights, disaster or beauty queens. When any assignment came up, if I was the man on deck, I covered it.

And there were times when I had reason to bitch and swear like everyone else about our common grievances—long periods of ridiculous nighttime hours, extra shifts on what was supposed to be a day off, and working with borrowed equipment in the office. It took me four and a half years to get a desk and a typewriter of my own.

All of this, disappointments as well as triumphs, had given me a sense of belonging. Also, a sense of having achieved a measure of fame and fortune on merit, not through somebody's charity. The money was damned good, too. And I was proud in the knowledge that my regular nightly appearances on the screen—talking about anything and everything—served to reinforce in literally millions of black people a belief that all black people harbor deep down: Anything they can do, we can do as well—if only they'll give us the same chance.

But all that is what I *should* have told that formidable array of company executives in refusing to go to Jersey City. During our tense confrontation, I suppose, none of those sentiments could break through my wall of resentment.

As the silence deepened in the room, I realized that it was too late now to retreat. I had told them flatly that I wanted no part of their so-called job-opportunity conference. And since retreat was out of the question, your daddy charged again.

"Furthermore," I said quietly, resigned to the worst, "I resent the whole idea right down to my toes. In the first place, I don't have any jobs to give. It seems to me that the people who do the hiring for this company are the ones to go. That's the only way to convince minorities that you mean business. Not just playing another game. It doesn't mean a thing to send a black example.

"And I resent being regarded as some kind of freak all of a sudden. To be trotted out on exhibit when it suits somebody else's purposes. I am not a freak. I am a man. I am a full-time employee of this company, and I'm doing a competent job. If I'm not, I should be fired."

Well, they didn't fire your daddy; and I have the feeling that nothing further will be said about my going to Jersey City or anywhere else. Except on regular news assignments.

As it always happens in your daddy's little combats, the world hasn't been changed. But I like to think that there are twelve more Charlies in the world who are beginning to understand this: Equal opportunity has nothing to do with conferences. What it's about is simply filling a job with the first capable man who comes along.

Starting Time: _____	Finishing Time: _____
Reading Time: _____	Reading Rate: _____
Comprehension: _____	Vocabulary: _____

VOCABULARY: The following words have been taken from the selection you have just read. Put an X in the box before the best meaning or synonym for the word as used in the selection.

1. **terrain**, page 46, column 1, paragraph 1
"...but extremely powerful in this terrain—"
□ a. weather
□ b. building
□ c. territory
□ d. situation

2. **reconnoitered**, page 46, column 1, paragraph 2
"Never before had I reconnoitered that sanctified stronghold."
□ a. entered
□ b. spied on
□ c. looked for
□ d. recognized

3. **probing**, page 46, column 2, paragraph 1
"...I felt controlled enough to try a probing counterattack."
□ a. probable
□ b. exploratory
□ c. measured
□ d. prodding

4. **ominous**, page 46, column 2, paragraph 3
"There was another ominous silence over the foxholes."
□ a. omnivorous
□ b. total
□ c. enormous
□ d. threatening

5. **formidable**, page 47, column 2, paragraph 6
"But all that is what I *should* have told that formidable array..."
□ a. exceptional
□ b. impressive
□ c. dangerous
□ d. informative

SELECTIONS FROM THE BLACK

Studies of good readers show that they are aware of the context of what they are reading. This means that they are anticipating what is coming next by what has gone before.

The many ways in which context functions to help the reader understand words are called contextual aids.

Contextual Aid 5. Words can be understood when they are compared or contrasted with known words. Similarly an unknown word in a phrase or clause can be understood when compared or contrasted with a word in another phrase or clause.

In the expression, **a question of life or _____** , the reader can easily fill in the correct word, **death**, the word in contrast to **life**.

In the following sentences, examples of this type of contextual aid have been used to compare with and contrast to nonsense words. Underline the nonsense word and write the correct word on the line following each sentence.

1. When she sees this, will she be happy or drill?

   _____

2. While most car thieves are amateurs, some are manderers.

   _____

3. It's true that some wear civilian clothes, but most wear dums.

   _____

4. If peace is not sought, then cern is inevitable.

   _____

5. For ceremonies the vessels should be gold or blumal.

   _____

6. Jobs which used to be done by hand are now done by riggess.

   _____

7. He was found guilty though he swore he was complesor.

   _____

8. One man sang while his partner dramced.

   _____

9. The difference is as obvious as night and yelp.

   _____

10. While most people today live in the city, some still live in the wasberg.

    _____

11. Check the clothes on the line to see if they are wet or glap.

    _____

We have seen how previewing is necessary for intelligent reading. The first three steps to previewing are 1) Read the Title, 2) Read the Subhead, and 3) Read the Illustration. Here are the last three steps:

4. Read the Opening Paragraph. The first paragraph is the author's opening, his first opportunity to address the reader. This paragraph is also called the introductory paragraph because it is precisely that—an introduction to the article or chapter. Opening paragraphs are used in different ways. Some authors announce what they plan to do in the following paragraphs. Other authors tell us why they are writing this article or chapter or why this is important for us to learn. Still other authors will do what speakers do—start with a story or anecdote to set the stage. This provides the setting or mood they need to present their material.

5. Read the Closing Paragraph. The next step in previewing: go to the end and read the last paragraph. This is the author's last chance to address the reader. If he has any closing remarks or final thoughts, here's where they'll come. If the author wishes to reemphasize or restate his principal thoughts or arguments, he'll do it here. Because this is the concluding paragraph, you'll find here the concluding or summarizing thoughts. This is where you'll see what the writer considers important—in his closing paragraph.

6. Skim Through. Finally, before completing your preview, skim quickly through the article or chapter to see what else you can learn. Be on the watch for headings and numbers, indicating important divisions in the author's presentation. You may learn that this material is divided into four or five major aspects, which will be helpful to know when reading.

COMPREHENSION: For each of the following statements and questions, select the option containing the most complete or most accurate answer.

1. The tone of Mr. Teague's letter to his son is
(i)
   - ☐ a. explanatory.
   - ☐ b. apologetic.
   - ☐ c. racist.
   - ☐ d. defeatist.

2. The author's behavior illustrates which of the
(g) following?
   - ☐ a. Charlie's hypocrisy must be unmasked.
   - ☐ b. Charlie favors whites over Blacks.
   - ☐ c. Violence is the only reaction Charlie understands.
   - ☐ d. Charlie must be forced into a defensive position.

3. Mr. Teague is
(j)
   - ☐ a. daring.
   - ☐ b. arrogant.
   - ☐ c. manly.
   - ☐ d. ungrateful.

4. The power structure on the fifty-second floor
(e) represents which of the following attitudes?
   - ☐ a. There are daggers in men's smiles.
   - ☐ b. The poor are the responsibility of the rich.
   - ☐ c. Sophistication and good breeding are always appreciated.
   - ☐ d. Duplicity lurks behind the mask of civility.

5. It might be inferred that Mr. Teague never
(h) wants his son to think of him as having been
   - ☐ a. overlooked.
   - ☐ b. violent.
   - ☐ c. exploited.
   - ☐ d. cheated.

6. The company Adam's father works for is
(f)
   - ☐ a. the largest in its field.
   - ☐ b. eager to hire minority talent.
   - ☐ c. unfair to its Black employees.
   - ☐ d. an equal opportunity employer.

7. A Black reporter or news commentator should
(c) be assigned to stories dealing with
   - ☐ a. Blacks.
   - ☐ b. anything.
   - ☐ c. whites.
   - ☐ d. riots.

8. Successful Black professionals should be
(c)
   - ☐ a. supervised and controlled.
   - ☐ b. taken for granted.
   - ☐ c. exhibited to the public.
   - ☐ d. preferred to whites.

9. After astonishing his bosses with his unex-
(k) pected reply, the author uses which of the following techniques?
   - ☐ a. Flashback
   - ☐ b. Rhetorical question
   - ☐ c. Euphemism
   - ☐ d. Tongue-in-cheek

10. More than anything else, the author's stand on
(c) the Jersey City conference
   - ☐ a. embarrassed his employers.
   - ☐ b. delayed minority progress.
   - ☐ c. increased his self-respect.
   - ☐ d. earned him a promotion.

Comprehension Skills: a—isolating details; b—recalling specific facts; c—retaining concepts; d—organizing facts; e—understanding the main idea; f—drawing a conclusion; g—making a judgment; h—making an inference; i—recognizing tone; j—understanding characters; k—appreciation of literary forms.

Funeral of a Whale

Tradition binds us to the sea and the whale is king of the elements there.

J. Benibengor Blay

There is great excitement in the ancient town of Missibi in Ghana.

The previous night had been wet and stormy and one which the fishermen were not likely to forget. Caught in the storm, their canoes had been dashed to pieces on the rocks and their nets swept away on the swift current. Only the fact that they were all strong swimmers had saved the men from drowning.

The sun is not yet up when they collect again on the shore to watch for their nets. The moon is still shining and little waves dance merrily on the strand, while the sea crabs scuttle among the scattered shells. But these things do not interest the fishermen, and even the search for nets is forgotten as they catch sight of a huge object, surrounded by a shoal of fish, tossing on the rolling sea. Their slow, questing advance is halted as a nauseating stench greets them. Fingers to their noses, they crane and peer. It is a whale—and judging by the smell, it has been dead for some days.

Now, such a sight is no mere spectacle to the people of Missibi. As descendants of a strong and virile race which long ago came by sea in great barge-like ships to settle in these parts, they hold to the tradition that the sea is their home and they worship it to this day. In any crisis—whatever its nature, whether drought or famine or war—they call upon the sea for help. The whale is the king of their sea. And it has been the custom, throughout their long history, to accord a ceremonial funeral to any whale that comes rolling ashore dead.

So, bound by tradition, the fishermen must bear the unhappy tidings to the ruler of the town. Their waists girdled with palm leaves and fingers to lips as signs that their news is urgent, and as yet secret, they go on their errand.

The chief's advisers are called together by the court messenger for a palaver. Now the fishermen are permitted to tell their news. Only after the chief's bodyguards have visited the beach to confirm this statement may the townsfolk be told. It is now past eight o'clock in the morning. The state drums boom out the warning of great calamity. The people from the busy market place, the farmers, coconut breakers and rice growers who have risen at cockcrow and gone to the farms, all come trooping to the palace yard, agog with excitement.

The chief comes to the courtyard with his advisers and sits on the landing of the dais. His face betokens sadness. His attendants bow and leave the palace. The drums are still booming. Outside are packed lorries and cars from up country bringing loads of hawkers and buyers to the market while the occupants move in with the still surging crowd.

The court messenger comes into the yard, bows to the chief and courtiers, commands silence and after giving a brief survey of the history of Missibi and her connection with the sea, makes his announcement to the assembled throng.

"The State is in mourning. A whale is dead and has been washed ashore. The funeral will be held at two o'clock at Aposika where the king of the sea now lies."

There is no whisper nor laughter nor cough as the great crowd moves from distant parts, out of the palace. The market day is postponed. The school bell's tolling stopped. All is sad silence. Yet it is a great day for the hawkers from distant parts, for now they will see something of which so far they have only heard. To the aged of the town it is history repeating itself, and the announcement seems to bring back pictures of half-forgotten times.

By order of a committee appointed by the chief's advisers, funeral preparations are put in hand at once. Cases of gin, beer, kola and palm wine are brought from the stores and cellars. A body of young men is engaged in the erection of bamboo huts, and the bush around the area is cleared, while musicians polish their instruments in readiness. Word is passed to neighboring places and more people arrive to swell the numbers.

At two o'clock the procession leaves for the scene of the funeral, guns booming, state guns rumbling, ivory horn blaring. The chief and his counselors are dressed in red. The womenfolk, besmeared with red clay and wearing pieces of red calico tied around their hair, are in front with the children. The men bring up the rear.

J. Benibengor Blay, Deputy Minister of Education and Minister of Arts and Culture in the Government of the First Republic of Ghana, has traveled extensively in Europe and America.

His short stories and poetry are popular in Ghana and other West African countries as well. He has written twenty-six books and pamphlets and numerous radio scripts and newspaper articles.

The tail of the column is as yet only at the outskirts of the town when its head reaches the place where a little off the beach, lies the great shapeless mass of the whale. Gallons of disinfectant have already been sprinkled around to kill the smell.

Now the chief's messenger calls for silence and orders the crowd to be seated. The chief steps forward followed by his advisers. Dropping the red cloth from his shoulder and gathering the folds in his left arm, with a glass of rum held in his right hand, he first raises his eyes to heaven then looks to the ground as he pours out a libation with these words: "Tradition binds us to the sea and the whale is king of the elements there. My people and I pay you homage and lament your death. How it happened we do not know. Whether it was in combat with your fellow kings, or whether it was inflicted by those who delight in making sport of you, or whether it was a natural death, we are afflicted all the same with a great sense of personal loss. We reaffirm our traditional ties with your descendants, will look to them in anxious days for help, and beg of you, who now belong to the ages, to release this land from starvation and sickness; leave in their place health and plenty. Rest in peace."

The funeral ceremony being declared open, the women like minstrels tell the story of the whale in parables; its connection with the state is recounted and the dead one praised. The chief and his advisers are head mourners and make themselves responsible for the fair distribution of drinks, providing food for those who have come from afar and recording donations received.

The young men keep order and play native instruments, while the old correct any departure from the traditional funeral procedure. Boys and girls play "Hunt the Slipper" and "Ampay." Hunters fire off guns and firecrackers at intervals in honor of the majesty of the dead. Fishermen fish in the waves and cast their nets on the beach; farmers sow their seeds on the strand, fetish priests play tom-toms and perform their feats of walking barefoot on broken bottles and gashing their stomachs with sharp knives. Everybody, in fact, is doing something. And all the men are partly or completely drunk.

As the celebration continues, weeping becomes the order of the day; there is competition among the womenfolk in pitch, tone and rendering of phrases, and prizes are offered to those who maintain the high standard of wailing set by their ancestors.

Further away from the crowds a great number of seagulls gather. Some are twittering, others are flying around the whale. The tide begins to rise and the waves are swelling high. Deep clouds overshadow the clear blue sky, and for a while the heavens are pouring rain. It seems that nature, too, is paying tribute to the king of the sea.

At six o'clock, as the sun is setting behind the clouds, the celebrations reach their climax—the solemn spreading of a long white sheet over the whale. Now each mourner takes a pebble, a shell, a stick, a coin or anything handy and, whispering a few words, whirls it around his head and throws it in the direction of the whale. Then without a further glance, all return to town.

The funeral of the king of the sea is over.

Starting Time: _____   Finishing Time: _____

Reading Time: _____   Reading Rate: _____

Comprehension: _____   Vocabulary: _____

"Funeral of a Whale" by J. Benibengor Blay. From *An African Treasury* edited by Langston Hughes. Reprinted by permission of J. Benibengor Blay.

SELECTIONS FROM THE BLACK

Photo: Dell Padgett

VOCABULARY: The following words have been taken from the selection you have just read. Put an *X* in the box before the best meaning or synonym for the word as used in the selection.

1. **strand**, page 51, column 1, paragraph 3
   "...little waves dance merrily on the strand,"
   ☐ a. strait
   ☐ b. shore
   ☐ c. rocks
   ☐ d. ocean

2. **questing**, page 51, column 1, paragraph 3
   "Their slow, questing advance is halted..."
   ☐ a. steady
   ☐ b. pursuing
   ☐ c. questionable
   ☐ d. searching

3. **crane**, page 51, column 1, paragraph 3
   "...they crane and peer."
   ☐ a. lower one's body
   ☐ b. recoil
   ☐ c. hesitate
   ☐ d. stretch one's neck

4. **accord**, page 51, column 1, paragraph 4
   "And it has been the custom, throughout their long history, to accord a ceremonial funeral..."
   ☐ a. bestow
   ☐ b. adapt
   ☐ c. accost
   ☐ d. inflict

5. **libation**, page 52, column 1, paragraph 2
   "...looks to the ground as he pours out a libation with these words:"
   ☐ a. purification
   ☐ b. liquid
   ☐ c. drink
   ☐ d. offering

ROOTS

Many English words consist of a base or root word to which prefixes (beginnings) and suffixes (endings) have been added. To the root word **agree** (a verb) we can add both a prefix and a suffix to get **disagreeable** (an adjective) which has an opposite meaning.

Roots are Latin and Greek stems on which our English words are based. For example, **bio** (life) is a Greek root on which our word **biology** (the study of plant and animal life) is built.

Two Roots

1. **clud, clus** are variants of the Latin root for **close** or **shut**. When a meeting has been **concluded**, it is closed.

2. **frag, fract** are variants of the Latin root which means **break**. A **fractured** arm is broken.

In the following sentences, roots have been left out. Space has been left indicating where the root belongs. Add one of these two roots and write your word on the line following the sentence.

1. He stepped on a —**ment** from the shattered vase.

   _____

2. An **in**—**ive** agreement takes everything into consideration.

   _____

3. Don't drop that; it's —**ile**.

   _____

4. In mathematics, —**ions** are less than whole numbers.

   _____

5. An **ex**—**ive** club shuts out many from membership.

   _____

6. A —**mentation** bomb explodes into many pieces.

   _____

7. A **se**—**ed** meeting place is private, shut off from outsiders.

   _____

8. **Con**—**ive** evidence settles the matter; it shuts out all doubt.

   _____

9. **In**—**ed** with the letter is the five dollars I owe you.

   _____

10. He was arrested for an **in**—**ion** of the law.

    _____

11. —**mentary** evidence consists of bits and pieces.

    _____

QUESTION THE AUTHOR

You've probably heard it said that you'll never learn if you don't ask questions.

Why is an inquisitiveness associated with learning? We speak of the student seeking knowledge, or of the inquiring mind, and both of these concepts imply asking or questioning.

This is because learning is not a passive process; it is something we do. Learning is an activity—it requires us to go after it, seek it out. This is why we say that questioning is part of learning.

A technique good students use is to question the author. We question following previewing by asking, "What can I expect to learn from this chapter or article? Based on my prereading what are some of the things to be covered or presented? What will the author tell me about this subject?" Questions like these "frame" the subject for us, give us an outline to fill in when reading.

Another thing we hope to discover from questioning is the author's method of presentation. There are many different methods the author can use in presenting his material. He may ask questions and answer them, adopting this technique to make his subject easier to learn. He may give details, or describe and illustrate, or he may use comparison and contrast. Whatever his method, discover it and put it to use when studying.

In many books the questions are already there waiting to be used. Check your textbooks. Are there questions following the chapters? If so, use them during previewing to instill the inquisitiveness so necessary to learning. These are special questions—these tell us what the author considers important in each chapter, what he really expects us to learn.

Develop the technique of questioning. Try whenever you study to create questions you expect to find answered.

SELECTIONS FROM THE BLACK

COMPREHENSION: For each of the following statements and questions, select the option containing the most complete or most accurate answer.

1. The excitement in the ancient town of Missibi
(d) was connected with

   □ a. the rescue.
   □ b. the whale.
   □ c. the competition.
   □ d. the market day.

2. The people of Missibi traced their ancestry to
(c)
   □ a. Egyptians.
   □ b. whales.
   □ c. Vikings.
   □ d. seafarers.

3. The whale is to the sea as
(g)
   □ a. royalty is to a kingdom.
   □ b. good fortune is to prosperity.
   □ c. fish is to water.
   □ d. size is to power.

4. The Missibians seem fond of
(h)
   □ a. sport and barter.
   □ b. surprises and adventure.
   □ c. market days and funerals.
   □ d. ceremony and symbolism.

5. The serious and detailed preparations for the
(g) unusual funeral may seem, to an outsider,

   □ a. degrading.
   □ b. outrageous.
   □ c. bizarre.
   □ d. hilarious.

6. The color red symbolizes
(h)
   □ a. authority.
   □ b. mourning.
   □ c. festivity.
   □ d. jealousy.

7. The funeral ceremony helps to dramatize the
(h) townspeople's

   □ a. promising future.
   □ b. extreme poverty.
   □ c. rich heritage.
   □ d. great sorrow.

8. The character of the individual contributions
(c) the townspeople made to the ceremonies was

   □ a. personal.
   □ b. monetary.
   □ c. religious.
   □ d. extraordinary.

9. The selection deals with
(e)
   □ a. current events.
   □ b. recorded history.
   □ c. primitive folklore.
   □ d. ancient superstition.

10. The people and the officials of Missibi are
(j)
   □ a. crude and common.
   □ b. pious and hospitable.
   □ c. open and natural.
   □ d. clever and calculating.

Comprehension Skills: a—isolating details; b—recalling specific facts; c—retaining concepts; d—organizing facts; e—understanding the main idea; f—drawing a conclusion; g—making a judgment; h—making an inference; i—recognizing tone; j—understanding characters; k—appreciation of literary forms.

The Interesting Narrative of the Life of

An Eleven-Year-Old African Boy, Sold into Slavery, Describes His Voyage to America

Gustavus Vassa

The first object which saluted my eyes when I arrived on the coast was the sea, and a slave ship, which was then riding at anchor, and waiting for its cargo. These filled me with astonishment, which was soon connected with terror, when I was carried on board. I was immediately handled, and tossed up to see if I were sound, by some of the crew; and I was now persuaded that I had gotten into a world of bad spirits, and that they were going to kill me. Their complexions too differing so much from ours, their long hair, and the language they spoke (which was very different from any I had ever heard), united to confirm me in this belief.

Indeed, such were the horrors of my views and fears at the moment, that, if ten thousand worlds had been my own, I would have freely parted with them all to have exchanged my condition with that of the meanest slave in my own country. When I looked round the ship too and saw a large furnace of copper boiling, and a multitude of black people of every description chained together, every one of their countenances expressing dejection and sorrow, I no longer doubted of my fate; and, quite overpowered with horror and anguish, I fell motionless on the deck and fainted.

When I recovered a little, I found some black people about me, whom I believed were some of those who had brought me on board, and had been receiving their pay; they talked to me in order to cheer me, but all in vain. I asked them if I were not to be eaten by those white men with horrible looks, red faces, and long hair. They told me I was not; and one of the crew brought me a small portion of spirituous liquor in a wine glass; but being afraid of him, I would not take it out of his hand. One of the blacks therefore took it from him and gave it to me, and I took a little down my palate, which, instead of reviving me, as I thought it would, threw me into the greatest consternation at the strange feeling it produced, having never tasted any such liquor before.

Soon after this, the blacks who brought me on board went off, and left me abandoned to despair. I now saw myself deprived of all chance of returning to my native country, or even the least glimpse of hope of gaining the shore, which I now considered as friendly; and I even wished for my former slavery in preference to my present situation, which was filled with horrors of every kind, still heightened by my ignorance of what I was to undergo.

I was not long suffered to indulge my grief; I was soon put down under the decks, and there I received such a salutation in my nostrils as I had never experienced in my life: so that with the loathsomeness of the stench and crying together, I became so sick and low that I was not able to eat, nor had I the least desire to taste anything.

I now wished for the last friend, death, to relieve me; but soon, to my grief, two of the white men offered me eatables; and, on my refusing to eat, one of them held me fast by the hands, and laid me across, I think, the windlass, and tied my feet, while the other flogged me severely.

I had never experienced anything of this kind before; and although, not being used to the water, I naturally feared that element the first time I saw it, yet nevertheless, could I have got over the nettings, I would have jumped over the side, but I could not; and, besides, the crew used to watch us very closely who were not chained down to the decks, lest we should leap into the water: and I have seen some of these poor African prisoners most severely cut for attempting to do so, and hourly whipped for not eating. This indeed was often the case with myself.

In a little time after, amongst the poor chained men, I found some of my own nation, which in a small degree gave ease to my mind. I inquired of these what was to be done with us. They gave me to understand we were to be carried to these white people's country to work for them. I then was a little revived, and thought, if it were no worse than working, my situation was not so desperate.

But still I feared I should be put to death, the white people looked and acted, as I thought, in so savage a manner; for I had never seen among any people such instances of brutal cruelty; and this not only shown towards us blacks, but also to some of the whites themselves.

One white man in particular I saw, when we were permitted on deck, flogged so unmercifully with a large rope near the foremast, that he died in consequence of it; and they have tossed him over the side as they would have done a brute. This made me fear these people the more; and I expected nothing less than to be treated in the same manner.

I could not help expressing my fears and apprehensions to some of my countrymen: I asked them if these people had no country, but lived in this hollow place (the ship). They told me they did not, but came from a distant one.

"Then," said I, "how comes it in all our country we 'never heard of them!' " They told me because they lived so very far off. I then asked where were their women. Had they any like themselves? I was told they had: "And why," said I, "do we not see them?" They answered, because they were left behind.

I asked how the vessel could go? They told me they could not tell; but that there were cloth put upon the masts by the help of the ropes I saw, and then the vessel went on; and the white men had some spell or magic they put in the water when they liked in order to stop the vessel. I was exceedingly amazed at this account, and really thought they were spirits. I therefore wished much to be from amongst them, for I expected they would sacrifice me: but my wishes were in vain; for we were so quartered that it was impossible for any of us to make our escape.

While we stayed on the coast I was mostly on deck; and one day, to my great astonishment, I saw one of these vessels coming in with the sails up. As soon as the whites saw it, they gave a great shout, at which we were amazed; and the more so as the vessel appeared larger by approaching nearer. At last she came to an anchor in my sight, and when the anchor was let go I and my countrymen who saw it were lost in astonishment to observe the vessel stop; and were now convinced it was done by magic.

Soon after this the other ship got her boats out, and they came on board of us, and the people of both ships seemed very glad to see each other. Several of the strangers also shook hands with us, black people, and made motions with their hands, signifying I suppose, we were to go to their country; but we did not understand them.

At last, when the ship we were in had got in all her cargo, they made ready with many fearful noises, and we were all put under deck, so that we could not see how they managed the vessel.

But this disappointment was the least of my sorrow. The stench of the hold while we were on the coast was so intolerably loathsome that it was dangerous to remain there for any time, and some of us had been permitted to stay on the deck for the fresh air; but now that the whole ship's cargo were confined together, it became absolutely pestilential.

The closeness of the place, and the heat of the climate, added to the number in the ship, which was so crowded that each had scarcely room to turn himself, almost suffocated us. This produced copious perspirations, so that the air soon became unfit for respiration, from a variety of loathsome smells, and brought on a sickness among the slaves, of which many died, thus falling victims to the improvident avarice, as I may call it, of their purchasers.

This wretched situation was again aggravated by the galling of the chains, now become insupportable; and the filth of the necessary tubs, into which the children often fell, and were almost suffocated. The shrieks of the women, and the groans of the dying, rendered the whole a scene of horror almost inconceivable.

Happily perhaps for myself I was soon reduced so low here that it was thought necessary to keep me almost always on deck; and from my extreme youth I was not put in fetters. In this situation I expected every hour to share the fate of my companions, some of whom were almost daily brought upon deck at the point of death, which I began to hope would soon put an end to my miseries. Often did I think many of the inhabitants of the deep much more happy than myself. I envied them the freedom they enjoyed, and as often wished I could change my condition for theirs.

Every circumstance I met with served only to render my state more painful, and heightened my apprehensions, and my opinion of the cruelty of the whites. One day they had taken a number of fishes; and when they had killed and satisfied themselves with as many as they thought fit, to our astonishment who were on the deck, rather than give any of them to us to eat, as we expected, they tossed the remaining fish into the sea again, although we begged and prayed for some as well as we could, but in vain. Some of my countrymen, being pressed by hunger, took an opportunity, when they thought no one saw them, of trying to get a little privately; but they were discovered, and the attempt procured them some very severe floggings.

One day, when we had a smooth sea and moderate wind, two of my wearied countrymen who were chained together (I was near them at the time), preferring death to such a life of misery,

From *The Interesting Narrative of the Life of Oloudah Equiano, or Gustavus Vassa.* (1789)

somehow made through the nettings and jumped into the sea: immediately another quite dejected fellow, who on account of his illness was suffered to be out of irons, also followed their example; and I believe many more would very soon have done the same if they had not been prevented by the ship's crew who were instantly alarmed.

Those of us that were the most active were in a moment put down under the deck, and there was such a noise and confusion amongst the people of the ship as I never heard before, to stop her, and get the boat out to go after the slaves. However, two of the wretches were drowned, but they got the other, and afterwards flogged him unmercifully for thus attempting to prefer death to slavery.

In this manner we continued to undergo more hardships than I can now relate, hardships which are inseparable from this accursed trade. Many a time we were near suffocation from the want of fresh air, which we were often without for whole days together. This, and the stench of the necessary tubs, carried off many.

At last we came in sight of the island of Barbados, at which the whites on board gave a great shout, and made many signs of joy to us. We did not know what to think of this; but as the vessel drew nearer we plainly saw the harbour, and other ships of different kinds and sizes; and we soon anchored amongst them off Bridge-Town.

Many merchants and planters now came on board, though it was in the evening. They put us in separate parcels, and examined us attentively. They also made us jump, and pointed to the land, signifying we were to go there. We thought by this we should be eaten by these ugly men, as they appeared to us; and, when soon after we were all put down under the deck again, there was much dread and trembling.

Starting Time: _____   Finishing Time: _____

Reading Time: _____   Reading Rate: _____

Comprehension: _____   Vocabulary: _____

VOCABULARY: The following words have been taken from the selection you have just read. Put an *X* in the box before the best meaning or synonym for the word as used in the selection.

1. **confirm**, page 56, column 1, paragraph 1
   "...united to confirm me in this belief."
   ☐ a. promise
   ☐ b. strengthen
   ☐ c. conform
   ☐ d. force

2. **meanest**, page 56, column 1, paragraph 2
   "...with that of the meanest slave in my own country."
   ☐ a. smallest
   ☐ b. most selfish
   ☐ c. cruelest
   ☐ d. most wretched

3. **consternation**, page 56, column 1, paragraph 3
   "...threw me into the greatest consternation..."
   ☐ a. conversation
   ☐ b. bewilderment
   ☐ c. composure
   ☐ d. excitement

4. **suffered**, page 56, column 2, paragraph 2
   "I was not long suffered to indulge my grief;"
   ☐ a. permitted
   ☐ b. tolerated
   ☐ c. suffused
   ☐ d. punished

5. **aggravated**, page 57, column 2, paragraph 3
   "This wretched situation was again aggravated by the galling of the chains,"
   ☐ a. alleviated
   ☐ b. agitated
   ☐ c. lessened
   ☐ d. intensified

SELECTIONS FROM THE BLACK

EXPECTANCY CLUES

The most important aids to word recognition and, therefore, fluency in reading are meaning clues. Good readers use these clues effectively and automatically. Meaning clues permit the reader to anticipate words before actually reading them.

Expectancy clues are one type of meaning clue. These refer to the sorts of words and concepts one might expect to encounter in a given subject. For example, in a story about big city life the reader should expect to meet words like *subway, traffic congestion, urban renewal, ghetto, high-rise apartments,* and so on. Anticipating, or expecting, these words enables the reader to move along the printed lines rapidly, with understanding.

Here are two exercises to help you develop your skill in using expectancy clues.

The following words except two all appeared in a story about children playing. Think first about the kinds of words you would find in such a story and then examine the words below. Underline the two words you would *not* expect to find in this story.

1. toys	6. laughing	11. tossing
2. jump rope	7. jumping	12. operation
3. happy	8. voting	13. shouts
4. skates	9. running	14. skipping
5. bikes	10. games	15. splashing

Which of the following phrases would you expect to read in a newspaper story about car racing? Put an *X* in the box before them.

☐ 1. the starter's flag	☐ 11. smell of burning rubber
☐ 2. revving up the engines	☐ 12. squealing around curves
☐ 3. dust and grime	☐ 13. rear-tire blowout
☐ 4. pit stop	☐ 14. green and yellow dress
☐ 5. using worms for bait	☐ 15. below decks
☐ 6. special fuel mixture	☐ 16. carburetor adjustment
☐ 7. crew springs into action	☐ 17. out of the race
☐ 8. flagging the winner in	☐ 18. reading the newspaper
☐ 9. approaching the final lap	☐ 19. record-breaking lap
☐ 10. a hit tune of the 70's	☐ 20. following the pace car

HOW TO CONCENTRATE, I

If you have trouble concentrating, consider yourself normal. This is the universal student complaint. And it is not restricted to just students. Everyone at some time encounters problems in concentrating.

Concentrating means giving your exclusive attention, shutting out everything else. The problem comes from distractions, the inability to shut out interfering matters and noises.

Are there ways to improve our ability to concentrate? Yes.

1. Increase Motivation. You've no doubt observed about yourself that concentration has come easily in the past on matters about which you were highly motivated. Motivation is one key to concentration; we don't become distracted when we're really interested in something.

Matters which have some immediate and specific goal are those which motivate us most. We study our local *Driver's Manual* when the goal of obtaining a driver's license is at hand. The goal of passing tomorrow's quiz often helps students concentrate quite effectively the night before.

Our task then, to increase motivation, is to formulate a goal which is meaningful enough to develop the kind of concentration we need. Even a short-range goal might be enough to give us the motivation we need at the moment.

2. Prepare to Study. Simple as this may sound, it works. Prepare yourself properly and completely for the task of studying. Distractions will obviously bother us if we don't make arrangements to remove them, or remove ourselves from them. No one can concentrate in a busy room or in an easy chair with noise around. Try to find a quiet, well-lighted spot equipped with a table and chair. Seated at the table, upright in the chair, you're in the best posture for studying and concentrating.

COMPREHENSION: For each of the following statements and questions, select the option containing the most complete or most accurate answer.

1. The theme of this selection can best be expressed by which of the following?
   (e)
   - □ a. Man's inhumanity to man.
   - □ b. History repeats itself.
   - □ c. Money is the source of all evil.
   - □ d. Do unto others before they do unto you.

2. The author's initial reaction was one of
   (i)
   - □ a. doubt.
   - □ b. terror.
   - □ c. anticipation.
   - □ d. intimidation.

3. Vassa soon realized that he
   (b)
   - □ a. had been sold by Blacks.
   - □ b. would be eaten by whites.
   - □ c. could not survive the stench.
   - □ d. would die from lack of fresh air.

4. Before his capture, Vassa had been
   (a)
   - □ a. a tribesman.
   - □ b. a chieftain.
   - □ c. a slave.
   - □ d. a farmer.

5. Vassa's homeland was
   (h)
   - □ a. in the interior.
   - □ b. on the coast.
   - □ c. in Barbados.
   - □ d. in North Africa.

6. Stripped of their humanity and reduced to a sub-human level, the captives
   (c)
   - □ a. fought among themselves.
   - □ b. defied their guards.
   - □ c. sought release in death.
   - □ d. surrendered to the inevitable.

7. The one factor which made life aboard ship particularly intolerable was the
   (f)
   - □ a. white men.
   - □ b. congestion.
   - □ c. floggings.
   - □ d. necessary tubs.

8. The slave ship was headed for
   (b)
   - □ a. Jamestown.
   - □ b. Barbados.
   - □ c. the Cape Verde Islands.
   - □ d. the New World.

9. The wild fear which spread through the captives after the Bridge-Town merchants examined them resulted from
   (g)
   - □ a. past treatment and new surroundings.
   - □ b. the cannibalistic reputation of the merchants.
   - □ c. heated arguments between the merchants and the captors.
   - □ d. sordid stories they had heard from other slaves.

10. The selection is written in the form of
    (k)
    - □ a. an essay.
    - □ b. a narrative.
    - □ c. a description.
    - □ d. a diary.

> Comprehension Skills: a—isolating details; b—recalling specific facts; c—retaining concepts; d—organizing facts; e—understanding the main idea; f—drawing a conclusion; g—making a judgment; h—making an inference; i—recognizing tone; j—understanding characters; k—appreciation of literary forms.

SELECTIONS FROM THE BLACK

Selections from the Black

Part Two
Selections 11-20

Nobody Knows My Name

All along the block, for anyone who knows it, are immense human gaps, like craters.

James Baldwin

Fifth Avenue, Uptown

There is a housing project standing now where the house in which we grew up once stood, and one of those stunted city trees is snarling where our doorway used to be. This is on the rehabilitated side of the avenue. The other side of the avenue—for progress takes time—has not been rehabilitated yet and it looks exactly as it looked in the days when we sat with our noses pressed against the windowpane, longing to be allowed to go "across the street." The grocery store that gave us credit is still there, and there can be no doubt that it is still giving credit. The people in the project certainly need it—far more, indeed, than they ever needed the project. The last time I passed by, the Jewish proprietor was still standing among his shelves looking sadder and heavier but scarcely any older. Farther down the block stands the shoe-repair store in which our shoes were repaired until reparation became impossible and in which, then, we bought all our "new" ones. The Negro proprietor is still in the window, head down, working at the leather.

These two, I imagine, could tell a long tale if they would (perhaps they would be glad to if they could), having watched so many, for so long, struggling in the fishhooks, the barbed wire, of this avenue.

The avenue is elsewhere the renowned and elegant Fifth. The area I am describing, which, in today's gang parlance, would be called "the turf," is bounded by Lenox Avenue on the west, the Harlem River on the east, 135th Street on the north, and 130th Street on the south. We never lived beyond these boundaries; this is where we grew up. Walking along 145th Street—for example —familiar as it is, and similar, does not have the same impact because I do not know any of the people on the block. But when I turn east on 131st Street and Lenox Avenue, there is first a soda-pop joint, then a shoeshine "parlor," then a grocery store, then a dry cleaners', then the houses. All along the street there are people who watched me grow up, people who grew up with me, people I watched grow up along with my brothers and sisters; and, sometimes in my arms, sometimes underfoot, sometimes at my shoulder—or on it— their children, a riot, a forest of children, who include my nieces and nephews.

When we reach the end of this long block, we find ourselves on wide, filthy, hostile Fifth Avenue, facing that project which hangs over the avenue like a monument to the folly, and the cowardice, of good intentions. All along the block, for anyone who knows it, are immense human gaps, like craters. These gaps are not created merely by those who have moved away, inevitably into some other ghetto; or by those who have risen, almost always into a greater capacity for self-loathing and self-delusion; or yet by those who, by whatever means—War II, the Korean war, a policeman's gun or billy, a gang war, a brawl, madness, an overdose of heroin, or, simply, unnatural exhaustion—are dead. I am talking about those who are left, and I am talking principally about the young. What are they doing? Well, some, a minority, are fanatical churchgoers, members of the more extreme of the Holy Roller sects. Many, many more are "moslems," by affiliation or sympathy, that is to say that they are united by nothing more—and nothing less—than a hatred of the white world and all its works. They are present, for example, at every Buy Black street-corner meeting—meetings in which the speaker urges his hearers to cease trading with white men and establish a separate economy. Neither the speaker nor his hearers can possibly do this, of course, since Negroes do not own General Motors or RCA or the A&P nor, indeed, do they own more than a wholly insufficient fraction of anything else in Harlem (those who *do* own anything are more interested in their profits than in their fellows). But these meetings nevertheless keep alive in the participators a certain pride of bitterness without which, however futile this bitterness may be, they could scarcely remain alive at all. Many have given up. They stay home and watch the TV screen, living on the earnings of their parents, cousins, brothers, or uncles, and only leave the house to go to the movies or to the nearest bar. "How're you making it?" one may ask, running into them along

Photo: Mottke Weissman

James Baldwin has received many literary honors. He is the winner of a Eugene F. Saxton Memorial Trust Award, a Rosenwald Fellowship, a Guggenheim Fellowship, a *Partisan Review* Fellowship, and a Ford Foundation Grant-in-Aid; and he is also a member of the National Institute of Arts and Letters.

Special honors have been awarded to two of his books: *Nobody Knows My Name* and *The Fire Next Time*. *Nobody Knows My Name* received a Certificate of Recognition from the National Conference of Christians and Jews. Both *Nobody Knows My Name* in 1961 and *The Fire Next Time* in 1963 were selected by the Notable Books Council of the American Library Association and both have been included in the ten best books list selected by the National Association of Independent Schools.

In August, 1972, The Dial Press published *No Name In the Streets,* James Baldwin's long-awaited personal statement on what has happened in and to America through the political and social agonies of her recent history. *No Name In the Streets* is Mr. Bladwin's first collection of essays since the publication of his prophetic *The Fire Next Time* in 1963.

the block, or in the bar. "Oh, I'm TVing it"; with the saddest, sweetest, most shamefaced of smiles, and from a great distance. This distance one is compelled to respect; anyone who has traveled so far will not easily be dragged again into the world. There are further retreats, of course, than the TV screen or the bar. There are those who are simply sitting on their stoops, "stoned," animated for a moment only, and hideously, by the approach of someone who may lend them the money for a "fix." Or by the approach of someone from whom they can purchase it, one of the shrewd ones, on the way to prison or just coming out.

And the others, who have avoided all of these deaths, get up in the morning and go downtown to meet "the man." They work in the white man's world all day and come home in the evening to this fetid block. They struggle to instill in their children some private sense of honor or dignity that will help the child to survive. This means, of course, that they must struggle, stolidly, incessantly, to keep this sense alive in themselves, in spite of the insults, the indifference, and the cruelty they are certain to encounter in their working day. They patiently browbeat the landlord into fixing the heat, the plaster, the plumbing; this demands prodigious patience; nor is patience usually enough. In trying to make their hovels habitable, they are perpetually throwing good money after bad. Such frustration, so long endured, is driving many strong, admirable men and women whose only crime is color to the very gates of paranoia.

One remembers them from another time—playing handball in the playground, going to church, wondering if they were going to be promoted at school. One remembers them going off to war—gladly, to escape this block. One remembers their return. Perhaps one remembers their wedding day. And one sees where the girl is now—vainly looking for salvation from some other embittered, trussed, and struggling boy—and sees the all-but-abandoned children in the streets.

Now I am perfectly aware that there are other slums in which white men are fighting for their lives, and mainly losing. I know that blood is also flowing through those streets and that the human damage there is incalculable. People are continually pointing out to me the wretchedness of white people in order to console me for the wretchedness of blacks. But an itemized account of the American failure does not console me and it should not console anyone else. That hundreds of thousands of white people are living, in effect, no better than the "niggers" is not a fact to be regarded with complacency. The social and moral bankruptcy suggested by this fact is of the bitterest, most terrifying kind.

The people, however, who believe that this democratic anguish has some consoling value are always pointing out that So-and-So, white, and So-and-So, black, rose from the slums into the big time. The existence—the public existence—of, say, Frank Sinatra and Sammy Davis, Jr. proves to them that America is still the land of opportunity and that inequalities vanish before the determined will. It proves nothing of the sort. The determined will is rare—at the moment, in this country, it is unspeakably rare—and the inequalities suffered by the many are in no way justified by the rise of a few. A few have always risen—in every country, every era, and in the teeth of regimes that can by no stretch of the imagination be thought of as free. Not all of these people, it is worth remembering, left the world better than they found it. The determined will is rare, but it is not invariably benevolent. Furthermore, the American equation of success with the big times reveals an awful disrespect for human life and human achievement. This equation has placed our cities among the most dangerous in the world and has placed our youth among the most empty and most bewildered. The situation of our youth is not mysterious. Children have never been very good at listening to their elders, but they have never failed to imitate them.

They must, they have no other models. That is exactly what our children are doing. They are imitating our immorality, our disrespect for the pain of others.

All other slum dwellers, when the bank account permits it, can move out of the slum and vanish altogether from the eye of persecution. No Negro in this country has ever made that much money and it will be a long time before any Negro does. The Negroes in Harlem, who have no money, spend what they have on such gimcracks as they are sold. These include "wider" TV screens, more "faithful" hi-fi sets, more "powerful" cars, all of which, of course, are obsolete long before they are paid for. Anyone who has ever struggled with poverty knows how extremely expensive it is to be poor; and if one is a member of a captive population, economically speaking, one's feet have simply been placed on the treadmill forever. One is victimized, economically, in a thousand ways—rent, for example, or car insurance. Go shopping one day in Harlem—for anything—and compare Harlem prices and quality with those downtown.

The people who have managed to get off this block have only got as far as a more respectable ghetto. This respectable ghetto does not even have the advantages of the disreputable one—friends, neighbors, a familiar church, and friendly tradesmen; and it is not, moreover, in the nature of any ghetto to remain respectable long. Every Sunday, people who have left the block take the lonely ride back, dragging their increasingly discontented children with them. They spend the day talking, not always with words, about the trouble they've seen and the trouble—one must watch their eyes as they watch their children—they are only too likely to see. For children do not like ghettos. It takes them nearly no time to discover exactly why they are there.

Starting Time: _____	Finishing Time: _____
Reading Time: _____	Reading Rate: _____
Comprehension: _____	Vocabulary: _____

VOCABULARY: The following words have been taken from the selection you have just read. Put an X in the box before the best meaning or synonym for the word as used in the selection.

1. **rehabilitated,** page 63, column 1, paragraph 1
   "This is on the rehabilitated side of the avenue."
   ☐ a. restored
   ☐ b. rebuilt
   ☐ c. reformed
   ☐ d. inhabited

2. **futile,** page 63, column 2, 7 lines from bottom
   "...however futile this bitterness may be,"
   ☐ a. unsuccessful
   ☐ b. effectual
   ☐ c. discouraging
   ☐ d. useless

3. **fetid,** page 64, column 1, paragraph 2
   "...and come home in the evening to this fetid block."
   ☐ a. stinking
   ☐ b. feverish
   ☐ c. uninviting
   ☐ d. disheartening

4. **prodigious,** page 64, column 1, paragraph 2
   "...this demands prodigious patience;"
   ☐ a. ordinary
   ☐ b. considerable
   ☐ c. unusual
   ☐ d. enormous

5. **complacency,** page 64, column 2, paragraph 1
   "...no better than the 'niggers' is not a fact to be regarded with complacency."
   ☐ a. satisfaction
   ☐ b. civility
   ☐ c. disparagement
   ☐ d. complaints

SYLLABICATION

Knowing how to reduce words to their syllables aids both reading and spelling. Frequently a long word can be recognized and understood if pronounced by syllables. And in spelling, of course, knowledge of syllables contributes to accuracy.

These are rules or generalizations which we can follow when dividing words. One such rule tells us that when a word ends in **le**, preceded by a consonant, the word is divided before that consonant. For example, the word **simple** is divided into **sim-ple** because the word is divided before the consonant **p** in front of **le**. An exception to this rule are words ending in **ckle**. The **ck** acts as a single letter—it cannot be split—so the word must be divided after the **k**. An example is **pickle**, which is divided into **pick** and **le** because of the **ck** combination.

The following sentences contain words of both types. In each sentence divide the words in bold print according to the rule or the exception. Write your word on the line following each sentence using hyphens to separate the syllables.

1. Meet me here at six and bring your fishing **tackle**.

   _____

2. Always **handle** glass carefully, especially in antique shops.

   _____

3. **Knuckle** down to your work; delay only makes it harder.

   _____

4. The flag shows a hammer and **sickle**.

   _____

5. The little kittens **nestled** against the old grey cat.

   _____

6. Chinese food tastes best with **noodles**.

   _____

7. When milk is added, the cereal goes snap, **crackle**, and pop.

   _____

8. I can't **gargle** after every meal.

   _____

9. Snow **crinkles** underfoot.

   _____

10. The prisoners were beginning to **grumble**.

   _____

11. Don't **dawdle**, practice your lesson.

   _____

12. Stars **twinkle** in the sky at night.

   _____

HOW TO CONCENTRATE, II

We've seen two techniques we can use to improve concentration: 1) increase motivation, and 2) prepare to study. Here are three other techniques.

3. Set a Time. Have you ever noticed how timing brings out peak efficiency? Almost every athletic event is closely timed; or else the participants are competing against time. In track events, the winner's time is what generates the interest, not the fact that he was first. Timing is a natural goal to competitive man—he can't resist the race. Try this when you've got an assignment to complete or a lesson to study. Set a time for the completion of the task; your inclination to beat the clock may bring the sustained concentration you need. Timing builds concentration.

4. Pace the Assignment. Trying to do too much too soon will destroy concentration, not increase it. We know that we cannot sustain full concentration for very long periods, especially when we're not in the habit. When an assignment is long, involved, or complex, it's best not to try to complete it at one sitting. Segment the task into twenty-minute parcels and spread out the periods of study. Returning to an unfinished task makes it easier for us to regain concentration—we want to see the job completed; we're anxious to get it done. All of these factors help build the kind of concentration we need.

5. Organize the Task. One major reason students can't concentrate is that they've nothing to concentrate on. The assignment is so unplanned and vague to them that it itself is a distraction. Through the skills of Previewing and Questioning any student should be able to organize his assignment into a series of related and specific tasks. Break the job down for yourself; list exactly what you wish to learn or accomplish in this next period of study.

COMPREHENSION: For each of the following statements and questions, select the option containing the most complete or most accurate answer.

1. The tone of the selection is
(i)
- ☐ a. hostile.
- ☐ b. pessimistic.
- ☐ c. guarded.
- ☐ d. prejudiced.

2. Poverty is described as
(c)
- ☐ a. a necessary predicament.
- ☐ b. a means to an end.
- ☐ c. a temporary condition.
- ☐ d. a vicious circle.

3. Harlem's "moslem" youth are united by
(b)
- ☐ a. brotherly love.
- ☐ b. opposition to whites.
- ☐ c. Allah's teachings.
- ☐ d. "turf" loyalties.

4. A common characteristic of ghetto dwellers
(h) is their feeling of
- ☐ a. pride.
- ☐ b. independence.
- ☐ c. commitment.
- ☐ d. frustration.

5. The author attributes the lack of orientation
(b) of ghetto children to
- ☐ a. the example of their elders.
- ☐ b. their need for counseling and supervision.
- ☐ c. the advice of their elders.
- ☐ d. their inability to rise above their present condition.

6. The rise of Frank Sinatra and Sammy Davis,
(b) Jr., from rags to riches is
- ☐ a. the result of rare self-determination.
- ☐ b. the result of community involvement.
- ☐ c. proof of the opportunities America offers.
- ☐ d. proof that Blacks and whites can work together.

7. The author implies that Harlem's poor
(h)
- ☐ a. do not get enough to eat.
- ☐ b. need federal assistance.
- ☐ c. suffer economic slavery.
- ☐ d. do not enjoy luxuries.

8. James Baldwin's descriptive analysis of the
(i) cause and effect relationships inherent to ghetto existence is
- ☐ a. brutally honest.
- ☐ b. shamelessly misleading.
- ☐ c. deliberately exaggerated.
- ☐ d. profoundly humiliating.

9. The cost of living in Harlem is
(b)
- ☐ a. regulated by the Better Business Bureau.
- ☐ b. higher compared to surrounding areas.
- ☐ c. average because neighborhood shops cater to the people.
- ☐ d. reasonable considering the high crime rate.

10. The last paragraph suggests that children
(c)
- ☐ a. know why they are prisoners of the ghetto.
- ☐ b. enjoy spending Sundays with friends and neighbors.
- ☐ c. are confused about ghetto existence.
- ☐ d. are a joy to their parents.

Comprehension Skills: a—isolating details; b—recalling specific facts; c—retaining concepts; d—organizing facts; e—understanding the main idea; f—drawing a conclusion; g—making a judgment; h—making an inference; i—recognizing tone; j—understanding characters; k—appreciation of literary forms.

Alternatives to Despair

We must accept the risk of failure if we are going to have the hope of success.

Leon H. Sullivan

I firmly believe that Black people must be integrated into the mainstream of American life. Black economic development has to be accomplished in terms of integration! There is no such thing as Black capitalism! There is no such thing as Black capital!

The economy in this country is tied into everything, everybody, and everything that happens. We can't have one economic system for the White man and another for the Black man. There must be one economic system and that has to be for everyone. Within that system Black people can develop their own business enterprises, just as the White population and various specific ethnic groups have often done over the years.

What the Black man is saying is that he must develop enterprises which are not just for Black people—just as White enterprises haven't been just for Whites. All over the country Black people buy Ford automobiles sold by Whites. All over the country Black people eat Kellogg's corn flakes produced in a factory owned and operated by Whites. The Black man, like his White brother, must be able to produce commodities that can be dispensed in the free markets of the country and the free markets of the world. He must be able to compete as an integral part of the system of free enterprise. The problem has been that the Black man hasn't even been in a competitive position; he hasn't even seen the side door of free enterprise so as to know what it involves.

His paramount need is to get inside the door in terms of management, in terms of knowing what the economic structure is, in terms of development and control of capital. Then he will be able to move step by step through the process of building economic strength. In the final analysis the country, in fact the world, is run on money. Although *people* run on spirit, the nation is run on money, enterprise is developed on money, communities are built on money. Communities are built to help the people utilize money.

Unfortunately, Blacks have not had the financial capital that they have needed to develop enterprises. They have always been on the consuming instead of the producing end. If you take all the businesses owned by the Blacks in America today, the total would comprise less than one-half of one percent of the business in the country. If all of the Black businesses were combined, their corporate net value would barely exceed one billion dollars. You can ride hundreds of miles before you find a single motel owned by a Black man today, or by a Black group or even by a group in which a Black man is a part. You can see hundreds of factories while traveling thousands of miles, and you will be hard put to find a single factory which is owned or controlled by Blacks or that would even have a Black man on the board. It is obvious; the Black man has been on the outside of the production and ownership of American industry. This is true although his people make up approximately 12 to 13 percent of the population in the United States today, and by the year 2000 this figure will be from 16 to 20 percent. In the year 2000, it is estimated that there will be 300 million people in America and these will include 60 million Blacks. Right now is the time when we have to move into Black ownership of businesses with the realization that we have to pay as we go.

Many of the Black businesses will not succeed, just as many of the White businesses have not succeeded. The majority of businesses fail, and many that continue to exist yield only minimal profit, really operating on a shoestring. However, we must accept the risk of failure if we are going to have the hope of success.

Black people are going to have to develop skills in merchandising. They need to develop the ability in sales management. Most of the money made in America is made on the sales market. If, for example, one is to realize a million dollars a year, one must make several big sales of large commodities in the excess of a million dollars. Such are the facts of life in the business community. A man who sells ten computers can make ten million dollars; a real estate man who sells two big office buildings can make a million dollars; a man who sells a ship can make four million dollars from the sale. However, a man must have adequate knowledge about merchandise; he must have developed a productive ability; and he must be able to conclude the sale.

A Black pastor who has become one of the most dynamic forces in the business life of American minority groups speaks out in this book. Leon H. Sullivan's dynamic creativity has been an exciting factor in the progress of the Black community toward economic self-reliance and stability.

As the founder of over a hundred Opportunities Industrialization Centers (OIC), he has provided an unequaled means of vocational training for all races.

This achievement requires the development of a class of Blacks who are oriented in terms of management, ownership, and sales.

At the present time there are a few Blacks who represent what we call the "top Black," and many times they do not relate to the rest of the Blacks but seek to become White. As a result, almost all of the big mass of Blacks remain in a disadvantaged state, living on their weekly or monthly wages. They are able to save very little. They comprise the big mass of Blacks in this country. They are locked in ghettos and are unable to get out. They don't have the money, the jobs, or the skills.

On the contrary, there are stories of White men who came to America from someplace else, or those who have been raised in this country who have become economically secure because they have developed businesses and sales. We are going to have to develop in this country parallel examples from the Black community. I say this not just to the Black community, but to the whole community, because we can't have an economy with only the Blacks or an economy with only the Whites. We must have a world economy and the Black man must be integrated into that economy. The modern world leans toward the integration of the Black man in the economy of all men.

Progress Plaza (our Black owned and operated shopping center in Philadelphia) and other economic ventures are cases in point. All of these programs are founded on this philosophy which I mentioned above.

Another factor in this approach to economic liberation is that we have to utilize the resources we have in order to be economically emancipated. Before we started the OIC, we began a program that would generate capital for Blacks so that they could develop businesses, enterprises, and housing programs of their own. I looked in the Bible one Saturday night and I was reading about the feeding of the five thousand (Mark 6:34-44). If Jesus himself could multiply a few loaves and fishes and feed five thousand people and have a few loaves left over, even that supernatural act would not have been as remarkable as the miracle of sharing that I believe really happened that day. The significant thing is that Jesus challenged the people to share what they had. Everybody—every man and every child and every woman—responded by doing just that. The miracle was the result of sharing. For the common good of all, they shared. Out of this sharing there was more than enough food for all. Jesus performed a miracle in getting the people to share what they had.

So I went to my church and after preaching a sermon on gathering the fragments of life, I asked fifty members to invest ten dollars a month. The money could be used in two ways, one for nonprofit purposes in which there would be no immediate return, such as to build health facilities, to finance nonprofit housing developments, to develop educational scholarship funds, and to provide care for the sick and the infirm. The other portion would go into a profit venture. Initially not fifty, but two hundred people responded. Their response formed the base for the 10-36 Plan. The idea was not that they would receive but that their children and their children's children would receive. This plan provides the basis of opportunity for those who are coming after us. Once a person puts his money in the pot, he knows it will come back; it will come back when he is sick or when he is old; it will come back in benefits to his heirs, his assignees, his children, his grandchildren, his great grandchildren, or to those friends who don't have children.

I told the people that many others would benefit from the sacrifices that they made. Ultimately, of course, they themselves would get benefits, once the ventures became profitable. Profit sharing encouraged them. Later they were to put their dividends back into the investment to expand the businesses. In 10-36 the common man was getting a part of the action while at the same time helping to build his community!

This activity is what I call the reverse syndrome of welfare. Instead of people continuing to be a drain on society, they were building up a reverse and giving input to persons and to the total community. I was trying to turn welfare around to become something that is positive. From programs and funds such as this the people would be able to help themselves. Through "reversal of welfare" the church and church people could, by their own resources, develop themselves and provide assistance by "helping themselves!"

Reprinted from *Alternatives to Despair* by Leon H. Sullivan. Used by permission of The Judson Press.

Here we were with two hundred people pooling their money to build a million-dollar apartment complex, the first built by Blacks in Philadelphia. Soon we had some six hundred people participating in the program, and we built a two-million-dollar shopping center—the first shopping center built by Blacks in America, perhaps the largest in the world built by Blacks. Then we opened the plan to five thousand people and as a result we built the first and largest aerospace company in the world owned by Blacks. Later we opened supermarkets where the Whites and the Blacks shopped together. We sought to develop a chain so that our food markets would be throughout Philadelphia and one day throughout America.

In this way we began to generate new capital. We began to buy office buildings. We worked the income from some of these into a charitable trust so that the income ultimately can improve education and provide scholarships. I call this money "Community Capital."

This effort began to move like a snowball so that by the time the Securities and Exchange Commission registered the "10-36 Plan" we could claim that this was the first time in history that stock issues which were both nonprofit and profit in nature had ever been registered by the federal government. Here is the plan:

Twenty thousand issues were placed on sale initially all over the country. We will have twenty thousand people giving ten dollars per month for thirty-six months. Our plan is to add up to as many as a half million shareholders all over the country, so that the kind of programs we developed in Philadelphia can be developed in up to one hundred cities.

The plan is for Blacks, Browns, Reds, and Whites. Everything I do is for all. I initiate the programs as a Black man with Black leadership but Whites can participate in anything I do, because I don't believe in a Black world or a White world. I believe in one world and in one America. I think Blacks must initiate; Blacks must lead in the ventures I conceive. I think that for long enough Whites have led Blacks in everything they have done. Now it is time for Black leadership, Black confidence, and the Black's turn, so that we can balance the system. But the White investors are welcome.

Starting Time: _____	Finishing Time: _____
Reading Time: _____	Reading Rate: _____
Comprehension: _____	Vocabulary: _____

VOCABULARY: The following words have been taken from the selection you have just read. Put an X in the box before the best meaning or synonym for the word as used in the selection.

1. **integral**, page 68, column 1, paragraph 3
"He must be able to compete as an integral part of the system..."
☐ a. honorable
☐ b. entire
☐ c. balanced
☐ d. necessary

2. **comprise**, page 68, column 2, paragraph 1
"...the total would comprise less than one-half of one percent..."
☐ a. consist of
☐ b. contain
☐ c. appeal to
☐ d. depend on

3. **oriented**, page 69, column 1, paragraph 1
"...a class of Blacks who are oriented in terms of management,"
☐ a. organized
☐ b. placed
☐ c. familiarized
☐ d. positioned

4. **ventures**, page 69, column 1, paragraph 4
"...other economic ventures are cases in point."
☐ a. undertakings
☐ b. adventures
☐ c. dangers
☐ d. businesses

5. **initiate**, page 70, column 2, paragraph 2
"I think Blacks must initiate;"
☐ a. conclude
☐ b. introduce
☐ c. lead
☐ d. imitate

SELECTIONS FROM THE BLACK

PREFIXES

Many English words are made up of a base or root word to which prefixes (beginnings) and suffixes (endings) have been added. To the root word **agree** (a verb) we can add both a prefix and a suffix to get **disagreeable** (an adjective) which has an opposite meaning.

A prefix is added to the beginning of a word and causes a change in the meaning of that word. We have just seen how the prefix **dis** reverses the meaning of **agree**. Most of the prefixes we will be examining in this book come from Latin.

Two Prefixes

1. anti- comes from Greek and means **against** or **opposing**. It appears in the word **antisocial**, referring to an unfriendly attitude.

2. trans- is from Latin and means **over** or **across**. In **translate** the prefix tells us that the words are being brought to another language.

In the following sentences the words in bold print need prefixes. Add one of these two prefixes to each word and write your word on the line following the sentence.

1. The peace marchers were violently **war**.

   _____

2. Be sure to put **freeze** in your car radiator before winter.

   _____

3. **Septic** washes are used to prevent the spread of infection.

   _____

4. Have your secretary **scribe** her notes and type them.

   _____

5. An **dote** was administered to counteract the poison.

   _____

6. He'll die without a blood **fusion**.

   _____

7. This hospital was the first to perform a heart **plant**.

   _____

8. **Biotics** are used in the treatment of infectious diseases.

   _____

9. **Lucent** glass is not transparent, but light passes through.

   _____

10. This was to be his first **atlantic** flight.

    _____

HOW TO REMEMBER

Just as there are ways to help build concentration, there are techniques we can employ to help us remember when we need to.

1. Plan to Remember. This is so obvious that we overlook its value, and yet it works. Tell yourself you want to remember something and you will. If you're like most people you have trouble remembering the names of those you just met. The next time you're introduced, plan to remember the person's name. Say to yourself, "I'll listen carefully; I'll repeat the name to be sure I've got it; and I'll remember it." You'll find there's nothing to it; you'll probably remember that name for the rest of your life.

We complain that we can't remember when the truth is we never tried or planned to remember. From now on, make up your mind before you read or study; tell yourself that you want to remember.

2. Review the Material. Most forgetting occurs shortly after the learning has been done. New material crowds out what we've just learned and we have trouble recalling. We overcome this by reviewing. A review does not have to be a total rereading of the entire assignment; you already know an excellent method of reviewing—your previewing skill. Previewing again and recalling your questions will give you enough of a review to help you remember.

3. Look for Principles. It's a fact that we cannot remember everything, and when we try, we end up remembering nothing. Don't think of the subject as lots of facts you've got to remember; generalize the subject into a few major ideas which you can easily recall.

This technique is especially true when studying for tests and exams. You waste time and actually minimize retention when you try to remember everything in a lesson or book.

COMPREHENSION: For each of the following statements and questions, select the option containing the most complete or most accurate answer.

1. Leon Sullivan's financial thinking is based on
(e) which of the following premises?

 ☐ a. Money is the root of all evil.
 ☐ b. Black Americans must initiate and direct cooperative, economic ventures.
 ☐ c. The white business community is willing to accept Black investors.
 ☐ d. Black owned and operated enterprises are financed by white capital.

2. Mr. Sullivan's economic involvement seems
(g) to be

 ☐ a. a plan for economic domination.
 ☐ b. a subtle form of racism.
 ☐ c. an exercise in collective deception.
 ☐ d. a means to an end.

3. Black business entrepreneurs must
(c)
 ☐ a. cross racial and ethnic lines.
 ☐ b. receive financial aid from white owned banks.
 ☐ c. develop their own economic system.
 ☐ d. resist absorption into the mainstream of American life.

4. The Black community can use men who
(d) understand

 ☐ a. the value of money.
 ☐ b. management and the economic structure.
 ☐ c. accounting and bookkeeping.
 ☐ d. production and distribution.

5. Leon Sullivan is
(j)
 ☐ a. a moralist.
 ☐ b. a dreamer.
 ☐ c. a realist.
 ☐ d. an opportunist.

6. Traditionally, Black people have been
(b)
 ☐ a. producers.
 ☐ b. capitalists.
 ☐ c. consumers.
 ☐ d. organizers.

7. Highly successful Blacks or the "top Black"
(g) should

 ☐ a. accept their responsibilities.
 ☐ b. cooperate with the white community.
 ☐ c. contribute money to interracial programs.
 ☐ d. command the respect and admiration of other Blacks.

8. The 10-36 Plan is
(f)
 ☐ a. a welfare assistance plan.
 ☐ b. a non-profit organization.
 ☐ c. a profit-sharing venture.
 ☐ d. a religious education program.

9. An unusual aspect of the 10-36 Plan is its
(d)
 ☐ a. profit stock issues.
 ☐ b. non-profit stocks.
 ☐ c. humble beginnings.
 ☐ d. "Community Capital."

10. Since the 10-36 Plan was religiously inspired
(f) (Mark 6:34-44), its growth and development calls to mind which of the following parables?

 ☐ a. The Good Samaritan
 ☐ b. The Mustard Seed
 ☐ c. The Laborers in the Vineyard
 ☐ d. The Sowers

> Comprehension Skills: a—isolating details; b—recalling specific facts; c—retaining concepts; d—organizing facts; e—understanding the main idea; f—drawing a conclusion; g—making a judgment; h—making an inference; i—recognizing tone; j—understanding characters; k—appreciation of literary forms.

SELECTIONS FROM THE BLACK

The Harlem Rat

"If you don't get me and my baby outta this rat trap, I will!"

John H. Jones

As Battle Young strode home along Harlem's Lenox Avenue on an October evening in nineteen-forty-eight, he scarcely noticed the chilly wind or the passersby. He was too absorbed in his own anger.

He swung a lunch pail as he walked, a tall, lithe man in Army clothes, thick-soled boots, khaki trench coat and knitted cap. His brown face was strong-featured, and his brown eyes mirrored an eternal hurt, frustration, or anger. He was a veteran, discharged only a year, after three bitter ones in the Army.

Crossing One Hundred and Thirty-fifth Street and heading north, his mind searched for the easiest way to tell Belle that he had failed again to get an apartment in the new project going up on Fifth Avenue. He thought of how she wanted to get out of those dismal three rooms on One Hundred and Thirty-eighth Street, so that Jean, their two-months-old baby, would have "a decent place to grow up in."

Belle had cried, threatened, pleaded, scolded, ridiculed and tried just about everything else in what she thought was the best method to make him get out and find a place! "Other vets are finding places. Why can't you?" she would cry out whenever she heard of someone else getting an apartment.

"We're lucky to find this hole." He told her over and over again, explaining that he wanted to get another place the same as she did. But she had always been a demanding woman, he thought, remembering their school days in Richmond, Virginia. It had been her strong persuasion after his Army discharge that brought them to New York.

And then, when the city-owned project started up giving priority to veterans, Belle had been certain they would get in. But just this evening he'd stood in line for an hour, only to have the interviewer tell him, "You're making too much money, Mr. Young. Your income is about three dollars a week more than the law calls for." He had argued at first and finally stalked out in anger. And now he had to face another one of those terrible arguments with Belle. God! How he hated to fight with her!

He walked around an unconscious Sneaky Pete drinker sprawled on the sidewalk at One Hundred and Thirty-sixth Street, crossed and glanced toward the Harlem Hospital as an ambulance turned east. Well, he had to go home, he thought, walking on in silence, swinging his lunch pail and staring in through the windows of the bars, the greasy cafes and the candy stores.

At the corner of One Hundred and Thirty-eighth Street, he turned east, walked past two tenements and entered the third. On the stoop stood a half dozen teen-age boys and girls. Climbing two flights of creaky stairs, he stopped just at the top of the landing, put his key in the lock, and went in the door.

Belle could see the answer in his grimy face when he came in, but she asked the question anyway, asked it hopefully, standing in the middle of the front room. "What did they say at the project, honey?" Her voice was soft but clear.

"Will you let me get outta these dirty clothes and catch a breath?" he snapped, and then turned away ashamed.

Belle took the pail from his hands, turned on her heel, and walked into the middle room. She was slender, and her skin was a delicate reddish tan. Her brown hair was held up neatly by a hair net. Brown eyes accented a snub nose and soft, full, unpainted lips. She wore a blue and red flowered house dress, and fuzzy blue slippers.

The small room was dimly lit. On an old-fashioned iron bed in the corner a tiny baby slept. This was Jean. Belle smiled anxiously as she peered at the baby. Satisfied that Jean was snug, she turned and inspected the small, round, black oil stove. The flame glowed through the vents in its side.

Belle shivered slightly, turned it up and silently cursed Kelly, the landlord, for not providing heat.

The ceilings were cracked and falling. The dirty gray plaster walls appeared to have once been buff. Ancient chandeliers had become loosened from the ceiling, and from time to time the crumbling electric wire insulation wore through and short-circuited, plunging the apartment into darkness.

Going down a short hall, Belle mashed a roach

with her foot as it scurried across the floor heading for the kitchen. She put Battle's pail on the top of a wooden icebox standing in a far corner and went to her stove. After half an hour, Battle came in wearing a tattered blue terrycloth bathrobe. His stiff, black hair was cropped short, and he carried an evening paper. His face, now clean, wore an annoyed expression as he walked to a cracked, porcelain-topped table, pulled out a rickety chair, and sat down with a sigh. He glanced at the paper's headlines while Belle stirred a pot. Both looked up knowingly as the steam pipe clanged a staccato beat of an overhead tenant calling for heat.

"That damn water is cold again. The day I leave this filthy hole I'm gonna kick that lousy Kelly right in his can!" Battle stormed. "Ain't no need of sayin' anything to the super. Kelly won't give him no coal!"

"Again?" Belle commented with sarcasm. "It's always cold." Then, "What did they say, Honey?" She reached back on the table for Battle's plate.

"I'm making too much," Battle said, looking hopefully as Belle dished up a sizzling pork chop, steaming lima beans, and kale.

Belle exclaimed, pushing the plate of food before Battle. "Whadda they mean? You making too much. We can hardly buy bread and meat!"

Battle chewed a mouthful and swallowed. "Well, there's this law against a guy making more than thirty-six dollars getting in city housing projects."

"Did you show 'em your discharge papers and tell 'em about me and Jean?"

"Sure. But that don't mean nothing."

"Well, since we got to stay here why don't you try to make Kelly fix up a few things and paint?" Belle said as she sat down to her own plate of food.

Battle slammed down his fork, and looked Belle straight in the eyes. "Now don't you go nagging at me again. Haven't I cussed and threatened ever since we been here? And Brown in I-E was here long before us, and Kelly ain't done anything in his apartment yet!" He picked up the fork, speared a piece of meat and started chewing savagely.

But Belle wasn't satisfied. She pushed the food about her plate without interest, contemplating an appropriate reply. "Well, can't you think of anything else? Can't you go see somebody? Isn't there a law for his kind? Or do you want me to do it?"

Battle had heard this before. She always managed to imply doubts of his ability to do things the way a man should, hitting his weakest spot. "Look," he muttered through a mouthful of food, "do you want me to kill that bastard, and go to Sing Sing? 'Cause if I get into one more argument with him and he gets smart, I'm gonna hit him with the first thing I get my hands on!"

"Fighting won't get the place painted, but

thinking out a few ways to make him do it might help a little!" she blazed. She hesitated a moment. "You never did go back to that tenants' meeting, like Mr. Brown asked you to. You and the rest of these folks ought to listen to Mr. Brown and get together. You can't do nothing by yourselves."

Battle glowered and broke off a bit of white bread. For a few minutes they both ate in silence. Noticing that Battle was almost finished with his food, Belle said, "There's no more meat or beans, just kale, but there's some rice pudding from yesterday, and—"

Battle sputtered suddenly, staring at the wall against which the table stood. A fat roach sluggishly made its way ceiling-wards, antennae waving.

"Well, knock him off for heavensake, and stop cussing!"

He reached down, pulled off a battered bedroom slipper and unceremoniously smashed the roach. They both looked disgustedly at the mess. Then, as Belle got up and turned towards the icebox, Battle tore a corner from the newspaper he had been reading and wiped the wall.

"I don't want any pudding now," he said just before she stooped to open the box.

"Well, why did you mash him, Mister nice-nasty?" She came back to the table, sat down, and pulled a pack of cigarettes from her dress pocket. Battle pushed his dishes back and continued to read.

Belle lit her cigarette and blew out the first puff. Her mind was busy trying to hit on the best way to mention their housing predicament again. Battle seemed to sense her thoughts, and he glanced at her from the corners of his eyes several times. "Honey—" she began. Battle stiffened physically and mentally, but he turned to the sports page as though he hadn't heard.

This always annoyed Belle. She reached over and snatched the paper from him. "I'm talking to you, man! If you don't get me and my baby outta this rat trap, I will!"

Battle suppressed a desire to shout back. Instead he just stared at her and then reached patiently for the paper. She jerked it out of his reach. "You can sit there like a knot on a log if you want to!" Belle blazed.

A whimper from the baby in the middle room went unheard by either of them. Battle raised himself half out of the chair, reached over and grabbed Belle's arm, twisting it, and pulled the paper loose. She began to scratch at him but stopped abruptly when an agonizing cry came from

Reprinted from *Harlem, U.S.A.*, John Henrik Clarke, Ed. Published in 1964 by Seven Seas Publications. Used with permission of the author.

SELECTIONS FROM THE BLACK

the baby. She released the paper, jumped up, and ran from the kitchen. The baby still shrieked while Battle shuffled the crumpled pages back into place.

"My God, Battle! Come here! It's a rat!"

As he dashed into the room, Belle held Jean in one arm, and inspected two rows of teeth marks on the baby's right cheek. Blood oozed from each mark.

"He bit her, Battle! Oh God! He bit her!" she wailed as her husband rushed in.

As Battle looked at the tiny blobs of blood, smothering anger rose.

"Better go and put some iodine on her," he told Belle.

He spun at a noise under the bed, and stomped viciously as a dirty gray rat the size of a kitten scampered across the room.

Gritting his teeth he looked into the bathroom where Belle painted Jean's bites.

"How late does Kelly stay in his office?" he asked so quietly it alarmed Belle.

"Eight. What you gonna do, Battle? Don't get into no trouble!"

"I ain't gonna start no fighting trouble, but I'm gonna make it hot for Kelly."

He went back in the room, opened a closet and pulled on his clothes. He glanced at a clock on a dresser that said seven-thirty p.m. He went back to the bathroom door.

"Then tomorrow I'm gonna go from door to door and tell everybody in the tenant council what happened."

Belle smiled as he kissed her lightly, and patted Jean's head.

He left and went to see the landlord.

Starting Time: _____   Finishing Time: _____

Reading Time: _____   Reading Rate: _____

Comprehension: _____   Vocabulary: _____

VOCABULARY: The following words have been taken from the selection you have just read. Put an X in the box before the best meaning or synonym for the word as used in the selection.

1. **priority**, page 73, column 1, last paragraph
"...the city-owned project started up giving priority to veterans,"
☐ a. order
☐ b. preference
☐ c. privilege
☐ d. rank

2. **contemplating**, page 74, column 1, paragraph 11
"...contemplating an appropriate reply."
☐ a. considering
☐ b. observing
☐ c. studying
☐ d. thinking

3. **glowered**, page 74, column 2, paragraph 2
"Battle glowered and broke off a bit of white bread."
☐ a. cowered
☐ b. stared
☐ c. glowed
☐ d. glared

4. **predicament**, page 74, column 2, paragraph 8
"...the best way to mention their housing predicament again."
☐ a. dilemma
☐ b. solution
☐ c. situation
☐ d. condition

5. **suppressed**, page 74, column 2, paragraph 10
"Battle suppressed a desire to shout back."
☐ a. expressed
☐ b. abolished
☐ c. withheld
☐ d. crushed

CONTEXTUAL AIDS: SYNONYMS

Studies of good readers show that they are aware of the context of what they are reading. Using the context as an aid to rapid understanding is a valuable tool to the reader.

Context is also an aid to word recognition. A word which is not well known to the reader or whose meaning is not too clear can become better known and understood through the context in which it is used.

The many ways in which context functions to help the reader recognize words are called contextual aids.

Contextual Aid 6. Words can be understood through synonyms provided in the context. In the example, **He _____ the note, concealing it from everyone**, the reader would correctly guess that the missing word is **hid** because of the synonym **concealing** which follows it.

In the following sentences nonsense words have been used with synonyms. Underline the nonsense word and write the correct word on the line following each sentence. The first one has been done for you.

1. I asked for his dralp and honest opinion.

   _____ *frank* _____

2. The prisoners are free; they were raseeded yesterday.

   _____

3. The amusing incident made us all perd.

   _____

4. You'd better hire a bilm to lead you through the woods.

   _____

5. It was a hard task, dampersil to perform.

   _____

6. They sang in falpency, blending their voices beautifully.

   _____

7. He is a humble man, colbad about his achievements.

   _____

8. He was one of the ones hurt but his funteresed was not great.

   _____

9. Pendelsy him; copy his every action.

   _____

10. He's immune to disease; he's built up a replasture.

    _____

11. She received the Dwlbxry Award in recognition of her one hundred years of service.

    _____

The saying goes that a mechanic is only as good as his tools. Implied is that he knows how to use them. What about the student? His tools of learning are textbooks, and his efficiency of work or study will depend in large measure on how well he uses them.

Fortunately, most textbooks today are well organized. The costs of producing a text are substantial, and publishers strive to ensure that their books are current, comprehensive, and concise. A publisher wants a text to be used and to last.

Because texts are well constructed, the student can capitalize on these very features.

Evaluate the Author

Of course he knows more about his subject than you; you cannot evaluate him on that basis. But you can try to discover his background and experience. Is he a lecturer, professor? Where does he teach? Is he a practitioner? Does he only teach or does he work in the field as well? This information may indicate his approach: theoretical or practical. The level at which he teaches or practices may tell you how specialized or broad his discussion may be.

Check too the copyright date. Is the text current? Today's student is different from yesterday's. The sciences accumulate new knowledge hourly — currency is essential in these fields.

Read the author's preface or introduction. Learn his approach to his subject. Does he consider his text an intensive discussion or a comprehensive survey? Does he plan to include illustrations gained from his experience in the field? Most importantly, examine the author's reason for writing. What does he expect of his readers? Why does he consider the subject useful or necessary for the reader?

His introduction is the first opportunity to address the reader. Anything of importance for you to keep in mind as you use the text will be covered here. These opening remarks are designed to get you off to a good start.

COMPREHENSION: For each of the following statements and questions, select the option containing the most complete or most accurate answer.

1. The tone of the selection is one of
(i)
    □ a. wishful thinking.
    □ b. fearful anxiety.
    □ c. depressing futility.
    □ d. deliberate oppression.

2. Belle can be described as
(j)
    □ a. a shrewish wife.
    □ b. hopelessly dejected.
    □ c. a careless housekeeper.
    □ d. impatient and frustrated.

3. The new Fifth Avenue apartments were given
(c) to families
    □ a. whose income was minimal.
    □ b. who could afford them.
    □ c. whose bread-winner was a veteran.
    □ d. who were displaced by renewal projects.

4. Battle refused the rice pudding because
(h)
    □ a. he had had enough to eat.
    □ b. he did not like desserts.
    □ c. he had lost his appetite.
    □ d. it was a day old.

5. Mr. Brown was
(c)
    □ a. a slum landlord.
    □ b. the superintendent.
    □ c. a welfare worker.
    □ d. a community organizer.

6. Belle tried to prod her husband to action by
(c)
    □ a. complaining to the landlord.
    □ b. attacking his manhood.
    □ c. joining the neighborhood council.
    □ d. looking for a job.

7. Which of the following best reflects Belle's
(g) thinking?
    □ a. Honest poverty hath no shame.
    □ b. In union there is strength.
    □ c. Problems are best resolved at home.
    □ d. Tomorrow is another day.

8. The conditions described in the selection
(g) should alert the establishment to
    □ a. the need for increased aid to education.
    □ b. the urgency of Black demands.
    □ c. the need to relax welfare regulations.
    □ d. the need to increase the size and strength of its security force.

9. Battle became an acitvist after
(f)
    □ a. his daughter was bitten by a rat.
    □ b. his wife hounded and nagged him.
    □ c. he set fire to Kelly's office.
    □ d. his apartment was overrun by roaches and rats.

10. The Harlem rat is
(e)
    □ a. Battle.
    □ b. the interviewer.
    □ c. Kelly.
    □ d. the rodent.

Comprehension Skills: a—isolating details; b—recalling specific facts; c—retaining concepts; d—organizing facts; e—understanding the main idea; f—drawing a conclusion; g—making a judgment; h—making an inference; i—recognizing tone; j—understanding characters; k—appreciation of literary forms.

The Revolt of the Evil Fairies

When the curtain rang down, the forces of Good and Evil were locked in combat.

Ted Poston

The grand dramatic offering of the Booker T. Washington Colored Grammar School was the biggest event of the year in our social life in Hopkinsville, Kentucky. It was the one occasion on which they let us use the old Cooper Opera House, and even some of the white folks came out yearly to applaud our presentation. The first two rows of the orchestra were always reserved for our white friends, and our leading colored citizens sat right behind them—with an empty row intervening, of course.

Mr. Ed. Smith, our local undertaker, invariably occupied a box to the left of the house and wore his cutaway coat and striped breeches. This distinctive garb was usually reserved for those rare occasions when he officiated at the funerals of our most prominent colored citizens. Mr. Thaddeus Long, our colored mailman, once rented a tuxedo and bought a box, too. But nobody paid him much mind. We knew he was just showing off.

The title of our play never varied. It was always *Prince Charming and the Sleeping Beauty,* but no two presentations were ever the same. Miss H. Belle LaPrade, our sixth-grade teacher, rewrote the script every season, and it was never like anything you read in the storybooks. Miss LaPrade called it "a modern morality play of conflict between the forces of good and evil." And the forces of evil, of course, always came off second best.

The Booker T. Washington Colored Grammar School was in a state of ferment from Christmas until February, for this was the period when parts were assigned. First there was the selection of the Good Fairies and the Evil Fairies. This was very important, because the Good Fairies wore white costumes and the Evil Fairies black. And strangely enough most of the Good Fairies usually turned out to be extremely light in complexion, with straight hair and white folks' features. On rare occasions a dark-skinned girl might be lucky enough to be a Good Fairy, but not one with a speaking part.

There never was any doubt about Prince Charming and the Sleeping Beauty. They were *always* light-skinned. And although nobody ever discussed those things openly, it was an accepted fact that a lack of pigmentation was a decided advantage in the Prince Charming and Sleeping Beauty sweepstakes.

And therein lay my personal tragedy. I made the best grades in my class, I was the leading debater, and the scion of a respected family in the community. But I could never be Prince Charming, because I was black.

In fact, every year when they started casting our grand dramatic offering my family started pricing black cheesecloth at Franklin's Department store. For they knew that I would be leading the forces of darkness and skulking back in the shadows—waiting to be vanquished in the third act. Mama had experience with this sort of thing. All my brothers had finished Booker T. before me.

Not that I was alone in my disappointment. Many of my classmates felt it, too. I probably just took it more to heart. Rat Joiner, for instance, could rationalize the situation. Rat was not only black; he lived on Billy Goat Hill. But Rat summed it up like this:

"If you black, you black."

I should have been able to regard the matter calmly, too. For our grand dramatic offering was only a reflection of our daily community life in Hopkinsville. The yallers had the best of everything. They held most of the teaching jobs in Booker T. Washington Colored Grammar School. They were the Negro doctors, the lawyers, the insurance men. They even had a "Blue Vein Society," and if your dark skin obscured your throbbing pulse you were hardly a member of the elite.

Yet I was inconsolable the first time they turned me down for Prince Charming. That was the year they picked Roger Jackson. Roger was not only dumb; he stuttered. But he was light enough to pass for white, and that was apparently sufficient.

In all fairness, however, it must be admitted that Roger had other qualifications. His father owned the only colored saloon in town and was quite a power in local politics. In fact, Mr. Clinton Jackson had a lot to say about just who taught in the Booker T. Washington Colored Grammar School. So it was understandable that Roger should have been picked for Prince Charming.

My real heartbreak, however, came the year they picked Sarah Williams for Sleeping Beauty. I had been in love with Sarah since kindergarten. She had soft light hair, bluish-gray eyes, and a dimple that stayed in her left cheek whether she was smiling or not.

Of course Sarah never encouraged me much. She never answered any of my fervent love letters, and Rat was very scornful of my one-sided love affair. "As long as she don't call you black baboon," he sneered, "you'll keep on hanging around."

After Sarah was chosen for Sleeping Beauty I went out for the Prince Charming role with all my heart. If I had declaimed boldly in previous contests, I was matchless now. If I had bothered Mama with rehearsals at home before, I pestered her to death this time. Yes, and I purloined my sister's can of Palmer's Skin Success.

I knew the Prince's role from start to finish, having played the Head Evil Fairy opposite it for two seasons. And Prince Charming was one character whose lines Miss LaPrade never varied much in her many versions. But although I never admitted it, even to myself, I knew I was doomed from the start. They gave the part to Leonardius Wright. Leonardius, of course, was yaller.

The teachers sensed my resentment. They were almost apologetic. They pointed out that I had been such a splendid Head Evil Fairy for two seasons that it would be a crime to let anybody else try the role. They reminded me that Mama wouldn't have to buy any more cheesecloth because I could use my same old costume. They insisted that the Head Evil Fairy was even more important than Prince Charming because he was the one who cast the spell on Sleeping Beauty. So what could I do but accept?

I had never liked Leonardius Wright. He was a goody-goody, and even Mama was always throwing him up to me. But above all, he, too, was in love with Sarah Williams. And now he got a chance to kiss Sarah every day in rehearsing the awakening scene.

Well, the show must go on, even for little black boys. So I threw my soul into my part and made the Head Evil Fairy a character to be remembered.

When I drew back from the couch of Sleeping Beauty and slunk away into the shadows at the approach of Prince Charming, my facial expression was indeed something to behold. When I was vanquished by the shining sword of Prince Charming in the last act, I was a little hammy perhaps—but terrific!

The attendance at our grand dramatic offering that year was the best in its history. Even the white folks overflowed the two rows reserved for them, and a few were forced to sit in the intervening one. This created a delicate situation, but everybody tactfully ignored it.

When the curtain went up on the last act, the audience was in fine fettle. Everything had gone well for me, too—except for one spot in the second act. That was where Leonardius unexpectedly rapped me over the head with his sword as I slunk off into the shadows. That was not in the script, but Miss LaPrade quieted me down by saying it made a nice touch anyway. Rat said Leonardius did it on purpose.

The third act went on smoothly, though, until we came to the vanquishing scene. That was where I slunk from the shadows for the last time and challenged Prince Charming to mortal combat. The hero reached for his shining sword—a bit unsportsmanlike, I always thought, since Miss LaPrade consistently left the Head Evil Fairy unarmed—and then it happened!

Later I protested loudly—but in vain—that it was a case of self-defense. I pointed out that Leonardius had a mean look in his eye. I cited the impromptu rapping he had given my head in the second act. But nobody would listen. They just wouldn't believe that Leonardius really intended to brain me when he reached for his sword.

Anyway, he didn't succeed. For the minute I saw that evil gleam in his eye—or was it my own—I cut loose with a right to the chin, and Prince Charming dropped his shining sword and staggered back. His astonishment lasted only a minute,

"The Revolt of the Evil Fairies" by Ted Poston. From *The Book of Negro Humor* edited by Langston Hughes. Published by Dodd, Mead & Company.

though, for he lowered his head and came charging in, fists flailing. There was nothing yellow about Leonardius but his skin.

The audience thought the scrap was something new Miss LaPrade had written in. They might have kept on thinking so if Miss LaPrade hadn't been screaming so hysterically from the side lines. And if Rat Joiner hadn't decided that this was as good a time as any to settle old scores. So he turned around and took a sock at the male Good Fairy nearest him.

When the curtain rang down, the forces of Good and Evil were locked in combat. And Sleeping Beauty was wide-awake and streaking for the wings.

They rang the curtain back up fifteen minutes later, and we finished the play. I lay down and expired according to specifications, but Prince Charming will probably remember my sneering corpse to his dying day. They wouldn't let me appear in the grand dramatic offering at all the next year. But I didn't care. I couldn't have been Prince Charming anyway.

Starting Time: _____	Finishing Time: _____
Reading Time: _____	Reading Rate: _____
Comprehension: _____	Vocabulary: _____

VOCABULARY: The following words have been taken from the selection you have just read. Put an *X* in the box before the best meaning or synonym for the word as used in the selection.

1. **intervening**, page 78, column 1, paragraph 1
"...our leading colored citizens sat right behind them—with an empty row intervening, of course."
☐ a. interfering
☐ b. coming between
☐ c. interviewing
☐ d. joining together

2. **ferment**, page 78, column 1, paragraph 4
"The Booker T. Washington Colored Grammar School was in a state of ferment from Christmas until February,"
☐ a. fervent
☐ b. anticipation
☐ c. excitement
☐ d. planning

3. **skulking**, page 78, column 2, paragraph 3
"...I would be leading the forces of darkness and skulking back in the shadows—"
☐ a. lurking
☐ b. retreating
☐ c. disappearing
☐ d. crawling

4. **purloined**, page 79, column 1, paragraph 3
"Yes, and I purloined my sister's can of Palmer's Skin Success."
☐ a. stole
☐ b. purchased
☐ c. borrowed
☐ d. used

5. **impromptu**, page 79, column 2, paragraph 6
"I cited the impromptu rapping he had given my head..."
☐ a. unplanned
☐ b. unexpected
☐ c. improper
☐ d. organized

ROOTS

Many English words consist of a base or root word to which prefixes (beginnings) and suffixes (endings) have been added. To the root word **agree** (a verb) we can add both a prefix and a suffix to get **disagreeable** (an adjective) which has an opposite meaning.

Roots are Latin and Greek stems on which our English words are based. For example, **bio** (life) is a Greek root on which our word **biology** (the study of plant and animal life) is built.

Two Roots

1. **mon** is a Greek root which means **one** or **single**. A **monosyllabic** word has just one syllable.

2. **psycho** is also a Greek root and it means **mind**. **Psychology** is the science which studies the workings of the mind.

In the following sentences, these roots have been left out. Space has been left indicating where the root belongs. Add one of these two roots and write your word on the line following the sentence.

1. A —**arch** rules alone.

    _____

2. Some mental disorders are called —**ses**.

    _____

3. A book or paper written on a single subject is a —**ograph**.

    _____

4. —**otony** is caused by a sameness or lack of variety.

    _____

5. Physical disorders are sometimes —**somatic**; they are emotional in origin.

    _____

6. In a —**drama** a patient acts out situations related to his mental problems.

    _____

7. —**aural** records and tapes contain just a single sound track.

    _____

8. Many patients undergo —**analysis** to reduce inner conflict.

    _____

9. Hypnosis is a popular form of —**therapy**.

    _____

10. A —**ologue** is delivered by an entertainer performing alone.

    _____

MASTERING THE TEXT, II

After checking on the author, examine some of the standard features of the text: the Table of Contents and the Bibliography.

Table of Contents

Next to the chapters themselves, this is the most important part of the text. This not only reveals the material covered; it also reveals how it is organized. Is the subject covered historically, chronologically? If so, you know that current thought will come at the end. You know that the early part of the text will present biographical data on previous contributors to this field.

The author's presentation may not be historical—it may be analytical. He may proceed from the simple to the complex. If so, this tells the reader that fundamental concepts will be discussed early in the text. The reader will need to know and understand these if he is to grasp material presented later.

Even though you may not know the field, you can determine how it will be presented. You may wish to preread a section of the text which interests you. This may contribute to your background in the field and may help you appreciate (or tolerate) material presented in the text.

The Bibliography

A bibliography is a list of books. At the end of a textbook, authors tell the reader which books they have referred to or obtained information from in presenting their subject. The listing tells the reader, too, which kinds of references and sources the author has used. Has the author referred to other textbooks or has he consulted original materials in the field? Examine the level of his sources. Are they comprehensive or do they appear to be highly specialized? Perhaps there's a book cited which you will want to read yourself for additional information.

COMPREHENSION: For each of the following statements and questions, select the option containing the most complete or most accurate answer.

1. The social life of Hopkinsville's Black population was
(h)
    ☐ a. rewarding.
    ☐ b. varied.
    ☐ c. limited.
    ☐ d. exciting.

2. The traditional standards governing role as-
(f) signments at the Booker T. Washington Colored Grammar School seem to be modeled after
    ☐ a. professional standards.
    ☐ b. white racism.
    ☐ c. amateur practices.
    ☐ d. intelligent policies.

3. The yearly variations on the school's produc-
(g) tion of the "Prince Charming and Sleeping Beauty" theme could have which of the following psychological connotations?
    ☐ a. Imaginary fantasies
    ☐ b. Obsessive fear
    ☐ c. Self-love
    ☐ d. Self-hatred

4. Rat Joiner's two comments are
(i)
    ☐ a. intentionally witty.
    ☐ b. wrily humorous.
    ☐ c. deliberately discouraging.
    ☐ d. sadly tragic.

5. The selection is obviously written in a light-
(e) hearted vein. Ted Poston, however, could be expressing which of the following views?
    ☐ a. Some Blacks can easily pass for white.
    ☐ b. Some Blacks resent their blackness and discriminate against other Blacks.
    ☐ c. Stage productions at Booker T. Washington fall below national standards.
    ☐ d. An all-Black school is inferior to an all-white school.

6. The faculty at Booker T. Washington was
(c)
    ☐ a. sensitive to the needs of Black students.
    ☐ b. impressed by the talent of Miss LaPrade.
    ☐ c. responsive to the needs of the Black community.
    ☐ d. partial to the ideologies of the white community.

7. Objectively, the empty row separating the
(k) audiences represents
    ☐ a. polite consideration.
    ☐ b. faculty nonconformity.
    ☐ c. Southern hospitality.
    ☐ d. historical divisions.

8. The Head Evil Fairy's decision to change dras-
(h) tically the outcome of the play was
    ☐ a. appreciated by the faculty.
    ☐ b. his moment of glory.
    ☐ c. resented by the audience.
    ☐ d. Rat Joiner's fault.

9. Prince Charming is to the Head Evil Fairy as
(g)
    ☐ a. antagonist is to protagonist.
    ☐ b. bystander is to observer.
    ☐ c. pedestrian is to driver.
    ☐ d. character is to play.

10. Which of the following expresses honest racial
(g) pride?
    ☐ a. "The title of our play never varied."
    ☐ b. "I couldn't have been Prince Charming anyway."
    ☐ c. "Yes, and I purloined my sister's can of Palmer's Skin Success."
    ☐ d. "As long as she don't call you a black baboon."

> Comprehension Skills: a—isolating details; b—recalling specific facts; c—retaining concepts; d—organizing facts; e—understanding the main idea; f—drawing a conclusion; g—making a judgment; h—making an inference; i—recognizing tone; j—understanding characters; k—appreciation of literary forms.

Up From Slavery

The Founder and First President of Tuskegee Institute Describes His Efforts to Obtain an Education

Booker T. Washington

One day, while at work in the coal-mine, I happened to overhear two miners talking about a great school for coloured people somewhere in Virginia. This was the first time that I had ever heard anything about any kind of school or college that was more pretentious than the little coloured school in our town.

In the darkness of the mine I noiselessly crept as close as I could to the two men who were talking. I heard one tell the other that not only was the school established for the members of my race, but that opportunities were provided by which poor but worthy students could work out all or a part of the cost of board, and at the same time be taught some trade or industry.

As they went on describing the school, it seemed to me that it must be the greatest place on earth, and not even Heaven presented more attractions for me at that time than did the Hampton Normal and Agricultural Institute in Virginia, about which these men were talking. I resolved at once to go to that school, although I had no idea where it was, or how many miles away, or how I was going to reach it; I remembered only that I was on fire constantly with one ambition, and that was to go to Hampton. This thought was with me day and night. . . .

In the fall of 1872 I determined to make an effort to get there, although, as I have stated, I had no definite idea of the direction in which Hampton was, or of what it would cost to go there. I do not think that any one thoroughly sympathized with me in my ambition to go to Hampton unless it was my mother, and she was troubled with a grave fear that I was starting out on a "wild-goose chase." At any rate, I got only a half-hearted consent from her that I might start. The small amount of money that I had earned had been consumed by my stepfather and the remainder of the family, with the exception of a very few dollars, and so I had very little with which to buy clothes and pay my travelling expenses. My brother John helped me all that he could, but of course that was not a great deal, for his work was in the coal-mine, where he did not earn much, and most of what he did earn went in the direction of paying the household expenses.

Perhaps the thing that touched and pleased me most in connection with my starting for Hampton was the interest that many of the older coloured people took in the matter. They had spent the best days of their lives in slavery, and hardly expected to live to see the time when they would see a member of their race leave home to attend a boarding-school. Some of these older people would give me a nickel, others a quarter, or a handkerchief.

Finally the great day came, and I started for Hampton. I had only a small, cheap satchel that contained what few articles of clothing I could get. My mother at the time was rather weak and broken in health. I hardly expected to see her again, and thus our parting was all the more sad. She, however, was very brave through it all. At that time there were no through trains connecting that part of West Virginia with eastern Virginia. Trains ran only a portion of the way, and the remainder of the distance was travelled by stage-coaches.

The distance from Malden to Hampton is about five hundred miles. I had not been away from home many hours before it began to grow painfully evident that I did not have enough money to pay my fare to Hampton. . . .

By walking, begging rides both in wagons and in the cars, in some way, after a number of days, I reached the city of Richmond, Virginia, about eighty-two miles from Hampton. When I reached there, tired, hungry, and dirty, it was late in the night. I had never been in a large city, and this rather added to my misery . . . . I was completely out of money . . . .

I must have walked the streets till after midnight. At last I became so exhausted that I could walk no longer. I was tired, I was hungry, I was everything but discouraged. Just about the time when I reached extreme physical exhaustion, I came upon a portion of a street where the board sidewalk was considerably elevated. I waited for a few minutes, till I was sure that no passers-by could see me, and then crept under the sidewalk and lay for the night upon the ground, with my satchel of clothing for a pillow. Nearly all night I could hear the tramp of feet over my head. The next morning I found myself somewhat refreshed,

Booker Taliaferro Washington was born a slave in Hale's Ford, Virginia, in 1856.

He was graduated from Hampton Institute in 1872 and, after teaching for a while, founded Tuskegee Institute in 1881.

In contrast to Frederick Douglass, the fiery Negro leader before him, Washington endorsed a more conciliatory policy of civil rights.

Because of his racially moderate viewpoint, Washington is sometimes regarded with little favor by today's militant Blacks even though his influence and self-help programs improved considerably conditions for Negroes of that time.

but I was extremely hungry, because it had been a long time since I had had sufficient food. As soon as it became light enough for me to see my surroundings I noticed that I was near a large ship, and that this ship seemed to be unloading a cargo of pig iron. I went at once to the vessel and asked the captain to permit me to help unload the vessel in order to get money for food. The captain, a white man, who seemed to be kind-hearted, consented. I worked long enough to earn money for my breakfast, and it seems to me, as I remember it now, to have been about the best breakfast that I have ever eaten.

My work pleased the captain so well that he told me if I desired I could continue working for a small amount per day. This I was very glad to do. I continued working on this vessel for a number of days. After buying food with the small wages I received there was not much left to add to the amount I must get to pay my way to Hampton. In order to economize in every way possible, so as to be sure to reach Hampton in a reasonable time, I continued to sleep under the same sidewalk that gave me shelter the first night I was in Richmond. . . .

When I had saved what I considered enough money with which to reach Hampton, I thanked the captain of the vessel for his kindness, and started again. Without any unusual occurrence I reached Hampton, with a surplus of exactly fifty cents with which to begin my education. To me it had been a long, eventful journey; but the first sight of the large, three-story, brick school building seemed to have rewarded me for all that I had undergone in order to reach the place. . . . It

seemed to me to be the largest and most beautiful building I had ever seen. The sight of it seemed to give me new life. I felt that a new kind of existence had now begun—that life would now have a new meaning. I felt that I had reached the promised land, and I resolved to let no obstacle prevent me from putting forth the highest effort to fit myself to accomplish the most good in the world. . . .

Life at Hampton was a constant revelation to me; was constantly taking me into a new world. The matter of having meals at regular hours, of eating on a tablecloth, using a napkin, the use of the bathtub and of the tooth-brush, as well as the use of sheets upon the bed, were all new to me. . . .

The charge for my board at Hampton was ten dollars per month. I was expected to pay a part of this in cash and to work out the remainder. To meet this cash payment, as I have stated, I had just fifty cents when I reached the institution. Aside from a very few dollars that my brother John was able to send me once in a while, I had no money with which to pay my board. I was determined from the first to make my work as janitor so valuable that my services would be indispensable. This I succeeded in doing to such an extent that I was soon informed that I would be allowed the full cost of my board in return for my work. The cost of tuition was seventy dollars a year. This, of course, was wholly beyond my ability to provide. If I had been compelled to pay the seventy dollars for tuition, in addition to providing for my board, I would have been compelled to leave the Hampton school. General Armstrong, however, very kindly got Mr. S. Griffitts Morgan, of New Bedford, Mass., to defray the cost of my tuition during the whole time that I was at Hampton. . . .

After having been for a while at Hampton, I found myself in difficulty because I did not have books and clothing. Usually, however, I got around the trouble about books by borrowing from those who were more fortunate than myself. As to clothes, when I reached Hampton I had practically nothing. Everything that I possessed was in the small hand satchel. . . .

In some way I managed to get on till the teachers learned that I was in earnest and meant to succeed, and then some of them were kind enough to see that I was partly supplied with second-hand clothing that had been sent in barrels from the North. These barrels proved a blessing to hundreds of poor but deserving students. Without them I question whether I should ever have gotten through Hampton. . . .

From *Up From Slavery* by Booker T. Washington. (1900)

SELECTIONS FROM THE BLACK

I was among the youngest of the students who were in Hampton at that time. Most of the students were men and women—some as old as forty years of age. As I now recall the scene of my first year, I do not believe that one often has the opportunity of coming into contact with three or four hundred men and women who were so tremendously in earnest as these men and women were. Every hour was occupied in study or work. Nearly all had had enough actual contact with the world to teach them the need of education. Many of the older ones were, of course, too old to master the textbooks very thoroughly, and it was often sad to watch their struggles; but they made up in earnestness much of what they lacked in books. Many of them were as poor as I was, and, besides having to wrestle with their books, they had to struggle with a poverty which prevented their having the necessities of life. Many of them had aged parents who were dependent upon them, and some of them were men who had wives whose support in some way they had to provide for.

The great and prevailing idea that seemed to take possession of every one was to prepare himself to lift up the people at his home. No one seemed to think of himself. And the officers and teachers, what a rare set of human beings they were! They worked for the students night and day, in season and out of season. They seemed happy only when they were helping students in some manner. Whenever it is written—and I hope it will be—the part that the Yankee teachers played in the education of the Negroes immediately after the war will make one of the most thrilling parts of the history of this country.

Starting Time: _____   Finishing Time: _____

Reading Time: _____   Reading Rate: _____

Comprehension: _____   Vocabulary: _____

VOCABULARY: The following words have been taken from the selection you have just read. Put an *X* in the box before the best meaning or synonym for the word as used in the selection.

1. **pretentious**, page 83, column 1, paragraph 1
"...that was more pretentious than the little coloured school in our town."
☐ a. aspiring
☐ b. ostentatious
☐ c. qualified
☐ d. presentable

2. **economize**, page 84, column 1, paragraph 2
"In order to economize in every way possible,"
☐ a. work profitably
☐ b. produce
☐ c. save money
☐ d. exist

3. **indispensable**, page 84, column 2, paragraph 3
"...so valuable that my services would be indispensable."
☐ a. absolutely necessary
☐ b. unessential
☐ c. highly acclaimed
☐ d. quite noticeable

4. **defray**, page 84, column 2, paragraph 3
"...to defray the cost of my tuition..."
☐ a. advance
☐ b. borrow
☐ c. pay
☐ d. defer

5. **prevailing**, page 85, column 2, line 1
"The great and prevailing idea that seemed to take possession of every one..."
☐ a. elusive
☐ b. overwhelming
☐ c. occasional
☐ d. dominant

CONTEXTUAL AIDS: SYNONYMS

Studies of good readers show that they are aware of the context of what they are reading. This means that they are anticipating what is coming next by what has gone before.

Using the context as an aid to rapid understanding is a valuable tool to the reader. Context is also an aid to word recognition.

The many ways in which context functions to help the reader recognize words are called contextual aids.

Contextual Aid 6. Words can be understood through synonyms provided in the context. In the example, **He _____ the note, concealing it from everyone**, the reader would correctly guess that the missing word is **hid** because of the synonym **concealing** which follows it.

In the following sentences nonsense words have been used with synonyms. Underline the nonsense word and write the correct word on the line following each sentence.

1. His promotion came and he scandered to the next rank.

    _____

2. I asked him for furness because his counsel is always valuable.

    _____

3. That machine makes metrons, putting out one facsimile every second.

    _____

4. That singer is ringbest, renowned throughout the world for his voice.

    _____

5. How anp did you go on that distant trip?

    _____

6. When it comes to style, she dresses in the latest itinons.

    _____

7. It was filmed on location, making a beautiful kenter.

    _____

8. In debutral matters, you should have a monitary adviser.

    _____

9. He marted the door open using all his strength.

    _____

10. Build a solid prondonture; a house must have a firm base.

    _____

11. Hire a lawyer to handle the prendle aspects of the case.

    _____

MASTERING THE TEXT, III

Another feature of the text you will want to explore is the index. Use it to obtain some cold, hard facts about your author and his presentation.

The Index

Every textbook contains a subject index. There may be other indexes too: for example, an author's index may be included so that you can look up by name those authorities mentioned throughout the text. Also listed will be their writings and works.

The subject index is likely to be the only one included in your texts. This index lists alphabetically aspects and topics which were discussed in the text. The page number is given with each listing.

Based on classroom lectures or on some previous knowledge of yours in this field, evaluate the author's treatment of one topic. Look through the index until you find a familiar listing. Go to the page given and read the material covered. What kind of job has the author done? Did he discuss what you expected? Or was his treatment too superficial? Make a couple of other checks if necessary to see if this same treatment occurs throughout the text. You may discover that the text covers the field in much greater depth than you wish or need; or the opposite may be true: this text is too sketchy for you. You may need a much more comprehensive discussion than what is presented here.

Granted you may be powerless to change texts and authors—this may be the assigned text for the course you are taking. You can, however, use other texts. Find one to supplement this, one you can read first to make the assigned text easier to understand. Or you may wish to read a more comprehensive text, along with the assigned one, to broaden your knowledge—feed your interest in the subject.

COMPREHENSION: For each of the following statements and questions, select the option containing the most complete or most accurate answer.

1. The selection can be classified as
(k)
  □ a. narrative.
  □ b. biographical.
  □ c. autobiographical.
  □ d. descriptive.

2. The tone of the selection is
(i)
  □ a. depressing.
  □ b. ironic.
  □ c. factual.
  □ d. hopeful.

3. Booker T. Washington was raised in
(a)
  □ a. Malden, West Virginia.
  □ b. Richmond, Virginia.
  □ c. Hampton, Virginia.
  □ d. Roanoke, Virginia

4. Washington's trip to the normal school was
(b) plagued by difficulties because
  □ a. there were no trains.
  □ b. the stage coaches were unreliable.
  □ c. walking was unsafe.
  □ d. he had very little money.

5. At the normal school, Booker T. Washington
(h) probably studied
  □ a. law.
  □ b. agriculture.
  □ c. medicine.
  □ d. economics.

6. The school administration provided financial
(h) assistance especially to those students who were
  □ a. young and orphaned.
  □ b. ambitious and determined.
  □ c. poor and Black.
  □ d. talented and eager.

7. The student body at Hampton could be com-
(g) pared to
  □ a. the leaven in the dough.
  □ b. non-violent demonstrators.
  □ c. militant activists.
  □ d. the frosting on the cake.

8. There is evidence to suggest that the Hampton
(h) Normal and Agricultural Institute received support from
  □ a. the federal government.
  □ b. Black organizations.
  □ c. the state of Virginia.
  □ d. Northern whites.

9. The selection suggests that Washington was
(j)
  □ a. remarkable, despite average ability.
  □ b. poor, hungry and lonely.
  □ c. ingenious, talented and industrious.
  □ d. insensitive to his family's needs.

10. Which of the following best expresses the
(e) theme of the selection?
  □ a. Slow and steady wins the race.
  □ b. To reap, one must sow.
  □ c. The truth shall set men free.
  □ d. Virtue is its own reward.

Comprehension Skills: a—isolating details; b—recalling specific facts; c—retaining concepts; d—organizing facts; e—understanding the main idea; f—drawing a conclusion; g—making a judgment; h—making an inference; i—recognizing tone; j—understanding characters; k—appreciation of literary forms.

No Name in the Street

Baldwin's Most Eloquent, Personal and Complete Expression on the Subject of His Times and Society

James Baldwin

I had heard a great deal about Malcolm, as had everyone else, and I was a little afraid of him, as was everyone else, and I was further handicapped by having been out of the country for so long. When I returned to America, I again went South, and thus, imperceptibly, found myself mainly on the road. I saw Malcolm before I met him. I had just returned from someplace like Savannah, I was giving a lecture somewhere in New York, and Malcolm was sitting in the first or second row of the hall, bending forward at such an angle that his long arms nearly caressed the ankles of his long legs, staring up at me. I very nearly panicked. I knew Malcolm only by legend, and this legend, since I was a Harlem street boy, I was sufficiently astute to distrust. I distrusted the legend because we, in Harlem, have been betrayed so often. Malcolm might be the torch white people claimed he was—though, in general, white America's evaluations of these matters would be laughable and even pathetic did not these evaluations have such wicked results—or he might be the hustler I remembered from my pavements. On the other hand, Malcolm had no reason to trust me, either—and so I stumbled through my lecture, with Malcolm never taking his eyes from my face.

It must be remembered that in those great days I was considered to be an "integrationist"—this was never, quite, my own idea of myself—and Malcolm was considered to be a "racist in reverse." This formulation, in terms of power—and power is the arena in which racism is acted out—means absolutely nothing: it may even be described as a cowardly formulation. The powerless, by definition, can never be "racists," for they can never make the world pay for what they feel or fear except by the suicidal endeavor which makes them fanatics or revolutionaries, or both; whereas, those in power can be urbane and charming and invite you to those which they know you will never own. The powerless must do their own dirty work. The powerful have it done for them.

Anyway: somewhat later, I was the host, or moderator, for a radio program starring Malcolm X and a sit-in student from the Deep South. I was the moderator because both the radio station and I

were afraid that Malcolm would simply eat the boy alive. I didn't want to be there, but there was no way out of it. I had come prepared to throw various camp stools under the child, should he seem wobbly; to throw out the life-line whenever Malcolm should seem to be carrying the child beyond his depth. Never has a moderator been less needed. Malcolm understood that child and talked to him as though he were talking to a younger brother, and with that same watchful attention. What most struck me was that he was not at all trying to proselytize the child: he was trying to make him think. He was trying to do for the child what he supposed, for too long a time, that the Honorable Elijah had done for him. But I did not think of that until much later. I will never forget Malcolm and that child facing each other, and Malcolm's extraordinary gentleness. And that's the truth about Malcolm: he was one of the gentlest people I have ever met. And I am sure that the child remembers him that way. That boy, by the way, battling so valiantly for civil rights, might have been, for all I can swear to, Stokely Carmichael or Huey Newton or Bobby Seale or Rap Brown or one of my nephews. That's how long or how short— *oh, pioneers!*—the apprehension of betrayal takes: "If you are an American citizen," Malcolm asked the boy, "why have you got to fight for your rights as a citizen? To be a citizen means that you have the rights of a citizen. If you haven't got the rights of a citizen, then you're not a citizen." "It's not as simple as that," the boy said. "Why not?" asked Malcolm.

I was, in some way, in those years, without entirely realizing it, the Great Black Hope of the Great White Father. I was *not* a racist—so I thought; Malcolm *was* a racist, so *he* thought. In fact, we were simply trapped in the same situation, as poor Martin was later to discover (who, in those days, did not talk to Malcolm and was a little nervous with me). As the GBH of the GWF, anyway, I appeared on a television program, along with Malcolm and several other hopes, including Mr. George S. Schuyler. It was pretty awful. If I had ever hoped to become a racist, Mr. Schuyler dashed my hopes forever, then and there. I can scarcely discuss this

Photo: Mottke Weissman

In August 1972, The Dial Press published *No Name In the Street*, James Baldwin's long-awaited personal statement on what has happened in and to America through the political and social agonies of her recent history. *No Name In the Street* is Mr. Baldwin's first collection of essays since the publication of his prophetic *The Fire Next Time* in 1963.

program except to say that Malcolm and I very quickly dismissed Mr. Schuyler and virtually everyone else, and, as the old street rats and the heirs of Baptist ministers, played the program off each other.

Nothing could have been more familiar to me than Malcolm's style in debate. I had heard it all my life. It was vehemently non-stop and Malcolm was young and looked younger; this caused his opponents to suppose that Malcolm was reckless. Nothing could have been less reckless, more calculated, even to those loopholes he so often left dangling. These were not loopholes at all, but hangman's knots, as whoever rushed for the loophole immediately discovered. Whenever this happened, the strangling interlocutor invariably looked to me, as being the more "reasonable," to say something which would loosen the knot. Mr. Schuyler often *did* say something, but it was always the wrong thing, giving Malcolm yet another opportunity. All I could do was elaborate on some of Malcolm's points, or modify, or emphasize, or seem to try to clarify, but there was no way I could disagree with him. The others were discussing the past or the future, or a country which may once have existed, or one which may yet be brought into existence—Malcolm was speaking of the bitter and unanswerable present. And it was too important that this be heard for anyone to attempt to soften it. It was important, of course, for white people to hear it, if they were still able to hear; but it was of the utmost importance for black people to hear it, for the sake of their morale. It was important for them to know that there was someone like them,

in public life, telling the truth about their condition. Malcolm considered himself to be the spiritual property of the people who produced him. He did not consider himself to be their saviour, he was far too modest for that, and gave that role to another; but he considered himself to be their servant and in order not to betray that trust, he was willing to die, and died. Malcolm was not a racist, not even when he thought he was. His intelligence was more complex than that; furthermore, if he had been a racist, not many in this racist country would have considered him dangerous. He would have sounded familiar and even comforting, his familiar rage confirming the reality of white power and sensuously inflaming a bizarre species of guilty eroticism without which, I am beginning to believe, most white Americans of the more or less liberal persuasion cannot draw a single breath. What made him unfamiliar and dangerous was not his hatred for white people but his love for blacks, his apprehension of the horror of the black condition, and the reasons for it, and his determination so to work on their hearts and minds that they would be enabled to see their condition and change it themselves.

For this, after all, not only were no white people needed; they posed, *en bloc*, the very greatest obstacle to black self-knowledge and had to be considered a menace. But white people have played so dominant a role in the world's history for so long that such an attitude toward them constitutes the most disagreeable of novelties; and it may be added that, though they have never learned how to live with the darker brother, they do not look forward to having to learn how to live without him. Malcolm, finally, was a genuine revolutionary, a virile impulse long since fled from the American way of life—in himself, indeed, he was a kind of revolution, both in the sense of a return to a former principle, and in the sense of an upheaval. It is pointless to speculate on his probable fate had he been legally white. Given the white man's options, it is probably just as well for all of us that he was legally black. In some church someday, so far unimagined and unimaginable, he will be hailed as a saint.

Starting Time: _____   Finishing Time: _____

Reading Time: _____   Reading Rate: _____

Comprehension: _____   Vocabulary: _____

VOCABULARY: The following words have been taken from the selection you have just read. Put an *X* in the box before the best meaning or synonym for the word as used in the selection.

1. **imperceptibly,** page 88, column 1, paragraph 1
"...I again went South, and thus, imperceptibly, found myself mainly on the road."
☐ a. invisibly
☐ b. impressively
☐ c. quickly
☐ d. gradually

2. **astute,** page 88, column 1, paragraph 1
"...I was sufficiently astute to distrust."
☐ a. unknowing
☐ b. honest
☐ c. shrewd
☐ d. wicked

3. **pathetic,** page 88, column 1, paragraph 1
"...would be laughable and even pathetic..."
☐ a. emotional
☐ b. pitiable
☐ c. tender
☐ d. hysterical

4. **stumbled,** page 88, column 1, paragraph 1
"—and so I stumbled through my lecture,"
☐ a. tripped
☐ b. fell
☐ c. hesitated
☐ d. hurried

5. **virile,** page 89, column 2, paragraph 2
"...a virile impulse long since fled from the American way of life—"
☐ a. pioneering
☐ b. virulent
☐ c. vigorous
☐ d. inflammatory

SUFFIXES

Many English words consist of a base or root word to which prefixes (beginnings) and suffixes (endings) have been added. To the root word **agree** (a verb) we can add both a prefix and a suffix to get **disagreeable** (an adjective) which has an opposite meaning.

A suffix is added to the end of a word and changes the part of speech of that word. We have just seen how the suffix **able** changes **agree** from a verb to an adjective.

Two Suffixes

1. **-ful** is an Old English adjective suffix. The verb **wonder** becomes an adjective, **wonderful**.

2. **-ness** is an Old English noun suffix. The adjective **happy** becomes a noun, **happiness**. Notice that the **y** in **happy** changed to **i** before the suffix.

In the following sentences, root words have been set in bold print. Add one of these suffixes to each root and write the new word on the line following the sentence. As you add suffixes to words, you may have to drop or change letters.

1. His **good** spread to those around him.

   _____

2. The **sudden** of the noise startled everyone.

   _____

3. There was great **sad** over his death.

   _____

4. Take a **teaspoon** of the green liquid before meals.

   _____

5. Having a tooth extracted is no longer **pain**.

   _____

6. The **fuzzy** of the photograph made him difficult to recognize.

   _____

7. Brotherhood fosters **together**.

   _____

8. Without a doubt, she is **beauty**.

   _____

9. His interpretation of the composition was **master**.

   _____

10. Remind him to bring his keys; he is so **forget**.

    _____

11. The **prompt** of the president's reply surprised us all.

    _____

MASTERING THE TEXT, IV

You know from earlier discussions that previewing is the wise reader's first step. Fortunately the organization of today's texts makes previewing rapid and rewarding. Here are the steps to follow when previewing a textbook chapter.

Preread the Chapter

1. **Read the Title.** As mentioned earlier, this is the author's announcement of what is to come — this may define the limits of the chapter.

2. **Read the Subhead.** The author's list of the three or four main points will be given here, or else a clue to the significance of the forthcoming material may be found. Either way, get the jump on the chapter.

3. **Read the Illustration.** Don't just look at it. Study it to see what it says. Graphs, maps, and charts appear in texts, too, to present visually data which may take hundreds of words to cover. At the very simplest, graphic aids demonstrate some relationship between two facts. This relationship may be the very heart of the chapter—the base which supports the entire discussion. If students are lacking, it is usually here. A false belief that time can be saved by overlooking graphic aids could decrease your understanding and increase your time spent trying to comprehend.

4. **Read the Opening Paragraph.** This helps you organize the material to come. Try to see what will be expected of you when you read.

5. **Read the Closing Paragraph.** Capitalize on the author's parting words— his statement which caps the chapter.

6. **Skim through the Chapter.** Get the feel of the presentation. Use typographical aids: roman numerals, headlines, italics, capital letters. Try to find the three or four main points to be covered. That's usually all there are in one lesson.

COMPREHENSION: For each of the following statements and questions, select the option containing the most complete or most accurate answer.

1. James Baldwin's reactions to Malcolm X
(i) ranged from
   - ☐ a. abuse to worship.
   - ☐ b. satisfaction to dissatisfaction.
   - ☐ c. trust to distrust.
   - ☐ d. uncertainty to admiration.

2. Taking time and place into consideration,
(g) Malcolm was
   - ☐ a. confused and unrealistic.
   - ☐ b. ahead of his time.
   - ☐ c. unique but narrow-minded.
   - ☐ d. accepted at face value.

3. Baldwin invokes personal background to ex-
(c) plain his insight into
   - ☐ a. the legend surrounding Malcolm X.
   - ☐ b. Malcolm X's attempts at hustling.
   - ☐ c. racism in reverse.
   - ☐ d. explaining Malcolm X's presence at his lecture.

4. The word which might explain Malcolm's
(h) presence at Baldwin's lecture is
   - ☐ a. who.
   - ☐ b. what.
   - ☐ c. where.
   - ☐ d. how.

5. James Baldwin would readily admit to having
(g)
   - ☐ a. regressed.
   - ☐ b. evolved.
   - ☐ c. surrendered.
   - ☐ d. accommodated.

6. White Americans looked upon Malcolm X as
(c)
   - ☐ a. a conformist.
   - ☐ b. a pacifist.
   - ☐ c. an incendiary.
   - ☐ d. a dreamer.

7. Racism can be reduced to a question of
(c)
   - ☐ a. power.
   - ☐ b. location.
   - ☐ c. legality.
   - ☐ d. knowledge.

8. The unfortunate position the powerless as
(h) opposed to the powerful are reduced to is
   - ☐ a. surrender.
   - ☐ b. compromise.
   - ☐ c. violence.
   - ☐ d. choice.

9. The potentially explosive radio interview was
(i) handled with
   - ☐ a. indifference.
   - ☐ b. cruelty.
   - ☐ c. firmness.
   - ☐ d. sensitivity.

10. Malcolm's ultimate objective was to
(e)
   - ☐ a. educate the white power structure.
   - ☐ b. provoke Black reaction.
   - ☐ c. undermine the white power structure.
   - ☐ d. foment revolution.

Comprehension Skills: a—isolating details; b—recalling specific facts; c—retaining concepts; d—organizing facts; e—understanding the main idea; f—drawing a conclusion; g—making a judgment; h—making an inference; i—recognizing tone; j—understanding characters; k—appreciation of literary forms.

A Love Song for Seven Little Boys Called Sam, I

It was just that every day they had to fight, and Reuben was sick of it.

C. H. Fuller, Jr.

The seven had been confined, since the first grade, to their own special section of the class. This year, as expected, their teacher, Miss Arnold, had seated them in the rear near the door. It was close to the lavatory, but otherwise it was the worse spot in the third grade. They were all eight years old, except for Reuben, who was eight-and-a-half. He sat at his desk, staring at Miss Arnold's wide nose, and recalling that his mother had promised a surprise for his birthday, *if* he got an "A" in Spelling. He didn't like his mother's surprises, or Miss Arnold. His mother always surprised him with clothes, and his teacher always complained about the way he dressed. But he did wish he was nine. When you're nine, you're bigger, and nobody messed with you; like the white boys did every afternoon.

He bet if he and his friends were all nine, the white kids would leave them alone. Not that the seven of them couldn't fight. Stevie, Billy, Allen, Francis, Harold, and Kenny were the best fighters he'd ever seen. It was just that *every day* they had to fight, and Reuben was sick of it. The bell in the Ingram Elementary School rang, and its only black pupils, seven little boys, picked up their schoolbags, and started outside into the afternoon chill.

No one talked to them. Even Miss Arnold, the lone colored teacher in the school, shunned them, except for the two times she complained about the way they talked. Reuben watched her now, crossing the street against the light, holding the hands of two little white boys. She never took his hand—he wouldn't let her either! If she didn't like them, he didn't like her. The seven of them waited at the corner, and sprinted across on the traffic lady's signal. Reuben sucked in a deep breath, and pivoted around. The daily trouble was just about to begin, and he wondered why, when they stopped the buses in the first grade, they didn't send them to a school in their own neighborhood.

"Hey Sams! Hey look 'et all the little black Sams!" A group of five second-graders shot past them, their schoolbags swinging, their white faces, red with excitement.

"Your mother's a Sam!" It was Billy. He always talked about people's mothers. Reuben didn't like that stuff, and if they played the "dozens" with him, somebody was gonna' get hurt.

"Your mother's a black dog," one yelled.

"When I catch you, I'ma' punch you in the mouth, hear? I don't play that stuff, boy!"

"Awwww, shut up, blackie! Old black Billy, and ole black Joe, must be niggers, 'cause they run so slow!"

"Old black Sams! Seven old black Sams!"

The white kids continued to run. When they reached the corner, they turned and headed west, but not before Allen picked up a stone, and threw it. It hit the boy on the leg; he stopped momentarily, looked at the bruise it had made, then kept going when he realized Allen was almost on top of him.

It was the same every day. Reuben had gotten used to it. There were three blocks of enemy territory. Every afternoon, the older white boys would send the little white boys darting past them, shouting "Sam," "blackie" or "nigger." Then, after the first block, they would meet a group of the older boys, who'd blame them for chasing the little boys, and after a fight, the seven of them would be chased home. Reuben hated it.

The white kids had been doing it every day for a month. He didn't understand white people. They sit next to you in school, and beat you up on the way home. They can't be trusted. Once they passed the graveyard they would be safe. Black people lived on the other side of those graves, and the white boys never chased them that far. "Over there, they wouldn' mess with me," Reuben thought, preparing himself for what would happen when they reached the next corner. "Billy! Billy Mayfield!" It was Miss Arnold. Reuben recognized the weak, scratchy voice. Her hard, black face was staring at Billy. She was a witch.

"Yes, Miss Arnold?"

"What did you say to those boys?"

"I didn' say nothin!"

"I heard you! You want me to send a note to your mother?"

"He had no business callin' me nigger! My name ain't no nigger!"

"Billy, sticks and stones may break my bones, but names will never harm me! You ought to be glad you can go to school with different kinds of people."

"My name ain't nigger—Mom told me to let nobody call me that!"

"Well, we'll see what your mother has to say!"

"I didn' do nothin'!"

"Goodbye, Billy."

"I didn' do nothin'!—and my mother ain't gonna' do nothin' to me either! 'Cause my name ain't no nigger!"

"Why they kept you kids in the school I'll never know—" She mumbled something else, but they didn't hear her. Harold Davis called her a black bitch behind her back. She disappeared into a store. "She don't never say nothin' to them," Reuben said, aware that this had a great deal to do with why he disliked her.

"My father said, she's prejudice," Harold Davis said, leaping out in front of them.

"What's that," Kenny asked.

"You don't know nothin' Kenny! My mother said only white people are prejudice. 'Cause white people don't like black people—and she said only white people do prejudice. I know all about that," Stevie put in.

"Well, Miss Arnold ain't white!" Kenny looked around at them. They were all silent for a moment.

"My father said, some colored people do it too, but white people do it all the time," Harold Davis said authoritatively. It satisfied Reuben. Harold Davis knew everything.

"Hey! What took you Sambos so long? You scared or something?" Reuben looked up at the corner and wanted to cry. There were a dozen white boys blocking the sidewalk, and swinging their schoolbags in a preparatory challenge. Reuben tried to slow down, and even wished he could leave his friends and run home, but he didn't do either. There was an attraction in this daily meeting. Something compelling in twisted expressions of the white boys made him want to take every opportunity to smash the ugliness from their faces. The sight of their hate for him made him angry. No one had a right to look at him that way! There was a moment of stillness. Suddenly everyone was moving. Harold was the first to run. He charged into the boy at the head of the gang, his schoolbag aimed at the white boy's head. Reuben felt himself running. Billy was screaming like an Indian, and swinging his fists at everything in his path. Everyone was yelling, and at one point, Reuben heard Francis crying, and knew his friend had been angered sufficiently enough to want to kill. Reuben ran straight at a blond-haired boy with large freckles, and bucked teeth. The boy made the mistake of charging forward, and when fear suddenly gripped him, trying to run away. He had already knocked down two boys, as he tried to get out of Reuben's way. Reuben instinctively followed through the escape path the white boy had made, swinging at the boy who was hollering hysterically. When he was through, Reuben turned around and kicked someone in the leg, and felt a schoolbag smash into his own face. It shocked him for a moment, and someone else punched him in the stomach before he had a chance to grab at one boy's hair and try to pull it out. Someone struck him with a stone on the hand, and he watched, horrified, as the skin curled up in a twisted black ball, and black flesh suddenly spurted red. He kicked his assailant, saw Francis spit on a red-haired boy's coat, and heard Harold screaming. They had knocked Harold down! One boy was leaning over him, and casually punching him in the face! An instant later, he and Kenny were pushing and kicking people off Harold and helping him up. Reuben punched someone in the nose, and watched another boy examine the sudden rush of blood before cursing him. They had almost made it. Kenny and Harold were already running, and the others were far ahead. Once they got started, the white boys could never catch them. The seven of them ran like the wind. Reuben, as he bolted away from the white gang, hadn't run far when Billy screamed "WATCH OUT, REUBEN!"

He tried to dodge what was behind him, and as he turned, he heard it. His coat was tearing. His three-month-old coat was being ripped by a sandy-haired white boy with a jagged can. Reuben swung, just as the boy turned and ran. He started after him but realized he would be running into the charging gang. He'd get the boy later, he thought, angry enough to cry. He turned and joined his friends in the one-block sprint to the graveyard. They crossed the street and stopped.

"You tore my coat! I'm a' git you for that!" He was staring at the boy.

"Why don'tcha come here and git me, blackie?"

"You black nigger!"

"You wait! I'm a' beat your ass!" He said the curse word softly, afraid someone his mother knew might hear him.

"Awwww, go on home, blackie! We can get you tomorrow!"

"You better run, Sambo!"

"Your mother better run," Billy shouted. They started home.

"A Love Song for Seven Little Boys Called Sam" by C. H. Fuller, Jr. From the *Liberator*, Vol. 6, No. 1, January 1966. Published by the Afro-American Research Institute.

SELECTIONS FROM THE BLACK

Reuben was worried. Not simply because of his torn coat. His mother's outrage was predictable, but the thought had just occurred to him, that if they didn't stop those white boys they'd be chased home for the rest of their lives. He didn't tell the others but it scared him, and he wished magically the white boys would disappear. If he had a machine gun, he bet they would leave him alone. But he didn't have one. He had a right to go home in peace. Why didn't they let him? His father had said, white people always bother Negro people, and when he had asked him why, he recalled his father saying, 'cause Negro people don't fight back! He and his friends fought back every day, and still got chased. His father had missed something. He said goodbye to his friends, and went into his house.

Starting Time: _____	Finishing Time: _____
Reading Time: _____	Reading Rate: _____
Comprehension: _____	Vocabulary: _____

VOCABULARY: The following words have been taken from the selection you have just read. Put an *X* in the box before the best meaning or synonym for the word as used in the selection.

1. **confined**, page 93, column 1, paragraph 1
"The seven had been confined, since the first grade, to their own special section of the class."
☐ a. confided
☐ b. restricted
☐ c. restrained
☐ d. allowed

2. **pivoted**, page 93, column 1, paragraph 3
"Reuben sucked in a deep breath, and pivoted around."
☐ a. centered
☐ b. looked
☐ c. backed
☐ d. spun

3. **authoritatively**, page 94, column 1, line 32
" '...but white people do it all the time,' Harold Davis said authoritatively."
☐ a. hesitantly
☐ b. autocratically
☐ c. positively
☐ d. respectfully

4. **compelling**, page 94, column 1, line 42
"Something compelling in twisted expressions of the white boys made him want to take every opportunity..."
☐ a. forceful
☐ b. repelling
☐ c. necessary
☐ d. compatible

5. **predictable**, page 95, column 1, paragraph 1
"His mother's outrage was predictable,"
☐ a. predicable
☐ b. understandable
☐ c. foreseeable
☐ d. unreliable

ROOTS

Many English words consist of a base or root word to which prefixes (beginnings) and suffixes (endings) have been added. To the root word **agree** (a verb) we can add both a prefix and a suffix to get **disagreeable** (an adjective) which has an opposite meaning.

Roots are Latin and Greek stems on which our English words are based. For example, **bio** (life) is a Greek root on which our word **biology** (the study of plant and animal life) is built.

Two Roots

1. **mis, mit** are variants of the Latin root for **send.** A **transmitted** message has been sent.

2. **sens, sent** are also Latin and mean **feel.** A **sensation** is a feeling.

In the following sentences, these roots have been left out. Space has been left indicating where the root belongs. Add one of these two roots and write your word on the line following the sentence.

1. —**sionaries** are those sent out by their church to spread the faith.

   _____

2. —**ory** impressions are highly pleasurable.

   _____

3. —**itivity** training is becoming popular; it encourages responsive feelings.

   _____

4. **Re**— your payment in the enclosed envelope.

   _____

5. His proposal was **sub**—**ted** for consideration.

   _____

6. The —**e** organs of the body receive stimuli.

   _____

7. —**imental** occasions arouse our emotions.

   _____

8. Troops were sent out on a combat —**sion.**

   _____

9. I was **dis**—**sed** from work because of illness.

   _____

10. A —**itive** person responds readily.

   _____

MARKING THE TEXT

If you own your textbook you will want to write in it. Marking the text as you read is creative reading—it is motivating and stimulating. It is the most profitable reading you will ever do.

Don't make the mistake of most students—that of frequent underlining. Many students feel that they should underline important facts and information. Unfortunately almost everything seems to be important and worthy of being underlined. Check the book of a student with this habit. You'll find a third of the chapter underlined—so distracting that the eye seeks out the unmarked passages to read.

You must mark selectively. If you wish to set off an important line or passage use brackets before and after. Better still, use the abbreviation *imp* in the margin.

Circles, brackets, numbers, and a few abbreviations are all that are needed to mark a text effectively.

1. Brackets are used four or five times to mark off very important statements. Look for these statements at the beginning of each new division. A strong summary statement at the end of a section or chapter may be bracketed, too. Use brackets sparingly.

2. Circles and numbers are used to indicate important series and enumerations. Circle the key word which introduces the series and number the items in the series. You do this to help you find the list later. Frequently a lot of explanations and details accompany a list, and the items may be sentences, paragraphs or even pages apart.

3. Abbreviations are used to indicate the principal statement *(imp)* of the whole lesson; a major illustration *(ill)* which helps the reader understand an essential concept; and a conclusion *(con)* based on facts and data included in the chapter.

COMPREHENSION: For each of the following statements and questions, select the option containing the most complete or most accurate answer.

1. One of Mr. Fuller's talents as a writer is his
(i) ability to elicit public
   - ☐ a. opposition.
   - ☐ b. concern.
   - ☐ c. rage.
   - ☐ d. contributions.

2. Major responsibility for the situation described
(h) by Mr. Fuller should be levelled at
   - ☐ a. the Blacks.
   - ☐ b. the children.
   - ☐ c. the families.
   - ☐ d. the school.

3. The seven were
(f)
   - ☐ a. aggressive.
   - ☐ b. abusive.
   - ☐ c. marked.
   - ☐ d. retarded.

4. At an early age, Reuben learned that
(c)
   - ☐ a. weapons make the difference.
   - ☐ b. education is freedom.
   - ☐ c. size commands respect.
   - ☐ d. clothes make the man.

5. The presence of the seven boys in an other-
(g) wise all-white school was an expression of
   - ☐ a. tokenism.
   - ☐ b. integrationism.
   - ☐ c. generosity.
   - ☐ d. acceptance.

6. The Black and white children in the story are
(e)
   - ☐ a. participants in an educational experiment.
   - ☐ b. enemies with irreconcilable differences.
   - ☐ c. youngsters with natural tendencies.
   - ☐ d. victims of a situation they do not fully understand.

7. The discussion as to what and who is "preju-
(c) dice" represents
   - ☐ a. accurate understanding.
   - ☐ b. confused thinking.
   - ☐ c. parental indifference.
   - ☐ d. eventual compromise.

8. It seems probable that if the clashes between
(f) Black and white children continue
   - ☐ a. officials will punish the troublemakers.
   - ☐ b. Black children will be bussed directly to their homes.
   - ☐ c. school integration will suffer a serious setback.
   - ☐ d. weapons will become progressively more lethal.

9. Miss Arnold is
(c)
   - ☐ a. a concerned teacher.
   - ☐ b. an Uncle Tom.
   - ☐ c. a white racist.
   - ☐ d. a strict disciplinarian.

10. The overall impact of the story leaves the con-
(g) cerned reader wrestling with which of the following questions?
   - ☐ a. Is human nature really perfectable?
   - ☐ b. Why do white parents encourage racism?
   - ☐ c. Will the Black community ever support integration?
   - ☐ d. Why do Black teachers support the majority position?

> Comprehension Skills: a—isolating details; b—recalling specific facts; c—retaining concepts; d—organizing facts; e—understanding the main idea; f—drawing a conclusion; g—making a judgment; h—making an inference; i—recognizing tone; j—understanding characters; k—appreciation of literary forms.

A Love Song for Seven Little Boys Called Sam, II

He had to think of something. It came to him, just before he fell asleep.

C.H. Fuller, Jr.

"Reuben, that you?"

"Yeah."

"What's the matter?" He didn't answer his mother. Instead, he took off his coat in the vestibule and placed it over his arm with the torn portion folded in, where she couldn't see it. "Reuben, what are you doing?"

"Nothin'!" He walked into the kitchen with his hands in his pockets.

"Mom, I don't wanna' go to that school no more."

"What?" His mother turned away from the sink and put potatoes on the stove, then wiped her hands on her green apron. "What's the matter, Reuben?"

"Them white boys is always fightin'."

She looked at him for a moment. "Reuben, what happened to your coat?"

"Nothin'."

"Reuben!" She grabbed the coat from his arm. "What?"

"I didn't do it, Mom! That white boy tore it!"

"Reuben, you let some boy tear your coat? What is wrong with you?" She shook him. Reuben was crying.

"It wasn't my fault, Mom! I couldn't help it! They chased us!" He heard his mother say, 'Dammit,' something she never said unless she was upset.

"What you let them chase you for?"

"They do it every day!"

"Well, can't you fight? Hit 'em back when they hit you!"

"It's too many."

"Go someplace! Go someplace before I whip you! Your father spends good money for a coat, and you let somebody tear it up? Go ahead, Reuben! Just go before I give you a beating! Wait 'til you father gets home. Get outta' my sight!"

"It wasn't my fault. It wasn't!" He went to his room, and slammed the door. For a moment he stood there, so angry he wanted to tear the door from its hinges. He couldn't help it if they chased him every day! He had tried to be friendly like his mother had told him, but they didn't want to be friends. All they wanted to do was fight, and call names. Now, they even had his own family against

him, and he hated them for it. If only he was bigger, stronger. It wasn't his fault! It wasn't! He fell across his bed in tears.

When he heard his father, he sat up on the bed. He was sure his mother was going to tell. She couldn't keep a secret, no matter what.

"Reuben! Reuben, come here!" He went downstairs crying. "What's this about lettin' some boy tear your coat?"

"They wanna' fight all the time, Daddy, an' call us names!"

"Who? What did they call you?"

"Them white boys—they called me nigger!"

"And what did you do?"

"I punched one in the nose, and bloodied his face!"

"I tol' you not to let him go to that damn school, Willa Mae! I told you! He don't need to go to no white school—and as long as he does, I want them to keep their damn hands off him! I'm sick of it! Reuben, don't come in here agin' with your clothes ripped up. You figure out somethin' to make them leave you alone, you hear? I'm not playin' either. Now eat your dinner!" Reuben ran to the kitchen.

"It's not his fault," his father said. "It's them damn white kids, Willa Mae! You think they'd have better sense than to teach that shit to their kids! Goddamn white people! No! You wanted him in there, and he's gonna' stay! Reuben's got to learn that you don't let people walk over you! If we take him out, he'll be runnin' all his life. Once he beats them, they'll leave him alone—I'm not gonna walk him from school, and neither are you!"

Reuben didn't eat much dinner, and when he went to bed, he lay there for a long time, trying to figure out something that would stop the fighting. He considered himself lucky. His father didn't whip him. Maybe Pop understood it wasn't his fault. He watched the white boys on his ceiling. They were standing in a gang, and the sandy-haired boy was out front, threatening him with another tin can. He cursed at Reuben, and Rueben swung at him, and the boy's face disappeared only to be replaced by an entire group that looked just like him. He pulled his blanket over his head. He had to think of something. It came to him, just before he fell asleep. When he took a final glance at the ceiling, the white boys were gone.

The following day, just before the bell sounded the end of the school, Miss Arnold spoke to the class. There was something hanging from her nose, and it annoyed Reuben that this woman, behind her big desk, could scold them, when she didn't have enough sense to blow her own nose. But she wouldn't bother him anymore, after today. Everything was going to change today.

"Now, children, someone told me that the white boys were fighting their colored friends. Is that true?"

"Yeah, teacher. That punk called me 'nigger'!" Billy stood and pointed to the blond-haired kid.

"I didn't!"

"You did—and I'm a' get you."

"I didn't!"

"I'm sure he didn't mean it, Billy. You didn't mean what you called Billy, did you Gavin?"

"Nooooo, Miss Arnold!"

"Oooo, you liar!"

"Billy, sit down!"

"I'm a' gitcha', hear? I don't take that stuff!"

"Sit down!" She shook her head.

When the bell rang, the seven of them bolted from the room. Reuben had told them his plan on the way to school, and they rushed from the class to execute it. It was going to be over—today. Miss Arnold came out of the building with two little white boys, as she always did. When she approached Reuben, she waved a warning finger at him. He waited until she had crossed the street, and with Billy and Harold Davis, followed behind her. Allen, Stevie, Francis and Kenny were out of sight now, and it was a part of the plan for the three of them to stay close to Miss Arnold.

"Hey, Sammy! Hey, black Sams!"

"Little black Sambo!" The little kids sprinted past them. Billy started to shout something but decided against it when Miss Arnold turned around and stared at him.

"Billy, remember, sticks and stones."

"Yes, Miss Arnold."

Reuben looked at her and laughed. She was a part of the plan, and didn't know it. She'd take them to the corner, and not only get an opportunity to see the boys waiting for them, but help, by her presence, to frighten them. The white boys were already gathering on the corner. "Hey, Miss Arnold! Look at them boys! See what I tol' you? All they wanna' do is fight, and call us names!"

The woman looked up suddenly, and her expression told Reuben that she was not only shocked, but afraid as well. The white boys were blocking the sidewalk, this time in a large circle. The first two boys held up tin cans menacingly.

Miss Arnold was speechless, and when she did open her mouth, she stuttered.

"You boys! You boys—what—what are you doing there? I don't want any fighting. Go home! You heard me! Go home before I report you." Several white boys backed up.

"You Sams is scared, aintcha'?"

"They gotta' go home wif' the teacher!"

"Did you boys hear me? I said go home!"

"Awww shut up!"

"Who said that? Who said it?—what grade—?"

"Black Miss Arnold, like a dirty carmel! Black Miss Arnold like a dirty carmel!"

"We don't want no black teacher!" One boy leaped away from the crowd his hands on his hips.

"Go back where you came from!"

Reuben was glad they'd hurt her. She stood in front of them, her mouth wide open, her eyes large and glassy. It serves her right, he thought. He was the first to run. While the white boys' attention was on Miss Arnold, Reuben, Billy and Harold charged, striking the first blow at the boy who stood with his hands on his hips. The sudden attack came as a surprise to the boys, and for a while they retreated. Harold was whooping like an Indian, and punching a tall, skinny boy in the back until the boy collided with a parked car, and skinned his face on the fender. The white boys didn't run far. Halfway up the block they scattered in every direction, running on stoops and hiding in doorways. Allen, Francis, Stevie and Kenny had been waiting for them, and the first white boy who approached them was slammed in the face with a rock. Reuben's plan worked, and he started swinging at them as they raced back trying to dodge stones. He grabbed one boy by the collar, and tripped him to the ground, kicking him in the leg. Another boy he garroted, and out the corner of his eye saw Harold pin a red-haired boy against a wall. He punched the boy he had tripped in the side, and ran by Harold, and slapped the red-haired boy in the face. It would end today, he was sure of it. The boy he slapped started crying, just as he saw the kid who had torn his coat. He noticed, momentarily, a panorama of screaming, crying white boys, running everywhere, and Stevie's foot going high in the air, and a fat boy running with his hands over his head, and no one chasing him. He sprinted after the sandy-haired boy, who, when he saw Reuben, started screaming "he didn't mean it." Reuben caught him at the corner right in front of Miss Arnold, and knocked him down. The boy was

"A Love Song for Seven Little Boys Called Sam" by C. H. Fuller, Jr. From the *Liberator,* Vol. 6, No. 1, January 1966. Published by the Afro-American Research Institute.

hysterical—screaming, kicking, and at one point, Reuben thought he might faint.

"I'm a' tear your coat!"

"I didn't mean it. I'm sorry, Reuben! I'm sorry! Please! I didn't—"

Reuben punched him once and stood. It had just occurred to him that the boy was deathly afraid, and for the first time since he had been in the Ingram School, a white boy had used his name. They were beaten. Reuben walked back to his friends.

"Did you tear his coat?"

"Nawwww."

"Why not? I'd a' tore his coat and bloodied his nose, man." Billy stuck his chest out.

"Man, I beat the piss outta' one guy," Allen said.

They turned around when they reached the graveyard. The white boys were going home in two's and three's. There were no names being shouted, no one throwing stones. Reuben knew why he felt good, but he wasn't sure why he suddenly liked his friends so much. They seemed different now. Stronger. Taller.

Miss Arnold was still on the corner, staring at them. Reuben didn't feel sorry for her. She hadn't shared in their victory, and tomorrow she'd punish them. He didn't understand her. At least the white boys had what they believed was a reason for disliking them.

But what about Miss Arnold? She was the same color as he was. Maybe she wanted to be white? The thought made him laugh. They put their arms around each other's shoulders, and started home.

"We're rough. We're tough. We black boys don't take no stuff!"

From that day on, they didn't.

VOCABULARY: The following words have been taken from the selection you have just read. Put an X in the box before the best meaning or synonym for the word as used in the selection.

1. **vestibule**, page 98, column 1, line 4
   "...he took off his coat in the vestibule..."
   ☐ a. passage
   ☐ b. vestry
   ☐ c. lobby
   ☐ d. hallway

2. **execute**, page 99, column 1, line 29
   "...they rushed from the class to execute it."
   ☐ a. pass judgment
   ☐ b. finish
   ☐ c. execrate
   ☐ d. carry out

3. **expression**, page 99, column 1, last paragraph
   "...her expression told Reuben that she was not only shocked,"
   ☐ a. voice
   ☐ b. language
   ☐ c. look
   ☐ d. statement

4. **menacingly**, page 99, column 1, last paragraph
   "The first two boys held up tin cans menacingly."
   ☐ a. fearfully
   ☐ b. defensively
   ☐ c. alarmingly
   ☐ d. threateningly

5. **panorama**, page 99, column 2, last paragraph
   "He noticed, momentarily, a panorama of screaming, crying white boys,"
   ☐ a. broad view
   ☐ b. picture
   ☐ c. panoply
   ☐ d. assortment

CONTEXTUAL AIDS: SETTING AND MOOD

Studies of good readers show that they are aware of the context of what they are reading. This means that they are anticipating what is coming next by what has gone before.

The many ways in which context functions to help the reader recognize words are called contextual aids.

Contextual Aid 7. Words can be understood through the setting and mood of the context. The reader's understanding of the impression created by the author can help him understand an unfamiliar word. In the example, **It was dark and gloomy;** _____ **was falling**, the reader guesses that the missing word is **rain**, the element that would add to the mood of the context.

The following sentences contain nonsense words which can be recognized from the mood and setting of the sentence. Underline the nonsense word and write the correct word on the line following each sentence.

1. In bastn the days are sunny and hot.

   _____

2. The odor of decaying flesh turned his cenblab.

   _____

3. Running from the bank and chased by the police, the dombes were caught.

   _____

4. At the top of the pole, the krelp fluttered in the breeze.

   _____

5. The speeding auto crashed through the guard rail of the brill and tumbled into the river.

   _____

6. The roses filled the air with their sadmart.

   _____

7. Dressed in their Sunday best, they paraded to crump.

   _____

8. A sinister look appeared on the villain's drul.

   _____

9. On Hallowe'en children go door to door dressed in flambots.

   _____

10. He hammered so hard that the slem bent.

    _____

11. In tamble, the icy condition of the roads makes driving dangerous.

    _____

HOW TO SUMMARIZE

Occasionally a student may want to (or have been told to) summarize an article or chapter. Summarizing means extracting just the essential information, leaving out all of the nonessentials.

Summaries must be brief. A paragraph should be summarized in one sentence. An entire page should be summarized in a paragraph. If your summary is longer than one third of the original, something's wrong.

Students hesitate to summarize because they fear leaving out something important. Following these few steps will help you write better summaries.

1. Preview to see the chapter or lesson as a whole. Try to list in your mind the main points—the ones that cannot be left out of a summary.

2. Read to determine what is important and what is not. From what you know about marking a book and prereading, you should be able to identify the main points as you read through.

3. Select the main points and include enough information about them so that they convey their essential idea.

4. Write compact sentences which cover the central thought and include necessary supplementary information.

Do not make the mistake of using the topic sentences of paragraphs for your summarizing statements. These might be sufficient to use in an outline because they do frequently state a topic. They do not, however, tell what the author has to say about that topic; they leave the reader hanging, waiting for more information.

Your sentence must include elements from the whole paragraph, so it is necessary to create a statement which is inclusive and concise. Practice doing this with simple paragraphs until you are able to state in a single sentence the essential thought of any paragraph.

COMPREHENSION: For each of the following statements and questions, select the option containing the most complete or most accurate answer.

1. Reuben's mother reveals her spirited nature
(j) when she says,
   - ☐ a. "Reuben, that you?...What's the matter?"
   - ☐ b. "Wait 'til your father gets home. Get outta' my sight!"
   - ☐ c. "Reuben, what happened to your coat?"
   - ☐ d. "Reuben, you let some boy tear your coat? What is wrong with you?"

2. Reuben's father urged his son
(c)
   - ☐ a. to use his head.
   - ☐ b. to seek revenge.
   - ☐ c. to change school.
   - ☐ d. to run faster.

3. Reuben's plan to expose the white boys came
(b) to him
   - ☐ a. in a vision.
   - ☐ b. in a dream.
   - ☐ c. before the start of class.
   - ☐ d. before he fell asleep.

4. "But she wouldn't bother him anymore after
(h) today. Everything was going to change today." The reader is left with the impression that
   - ☐ a. brains will win over brawn.
   - ☐ b. violence and vengeance will rule the day.
   - ☐ c. Miss Arnold will be reassigned.
   - ☐ d. Reuben and his friends will transfer to another school.

5. Miss Arnold's form of questioning in the class-
(g) room was
   - ☐ a. partial.
   - ☐ b. astute.
   - ☐ c. devious.
   - ☐ d. honest.

6. Miss Arnold "saw the light" when
(f)
   - ☐ a. Reuben's coat was ripped.
   - ☐ b. she was defended by the Black students.
   - ☐ c. her illusions were shattered.
   - ☐ d. Billy shouted, "I'm a' gitcha', hear?"

7. The successful execution of Reuben's plan
(h) was due largely to
   - ☐ a. Miss Arnold's intervention.
   - ☐ b. discipline and timing.
   - ☐ c. numbers and strength.
   - ☐ d. the opposition's leadership.

8. Reuben's final analysis of Miss Arnold's po-
(g) sition was
   - ☐ a. hasty and immature.
   - ☐ b. exaggerated and unfounded.
   - ☐ c. accurate and insightful.
   - ☐ d. cruel and petty.

9. The selection ends on a note of
(i)
   - ☐ a. arrogance and determination.
   - ☐ b. discouragement and regret.
   - ☐ c. triumph and hope.
   - ☐ d. threat and violence.

10. The problem of "The Seven" was handled
(e) with boldness and
   - ☐ a. applied intelligence.
   - ☐ b. violent determination.
   - ☐ c. superior strength.
   - ☐ d. prudent strategy.

> Comprehension Skills: a—isolating details; b—recalling specific facts; c—retaining concepts; d—organizing facts; e—understanding the main idea; f—drawing a conclusion; g—making a judgment; h—making an inference; i—recognizing tone; j—understanding characters; k—appreciation of literary forms.

A Time to Speak, A Time to Act

Bond Warns the Country that It Has a Last Chance before Blacks and Radicals Give Up on Electoral Politics

Julian Bond

I must admit to a certain prejudice, a bias. That is race. Most of my life has been colored by race, so much of my thinking focuses on race.

In Atlanta I represent an urban constituency, people who are poor and black and old, so one may perhaps understand why the problems of the cities seem to me significant.

Black Americans are becoming, along with much of the rest of America, an urban population. In Washington, D.C., where we can't elect the mayor, we are more than 60 per cent of the population. In Richmond, Nashville, New Orleans, Jacksonville, and Birmingham we are more than 40 per cent of the population. Atlanta, Compton (California), Baltimore, Gary, St. Louis, Newark, Detroit, and Trenton have in the last decade become cities that have majority black populations.

Some things in America over the past several years have gotten better for some few of us. We can eat where we never ate before and go to school where we never went to school before and sit in the front of buses. There are more Negroes holding elective office today in all parts of this country and more Negroes making more money now than ever before, and more of us are registered to vote.

But for most of us, things have not gotten better. Let me quote the late President Lyndon B. Johnson:

In 1948 [said Johnson, before leaving office], the 8 per cent unemployment rate for Negro teen-age boys was actually less than that of whites. By 1964, the rate for Negroes had grown to 23 per cent as against 13 per cent for whites. Between 1949 and 1959, the income of Negro men relative to white men declined in every section of the country. From 1952 to 1963, the median income of Negro families compared to white actually dropped from 57 to 53 per cent. Since 1947, the number of white families living in poverty has decreased 27 per cent, while the number of non-white families living in poverty has decreased by only 3 per cent. The infant mortality of non-whites in 1940 was 70 per cent greater than whites. In 1962, it was 90 per cent greater.

To use former President Johnson's figures, the rate of unemployment for Negroes and whites in 1930 was about the same. In 1965, the Negro rate was twice as high.

Since the typical black person is poor, he faces all of the problems of poverty. For example, although there are more than five and one-half million units of substandard housing in the United States, and although congressional declarations in 1949 insisted that every American has a right to a decent home, in the better than two decades since 1949, urban renewal, highway construction, and other forces have destroyed 100,000 more homes for low-income people than have been built.

At the end of the Second World War, the median income for white families was $3,150; for blacks, a little more than $1,600. Today the average white family has an income of more than $6,500 a year, while the black family's income is about $3,500. The white family, in other words, has gained about $3,400, while the black family has gained about $1,800. In spite of laws and courts and marches and summer urban disruptions, the white family has moved twice as far ahead of its black counterpart than it was twenty years ago. Low-income black people suffer four times the national incidence of heart disease, ten times the incidence of defective vision. In black urban America, 30 per cent of the people have never seen a doctor; half of the expectant mothers never have prenatal care.

Statistics and figures are boring enough, as a rule. But the figures describing the plight of black people in America paint an unrelievedly gloomy picture.

In November 1971 the National Urban League made public an updated report on the black aged in this country, taking as starting point the League's pioneering study of elderly black people first published in 1960. Dr. Robert Hill, deputy director of the League's research department, concluded that the situation for aged blacks in the United States had "not improved significantly since 1960."

Life expectancy for black men actually declined from 61.1 years to 60.1 years, in contrast to a 67.5-year life expectancy for white males between 1960 and 1968, compounding an already unhappy truth: black men have far greater difficulty getting retirement benefits than white men. Most jobs held by blacks were not covered by Social Security until recently, and with a life expectancy under sixty-five, elderly blacks tend to receive minimal or nonexistent Social Security benefits. Moreover, the League report adds, more than two-thirds of the black elderly do not benefit from Medicare because of the high cost of that insurance.

More than three-fourths of the black elderly living alone had less than a $2,000 income in 1969; a third had less than $1,000. White elderly poor had on the average almost twice as much to spend.

Poverty is not the exclusive province of America's blacks. There are poor white people as well. They, however, enjoy the dubious pleasure of knowing they are not poor simply because they are white, but rather are poor in spite of their whiteness. We must, then, assume that the racial problem in this country is one of race and class. Millions of Americans are right now looking for work they won't find as unemployment hovers near 6 per cent. And another million more, no one knows how many for sure, have given up looking and are therefore no longer even counted as "unemployed" by the Labor Department. Unemployment in the black ghetto runs between 30 and 50 per cent, as compared with about 4 to 6 per cent for America as a whole during the last decade. One recent survey showed 357,000 black men and 419,000 black women officially out of work, with another 300,000 to 400,000 of the "hidden jobless" not even counted. Unemployment among black youth between the ages of sixteen and twenty-one is six times higher than for whites in the same age group.

These are awful facts and figures. They are all the more awful because they are familiar to most literate Americans and have been for more than ten years and because most literate Americans have chosen to do nothing about them.

The typical black ghetto dweller is a young adult with better than a 50 per cent chance of dropping out of high school. He is not only unemployed, but by current standards he is unemployable. He has no salable skill. Neither of his parents went beyond the eighth grade. He entered school at six but, because of overcrowding, had to attend half-day sessions. During his six years in elementary school, he attended four different schools.

What is his history and the history of his parents? What sorts of efforts have they made to improve their condition?

Since 1917, this country has had sporadic racial violence. Interestingly, it has always occurred during periods of war: 1917 to 1919, in 1943, and from 1965 into 1968. Since 1954, there have been various sorts of methods and techniques directed at solving America's white problem. These include the sit-in demonstration and nonviolent march,

the pursuit of education as a barrier breaker, the use or threat of violence as inducement to change, the challenging in the courts of segregation by law, and the thrust for power through direct political action.

Legal action brought us in 1954 a statement from the nation's highest court that segregation was illegal. Almost two decades later, there are more black children attending all-black schools north of the Mason-Dixon line than there were in 1954. And, there is evidence that in 1972 there is more segregation in the North than in the South.

Each of these victories of the '60's had little meaning for most black people and the last won, the right to vote, has yet to win bread-and-butter victories for the millions now voting for the first time.

Education as a means of improving conditions for the masses dies every day that ghetto schools continue to teach that whiteness is rightness. Education is a useless tool when education systems become so large and so impersonal as to deny either parent or student or teacher the right to participate in educational decisions.

Violence as a political technique has not had a real test in this country, and the present national mood seems to suggest too that only continued repression can follow another long, hot summer.

In the immediate past few years of the life of our imaginary ghetto dweller, the country at large has begun to change, not by any means always for the better. In 1964, his community was promised that poverty would end. By 1967, a foreign war had rendered that promise, if it was ever meant, nearly useless. Between 1961 and 1964, the country officially denounced violence and war as a means of settling disputes between persons or nations. From 1965 to the present, violence has been the official policy of the government of the United States in settling her own disputes with other nations, and that belief has seeped into the police stations and slums across the land.

In 1964, our young black slum dweller thought he might get a job, but in 1972, the only job open to him was being a soldier. War has brewed anger in the black community, and it gave birth to the belief that nonviolence was only a joke to be played on or played by the black community.

It is curious to note the similarities of the national response to problems here and abroad. First one tries a little economic aid, and urges local authorities to give the peasants a bone of reform. In Vietnam this is called pacification; at home it is the poverty program. Next, when trouble erupts, counterinsurgency is used; in Vietnam, the local militias; in America, the police. When the peasants shoot back, we bomb the hell out of them. Following this thought to a logical and local ending, we might next expect to see in America the "resettlement" of Negroes into well-policed villages. In fact, that resettlement has already begun. We do live in villages and compounds within the city, policed well when police action is aimed against us, policed poorly to contain the violent and criminal forces that operate in our lives daily.

Is not the status quo as violent as any Watts or Newark or Detroit? Is it not violent to condemn to death twice the proportion of black babies as white babies in their first year? Was it not violent to send a higher proportion of black men to white men to Vietnam every year?

There are those in America who believe that a nonviolent confrontation will force a reluctant government to turn its attention homeward and toward a real solution of the white problem in America. There are those who believe that progress of a sort is being made and will be made, and, like Scarlett O'Hara, believe tomorrow will be another—and perhaps a better—day. There are those who believe that giving some small power—the appearance of control of neighborhood schools, decision making in some forms of government—will hold off the day of Armageddon that many think is coming.

And there are those for whom the major problem has become the right to smoke pot or to throw flowers, while for others the fight is for the right to breathe clean air or to throw bombs.

Starting Time: _____	Finishing Time: _____
Reading Time: _____	Reading Rate: _____
Comprehension: _____	Vocabulary: _____

VOCABULARY: The following words have been taken from the selection you have just read. Put an *X* in the box before the best meaning or synonym for the word as used in the selection.

1. **focuses**, page 103, column 1, paragraph 1
"...so much of my thinking focuses on race."
☐ a. concentrates
☐ b. depends
☐ c. works against
☐ d. results from

2. **counterpart**, page 103, column 2, paragraph 3
"...the white family has moved twice as far ahead of its black counterpart than it was twenty years ago."
☐ a. companion
☐ b. counterpane
☐ c. complement
☐ d. equivalent

3. **province**, page 104, column 1, paragraph 3
"Poverty is not the exclusive province of America's blacks."
☐ a. domain
☐ b. business
☐ c. providence
☐ d. concern

4. **dubious**, page 104, column 1, paragraph 3
"They, however, enjoy the dubious pleasure of knowing they are not poor simply because..."
☐ a. decided
☐ b. questionable
☐ c. hesitant
☐ d. duplicate

5. **sporadic**, page 104, column 1, paragraph 7
"Since 1917, this country has had sporadic racial violence."
☐ a. frequent
☐ b. continuous
☐ c. occasional
☐ d. isolated

EXPECTANCY CLUES

The most important aids to word recognition and, therefore, fluency in reading are meaning clues. Good readers use these clues effectively and automatically. Meaning clues permit the reader to anticipate words before he actually reads them.

Expectancy clues are one type of meaning clue. These refer to the sorts of words and concepts one might expect to encounter in a given subject. For example, in a story about big city life, the reader should expect to meet words like *subway, traffic congestion, urban renewal, ghetto, high-rise apartments,* and so on. Anticipating or expecting these words enables the reader to move along the printed lines rapidly, with understanding.

Here are two exercises to help you develop your skill in using expectancy clues.

The following words, except two, all appeared in a story about winter. Think first about the kinds of words you would find in such a story and then examine the words below. Underline the two words you would *not* expect to find in this story.

1. cold	6. overcoats	11. icy
2. scarves	7. freezing	12. flowers
3. umbrellas	8. snowy	13. skidding
4. windy	9. snowshoes	14. blustery
5. swimsuits	10. shoveling	15. earmuffs

Which of the following phrases would you expect to read in a newspaper story about an automobile accident? Put an *X* in the box before them.

□ 1. crowds gathered around   □ 11. unsafe driving conditions

□ 2. flashing red lights   □ 12. typing copies of the letter

□ 3. galloping on the sand   □ 13. traveling at high speed

□ 4. backed up for miles   □ 14. in the passenger seat

□ 5. animals on the farm   □ 15. reverse to the fullback

□ 6. police report   □ 16. painting a chair

□ 7. mechanical defects   □ 17. through the windshield

□ 8. witnesses at the scene   □ 18. carrying the stretcher

□ 9. table set for dinner   □ 19. pieces of metal and glass

□ 10. trail of skid marks   □ 20. ambulances with sirens

HOW TO TAKE NOTES

It is a disconcerting experience to attend our first lecture and discover that we cannot possibly write fast enough to keep up with the speaker. Actually the experience should not be terrifying or frustrating, because a verbatim copy of the lecturer's words is neither useful nor necessary.

Notetaking means simply that: taking notes on what the speaker is saying—not making a transcript. To be able to make notes on what is being said, we must be listening—not hearing and copying, but listening, and understanding the presentation.

A common student fault is that of writing instead of listening. If you do not understand the lecture in the classroom, you'll never piece it together meaningfully from your notes. The first task of the notetaker, then, is to listen.

The value of notes taken in the classroom lies in their association or recall power. Learn the topic of the lecture and make a note of it. Next as the speaker progresses, listen to what he has to say on his topic and, while listening, jot on paper the gist of his words, enough to trigger later recall of the ideas.

The way you arrange your notes should indicate the organization of the lecture. You should begin with a title for the lecture; this goes at the top of the page. When the speaker changes topics, start a new page.

Record your notes in outline style. Main points are listed at the margin, followed by a sentence or two about them. Secondary ideas on the same point should be indented and followed by a sentence of explanation. Further indentions indicate more subordinate ideas. When reviewing your notes, a glance down the left-hand margin will reveal all the main points of the lecture.

SELECTIONS FROM THE BLACK

COMPREHENSION: For each of the following statements and questions, select the option containing the most complete or most accurate answer.

1. The selection is
(i)
   □ a. factual.
   □ b. defeatist.
   □ c. racist.
   □ d. incendiary.

2. The selection is written in the form of
(k)
   □ a. a survey.
   □ b. a complaint.
   □ c. an exposé.
   □ d. a summary.

3. Julian Bond admits to prejudice and bias and
(c) traces his attitude to his
   □ a. background.
   □ b. family.
   □ c. politics.
   □ d. profession.

4. The civil rights victories improved the quality
(f) of life for
   □ a. a majority of Black Americans.
   □ b. a minority of Black Americans.
   □ c. militant Black Americans.
   □ d. typical Black Americans.

5. Julian Bond's extensive use of dates and sta-
(g) tistics is especially
   □ a. interesting.
   □ b. educational.
   □ c. accurate.
   □ d. boring.

6. The conclusions resulting from the depressing
(e) facts and figures are compounded because they are
   □ a. understandable and justified.
   □ b. recognized but overwhelming.
   □ c. obvious but misunderstood.
   □ d. known and ignored.

7. Mr. Bond concludes that the racial problem in
(b) the United States is one of
   □ a. skin color.
   □ b. race and poverty.
   □ c. race and class.
   □ d. family background.

8. Considering the facts and figures advanced by
(g) the author, the young, Black ghetto adult is
   □ a. a dropout.
   □ b. an exception.
   □ c. a victim.
   □ d. a delinquent.

9. Violence as a means of settling United States
(g) problems abroad has
   □ a. corrupted the fabric of American society.
   □ b. led to the use of sophisticated weaponry.
   □ c. created jobs and opportunities at home.
   □ d. extended United States influence in foreign lands.

10. Essentially, national responses to foreign and
(c) domestic problems are
   □ a. imaginative.
   □ b. diplomatic.
   □ c. similar.
   □ d. compassionate.

Comprehension Skills: a—isolating details; b—recalling specific facts; c—retaining concepts; d—organizing facts; e—understanding the main idea; f—drawing a conclusion; g—making a judgment; h—making an inference; i—recognizing tone; j—understanding characters; k—appreciation of literary forms.

Die, Nigger, Die

"We see america for what it is . . . and we recognize our course of action."

H. Rap Brown

While I was in jail in Alexandria, I wrote what was to become a series of Letters from Jail. I didn't plan it like that but that's how it's been working out. I feel when I'm in jail that the people should understand very clearly that the reason I'm in jail is because my crime is political, because I've spoken out against injustices. When I was arrested after Cambridge, the press tried to portray me as some kind of dangerous outlaw. So in my Letters from Jail, I raised the question: Who Are the Real Outlaws?

Brothers and Sisters,

White people are saying that the uprisings of our people in almost 100 american cities "must be a conspiracy." Where is the real conspiracy? *Black people across this country have known that the real conspiracy in this country is to run us out, keep us down or kill us, if we can't act like the honky wants us to act.*

We're fighting for our survival and for this we are called criminals, outlaws and murderers. Who are the real criminals? *Who stole us from Africa? Who has been stealing our labor these past 400 years to build this country?* Who are the real murderers? *Why don't they call the police who gun us down in the streets every day, all year 'round. . .why don't they call them murderers?*

Why don't they call Lyndon Johnson a murderer and an outlaw? He fights an illegal war with our brothers and our sons. He sends them to fight against other people of color who are also fighting for their freedom.

Who are the real outlaws in this country? *They say I am an outlaw. I am charged with inciting Black people to "riot." It is against the "law" to riot. But did you or I have any say in passing this law? Do we have much of a say in any of the laws passed in this country? I consider myself neither morally nor legally bound to obey laws that were made by a group of white "lawmakers" who did not let my people be represented in making those laws.*

That government which makes laws that you and I are supposed to obey, without letting us be a part of that government. . .is an illegal government. The men who pass those laws are outlaws; the police who enforce those laws are outlaws and murderers.

It should be understandable that we, as Black people, should adopt the attitude that we are neither morally nor legally bound to obey laws which were not made with our consent and which seek to keep us "in our place." Nor can we be expected to have confidence in the white man's courts which interpret and enforce those laws. The white man makes all the laws, he drags us before his courts, he accuses us, and he sits in judgment over us.

White america should not fool itself into believing that if it comes down harder on us that that will keep us from doing what we believe is right. History has shown that when a man's consciousness is aroused, when a man really believes what he is doing, threats of jail and death cannot turn that man back. The threat of jail or death will not turn me nor others like me from the path we have taken.

We stand on the eve of a Black revolution. These rebellions are but a dress rehearsal for real revolution. For to men, freedom in their own land is the pinnacle of their ambitions, and nothing can turn men aside who have conviction and a strong sense of freedom.

More powerful than my fear of what could happen to me in prison is my hatred for what happens to my people in those outside prisons called the Black ghettoes of this country. I hate the practice of race discrimination, and in my hatred I am supported by the fact that the overwhelming majority of mankind hates it equally. There is nothing any court can do to me that will change that hatred in me; it can only be changed by the removal of the racism and inhumanity which exists in this country.

A society which can mount a huge military action against a Black youth who breaks a window, and at the same time plead that it is powerless to protect Black youths who are being murdered each year because they seek to make democracy in america a reality, is a sick, criminal and insane society. They talk about

SELECTIONS FROM THE BLACK

Photo: Scott

H. Rap Brown, the most revolutionary of the leaders of the Student Nonviolent Coordinating Committee, was born in Louisiana in 1943 and raised in an orphanage by white missionaries. At fifteen he entered Southern University and became active in the civil rights movement.

Brown replaced Stokely Carmichael as chairman of S.N.C.C. in May 1967. He immediately made almost every ghetto scene, North and South, preaching his fiery rhetoric to Blacks grown impatient over delays on various civil rights pledges. He expressed his views on the black liberation struggle in Detroit: "Violence is as American as cherry pie."

This is one of his letters from jail, written when he was held in Alexandria, Virginia, pending a hearing to extradite him to Maryland where he was charged with instigating arson and riots in the city of Cambridge.

violence in the country's streets! Each time a Black church is bombed or burned, that is violence in our streets! Where are the troops?

Each time a Black body is found in the swamps of Mississippi or Alabama, that is violence in our land! Where are those murderers?

Each time Black human rights workers are refused protection by the government, that is anarchy!

Each time a police officer shoots and kills a Black teenager, that is urban crime! Where is the national leader who will go on t.v. and condemn police crime?

Black people see america for what it is. It is clear now that white america cannot condemn itself, cannot see the reality of its crimes against mankind. We see america for what it is: the Fourth Reich. . .and we recognize our course of action.

The repeated attempts that the government has made to silence me represent just one level of genocide that is practiced by america. This genocide can be seen on many different levels. It can be seen actively in Vietnam where 45 percent of the frontline casualties are Black. That's no accident. Another level of genocide can be seen operating in the South, where many Black people live on a starvation level. Over 500 Black people die in Alabama each year for lack of proper food and nourishment. This is happening in a country that sends people to the moon. Yet another level of genocide can be seen in the courts. Any Black man across america who faces a white judge or who faces any court procedure can expect the maximum fine and the maximum sentence. Muhammad Ali, LeRoi Jones, Huey Newton, Ed Oquenda, myself, and thousands of Black men and women across the country have been thrown into prison because we have stood up and challenged the system. Some of the best minds in the Black community are in jail and that's genocide. The most obvious example of genocide is in the concentration camps that america has prepared for Black people. This came about as a result of the McCarran Act of 1950, a law that establishes concentration camps. There is a part, Title II, which suspends the right of due process. That means that there goes the dissolution of all machinery whereby you would be entitled to see a lawyer or go to court. You're arrested and taken off to the camp, without having had an opportunity to state your side of the case. Not that the presentation of your case matters.

At the present time, america still lets us use her "legal" machinery and, through legal maneuvers, my attorney was able to get me freed. But this was only after the court set ridiculously high bail. This is nothing short of ransom. I anticipate one day, however, that I will be arrested and there will be no legal procedure any lawyer will be able to use to secure my release. In fact, the first question will not be, Let's get Rap out of jail. It'll be, Where is Rap?

Starting Time: _____   Finishing Time: _____

Reading Time: _____   Reading Rate: _____

Comprehension: _____   Vocabulary: _____

VOCABULARY: The following words have been taken from the selection you have just read. Put an *X* in the box before the best meaning or synonym for the word as used in the selection.

1. **political**, page 108, column 1, paragraph 1
   "...because my crime is political,"
   ☐ a. pertaining to citizens
   ☐ b. duly elected
   ☐ c. against the state
   ☐ d. concerned with politics

2. **bound**, page 108, column 2, paragraph 2
   "...neither morally nor legally bound..."
   ☐ a. tied
   ☐ b. determined
   ☐ c. destined
   ☐ d. obliged

3. **consciousness**, page 108, column 2, paragraph 3
   "...when a man's consciousness is aroused,"
   ☐ a. awareness
   ☐ b. sensations
   ☐ c. feelings
   ☐ d. thoughts

4. **genocide**, page 109, column 2, paragraph 1
   "...are in jail and that's genocide."
   ☐ a. killing of genes
   ☐ b. execution
   ☐ c. racial extinction
   ☐ d. systematic extermination

5. **dissolution**, page 109, column 2, paragraph 1
   "...the dissolution of all machinery..."
   ☐ a. termination
   ☐ b. solution
   ☐ c. dispersal
   ☐ d. undoing

SELECTIONS FROM THE BLACK

SYLLABICATION

Knowing how to reduce words to their syllables aids both reading and spelling. Frequently a long word can be recognized and understood if pronounced by syllables and in spelling, of course, knowledge of syllables contributes to accuracy.

There are rules or generalizations which we can follow when dividing words. One such rule tells us that a suffix is usually regarded as a separate syllable. Thus the word **hunter** is divided into **hunt** and **er** because **er** is a suffix added to the base word **hunt**.

The following sentences contain similar words. Find them and write them on the lines following each sentence, separating the base words from the suffixes with hyphens (-).

1. He's an expert finisher.

   _____

2. The skies are cloudy before rain.

   _____

3. The star made a great comeback.

   _____

4. He has reached the rank of commander.

   _____

5. Twelve conferees were given medals.

   _____

6. Fight back; don't be a defeatist.

   _____

7. Build it on this framework.

   _____

8. The puck got past the goalie for a score.

   _____

9. The linkage system is weak.

   _____

10. Use that marker as a guide.

    _____

11. A graphic display showed the extent of the problem.

    _____

12. The wooden seats were hard to sit on.

    _____

13. He was released after a year of confinement.

    _____

SIGNS AND SIGNALS

In today's well-written texts you'll find many signs placed there to guide the reader. Signs are such obvious guides that we distinguish them from signals which we will discuss later.

Signs refer to the use of numbers and letters to indicate the importance or sequence of thoughts. The most obvious of these are the numbers *1, 2, 3,* etc. (Or, of course, the Roman numerals *I, II, III,* etc.) Frequently these are introduced by another sign: "There are *three* major causes of baldness." The reader, seeing the word *three* knows to look for numbers to follow.

Letters, too, are used like numbers. *A, B* and *C* or *a, b* and *c* appear consistently throughout texts to guide the reader. In marking a text, it is frequently wise to circle such signs.

In addition to numbers and letters, words are used unmistakably as signs. We often see the words *one, two, three;* or *first, second,* and *third.* These have the same value and significance to the reader even though typographically they are not so prominent. These should be numbered by the reader who is marking his text, so that they will not become lost among the other words.

Still another set of signs are the phrases *in the first place, in the second place,* and so on. These also signal the reader that an enumeration is occurring although the reader may not be as aware of it. It is almost essential that they be numbered by the reader if they are to have the significance the author intended.

Signs are more likely to appear in certain places in the chapter. Often they are used at the beginning to list the important elements.

Another place to look for signs is at the end of a chapter or section. Here they are used as a summary enumeration of important elements covered in the preceding material

COMPREHENSION: For each of the following statements and questions, select the option containing the most complete or most accurate answer.

1. The tone of the selection is
(i)
   - ☐ a. dispassionate.
   - ☐ b. objective.
   - ☐ c. restrained.
   - ☐ d. militant.

2. The misspelling of the word "america" seems
(h) to be
   - ☐ a. careless.
   - ☐ b. a misprint.
   - ☐ c. defiant.
   - ☐ d. unpatriotic.

3. In his letter Rap Brown identifies "outlaws"
(c) as the members of the
   - ☐ a. legislative branch of the government.
   - ☐ b. judiciary branch of the government.
   - ☐ c. executive branch of the government.
   - ☐ d. all of the above.

4. The use of such words as "genocide," "con-
(i) centration camps," and "Fourth Reich" is
   - ☐ a. emotional and inflammatory.
   - ☐ b. precise and logical.
   - ☐ c. judicious and guarded.
   - ☐ d. loose and indiscreet.

5. The statement "For to men, freedom in their
(g) own land is the pinnacle of their ambitions" is
   - ☐ a. without precedent in history.
   - ☐ b. an unrealistic goal.
   - ☐ c. supported by white America.
   - ☐ d. a legitimate aspiration.

6. The reference to Muhammed Ali, LeRoi Jones
(g) and others
   - ☐ a. substantiates Rap Brown's position.
   - ☐ b. weakens Rap Brown's argument.
   - ☐ c. has no bearing on the author's position.
   - ☐ d. offends the reader's sensitivity.

7. Given that the McCarran Act of 1950 was
(g) specifically designed to protect America from the threats of a violent overthrow of the government by Communist-inspired groups, it can be assumed that Rap Brown
   - ☐ a. was justified in the use he made of it.
   - ☐ b. may have used it out of context.
   - ☐ c. was unaware of the content of the act.
   - ☐ d. tried to arouse the sympathy of white America.

8. The author's style is
(k)
   - ☐ a. formal.
   - ☐ b. wordy.
   - ☐ c. bombastic.
   - ☐ d. informal.

9. In this selection Rap Brown shows evidence of
(k)
   - ☐ a. skill and competence as a writer.
   - ☐ b. an uncertain grasp of grammar and usage.
   - ☐ c. thorough documentation and research.
   - ☐ d. formal training in the rules of logic and debate.

10. Which of the following Black leaders can best
(g) be compared to the author?
   - ☐ a. Malcolm X
   - ☐ b. Muhammed Ali
   - ☐ c. Roy Wilkins
   - ☐ d. Martin Luther King, Jr.

Comprehension Skills: a—isolating details; b—recalling specific facts; c—retaining concepts; d—organizing facts; e—understanding the main idea; f—drawing a conclusion; g—making a judgment; h—making an inference; i—recognizing tone; j—understanding characters; k—appreciation of literary forms.

SELECTIONS FROM THE BLACK

Selections from the Black

Part Three
Selections 21-30

The Spook Who Sat By the Door, I

The Most Powerful Nation in History Stood on the Brink of Panic and Chaos

Sam Greenlee

Oakland blew first, then Los Angeles, then, leapfrogging the continent, Harlem and South Philadelphia. After years of crying conspiracy, the witch hunters found, to their horror, there was a conspiracy afoot among the black masses. Every city with a ghetto wondered if they might be next. The most powerful nation in history stood on the brink of panic and chaos. The Freedom Fighters fought first the police, then the National Guard and finally, the elite troops of the army and marines. Within a week there were major guerrilla uprisings in eight major cities in the United States and efforts to eliminate them had proven futile.

Several days of heavy rain, followed by a cool air mass moving down from Canada, broke the Chicago heat. The city lay under a bright warm sun and at night there was a cool breeze from the lake. The birds began their southern journey and the leaves of the cottonwood, poplar and maple trees began to change color, some of them reluctantly releasing from the limbs to trace a lazy descent to the ground, to be gathered and burned at the curb and produce the pungent smell of autumn come to Chicago. At night the city's silence would be broken by the explosion of grenades, the staccato message of automatic fire. The FF moved easily and silently through the ghetto which offered them affection and support, their coloration finally protective.

The curfew had silenced the streets below and a cleansing breeze from the lake stirred through Freeman's apartment. Miles Davis, mute meeting mike in a sexless kiss, blew bittersweet chocolate tones through the speakers, "My Funny Valentine" becoming a poignant poem of lonely love.

Freeman and Joy sat on the couch, the lights low, the dishes in the sink, an empty wine bottle in the trash, slowly sipping their drinks and Miles in the room, brooding, black and beautiful, saying his thing on his horn. In the sudden silence as the record changed, Freeman turned to Joy.

"Joy," he asked, "what's bugging you tonight?"

"Those damn Freedom Fighters, as they call themselves. You can't go to a cocktail party nowadays without running into someone who has lost his integrated job.

"My husband," she said with bitterness, "has lost his staff appointment at the hospital, and he was the only Negro doctor in a white hospital in the city."

"What did he have to do with the riots?"

"That's the point: decent, innocent people are suffering. Now they want to get rid of me at the store, I can smell it."

"They can't let you go, baby, you're the best-looking buyer with any department store in the Loop."

"It's nothing to joke about." She took a long swallow of her drink. "People are losing jobs they worked and sacrificed to get, all because of ignorant niggers who know nothing but hate."

Freeman rose to put another record on the changer and John Coltrane's soprano sax gave an oriental flavor to "My Favorite Things."

"Can't you remember, Joy, how it was to live like they do?"

"Don't defend those hoodlums. Those Freedom Fighters," she spat out the words in contempt, "are shooting real guns."

"Didn't figure to take long before some of them realized there's no win in throwing a brick at a man with a gun." Joy took a slow sip of her drink, watching him carefully over the rim of her glass.

"Dan," she asked quietly, "are you mixed up in this?"

"Baby, you got to be kidding," he laughed. "You think I'm stupid enough to get involved in a scene like that? They don't stand a chance."

"You used to talk about this kind of thing when we were in East Lansing. You insisted when everything else failed, Negroes would have to fight."

"Honey," he said reasonably, "I was a kid in college then. And besides, everything else hasn't failed. We're both examples of the kind of progress Negroes have made in the last few years." She searched his face for some clue and he told her what she wanted to hear, calmed, reassured her.

"Look at all the Negroes we have in influential positions: a member of the presidential cabinet, a Supreme Court justice, a senator. And look at me," he smiled, his arm swept his Playboy pad, "I've been poor and, believe me, this is better."

Sam Greenlee was born in Chicago in 1930, a second-generation immigrant from the Deep South. Despite the worst efforts of Chicago's ghetto schools, he succeeded in qualifying for the University of Wisconsin, later studying at the University of Chicago and the University of Salonica, in Greece, where he recently spent four years writing. He served with the United States Information Service in Iraq, Pakistan, Indonesia, and Greece, and was officially honored for his activities during the 1958 Kassem revolution in Baghdad. He came back to Chicago to work for an otherwise white civil-rights organization. "My job," he says, "is to sit by the door."

"Honey," she smiled, "I'm being silly. This thing has us all nervous and on edge." She rose gracefully and walked to the door leading to the bedroom. She turned and took off her wig.

"Fix us some more drinks while I get comfortable," and with a smile, she turned and walked into the bedroom. Freeman smiled with some relief. It had been close for awhile, but he was sure he had convinced her. A short time later, lying bathed in sweat, her head on his shoulder, he was certain.

It was hot the next afternoon, but the thick walls of the precinct police station made it cool and comfortable inside and the desk sergeant sat, oblivious to the station smells, working the crossword puzzle in the *Chicago Tribune.* The door opened and a bit of the hot day outside followed a woman who seemed immune to the heat. She walked to the sergeant's desk much like the models he had seen displaying fashions on television and in the newsreels. She wore a small white hat, white gloves and a pale green summer suit of shantung silk. The sergeant could not identify the material, but he knew it was expensive, so he spoke to her with far more respect than was usual for the colored women who normally entered his domain.

"Yes, lady; can I help you?"

"I want to speak with someone," she replied, "about 'Uncle Tom.'"

That evening, Freeman, entering his lobby, found a coded message in his mailbox. It was from one of his double agents on the police force, indicating the police planned a shakedown of the block in which the FF had one of its arms caches. Because there was not much time, he ignored telephone security and, hurrying to his apartment, he phoned from his bedroom, the room lit only by the light in the hallway.

"Daddy? Turk. Listen carefully. The fuzz are shaking down the block where we have a stash, safe house three. Move it right away to safe house six. Cancel tonight's hit if you have to, but get that stuff moved and check back with me." He hung

up and light burst into the room from the floor lamp in the corner. In one motion, Freeman whirled, dropped to the floor next to the bed and reached for the pistol he kept beneath the pillow, but the gun was not there.

"Freeze, Freebee," ordered Dawson, "or should I call you 'Uncle Tom.'" He sat in the Saarinen womb chair next to the teak floor lamp, his service Smith & Wesson .38 Police Positive held with easy competence and resting on the right knee of his crossed legs.

"The heat's not under the pillow. I have that one and the rest you had stashed here. You got quite an arsenal for a playboy—that how you get so much trim?"

"Uncle Tom? Not me, baby. You trying to put me on?" and suddenly indignant: "What the hell you doing in my pad pointing a gun at me? I hope you got a search warrant, man."

"Martial law, remember? I don't need a warrant."

"Now you fuzz can continue to do what you always have in the ghetto, only for a change, it's legal. That must take all the kicks out of it." Freeman, his eyes on those of Dawson, began to rise carefully. He had fired on the police range with Dawson; he knew what he could do with that revolver.

"Like I said, Freebee: freeze." Dawson rose from his seat, the gun never wavering. "OK, now stand up very slow and keep your hands where I can see them. Good, now walk over to that wall. Hands as high as you can reach, flat against the wall, you know the drill. Now hold it and don't move." Freeman stood, his weight on his hands flat against the wall and to either side of a Saito woodblock he had purchased in Tokyo. Dawson approached him, deftly searched him, then retreated slowly to the womb chair.

"OK, you can sit on the bed." Freeman walked slowly to the bed and seated himself as close to Dawson as he dared.

"Man, you sure had my nose open, Freebee. Out of all the people in Chicago, I never figured you for Uncle Tom. Cool Dan Freeman, the South Side playboy, nothing on your mind except chicks, clothes, good whiskey and sports cars. A beautiful cover, now I think about it."

"You think I'd risk all this for . . ."

"Save it. I don't know if you are or if you're not Uncle Tom and it's not my job to decide. I have enough evidence to take you in and that's what I'm going to do."

"What evidence?"

From *The Spook Who Sat by the Door* by Sam Greenlee. Published by Richard W. Baron Publishing Co., Inc.

"This reel of tape I found here. One of Uncle Tom's propaganda broadcasts you cats run all over the neighborhood from booby-trapped recorders."

"I don't know anything about that."

"You know, right up until I found this I didn't believe it. Didn't even bother to bring my partner along. After I searched the place I was going to wait for you and apologize for having to check out the lead."

"That's mighty white of you."

Starting Time: _____   Finishing Time: _____

Reading Time: _____   Reading Rate: _____

Comprehension: _____   Vocabulary: _____

VOCABULARY: The following words have been taken from the selection you have just read. Put an X in the box before the best meaning or synonym for the word as used in the selection.

1. **futile**, page 115, column 1, paragraph 1
"...efforts to eliminate them had proven futile."
□ a. dangerous
□ b. effective
□ c. useless
□ d. unimportant

2. **poignant**, page 115, column 1, paragraph 3
" 'My Funny Valentine' becoming a poignant poem of lonely love."
□ a. pointed
□ b. mild
□ c. sharp
□ d. sorrowful

3. **oblivious**, page 116, column 1, paragraph 3
"...the desk sergeant sat, oblivious to the station smells,"
□ a. conscious
□ b. unaware
□ c. absent-minded
□ d. obligative

4. **domain**, page 116, column 1, paragraph 3
"...far more respect than was usual for the colored women who normally entered his domain."
□ a. territory
□ b. door
□ c. empire
□ d. domicile

5. **deftly**, page 116, column 2, paragraph 7
"Dawson approached him, deftly searched him,"
□ a. carefully
□ b. cleverly
□ c. skillfully
□ d. eagerly

PREFIXES

Many English words consist of a base or root word to which prefixes (beginnings) and suffixes (endings) have been added. To the root word **agree** (a verb) we can add both a prefix and a suffix to get **disagreeable** (an adjective) which has an opposite meaning.

A prefix is added to the beginning of a word and causes a change in the meaning of that word. We have just seen how the prefix **dis** reverses the meaning of **agree**. Most of the prefixes we will be examining in this book come from Latin.

Two Prefixes

1. **ab-** is a Latin prefix which means **from** or **away**; it appears in words like **absent** and **abnormal**.

2. **tri-** is also a Latin prefix and it has the meaning of **three** or **thrice**. It is used in words like **triangle** and **tricycle**.

In the following sentences the words in bold print need prefixes. Add one of these two prefixes to each word and write your word on the line following the sentence.

1. The **plets** look so much alike I cannot tell them apart.

    _____

2. A brief statement containing the essential thoughts is an **stract.**

    _____

3. Until you're fully recovered, try to **stain** from coffee.

    _____

4. One transit system serves the **-city** area.

    _____

5. Three **sences** will result in your being dropped.

    _____

6. In geometry I learned how to **sect** an angle.

    _____

7. It was obvious that her belligerent behavior was **normal.**

    _____

8. Grab a sponge and try to **sorb** the spilled water.

    _____

9. Mount your camera on a **pod** to keep it steady.

    _____

10. The league champion hit two singles, a **ple** and a home run.

    _____

11. The courts **solved** the defendant of all blame.

    _____

FORWARD SIGNALS

Another kind of guide for the reader are signals—these can be just as useful, but are not so apparent, as signs. The first of these that we are going to look at are called Forward Signals.

Forward Signals

This group of signals tells the reader to advance with the thought. They indicate that more of the same is coming and the reader should continue forward.

The more common forward signals are *and, more, moreover, more than that, furthermore, also* and *likewise.*

The most frequently used one of this group is *and;* it signals the reader that another item of equal importance is following, or that this is one of a series. It indicates that the reader will not be faced with an opposing or reversing thought—he can go right on for more of the same.

The signals *more, moreover, more than that, furthermore* all indicate that new and even stronger thoughts along this same line are coming up: "He's clever all right; *more than that* he's a genius." Observe how these signals reinforce the previous idea and add more to it.

The signal *also* means "all in the same manner." Along with *likewise,* these two signals indicate that something quite similar to what has preceded is about to follow: "Along with signs, authors *also* use signals." The use of *also* indicates that what is coming has a similarity to what has gone before.

Signals are unlike signs in several ways. Signs as you recall stand out in the text; most of them are easy to identify—they are almost impossible to overlook. Signs are used in front, apart from the enumeration.

Signals on the other hand are words, and they appear in the context—they are not set off from the rest of the copy. For this reason, they are not so readily recognizable and, therefore, require the reader to be alert for their use.

SELECTIONS FROM THE BLACK

COMPREHENSION: For each of the following statements and questions, select the option containing the most complete or most accurate answer.

1. The event in Oakland triggered
(c)
- [ ] a. a national disgrace.
- [ ] b. a military victory.
- [ ] c. a white conspiracy.
- [ ] d. a nationwide alarm.

2. The FF were to the establishment as
(g)
- [ ] a. Helen was to Troy.
- [ ] b. Caesar was to Rome.
- [ ] c. Moses was to the Burning Bush.
- [ ] d. David was to Goliath.

3. The passage "The FF moved easily and silent-
(k) ly...their coloration finally protective" is an example of
- [ ] a. irony.
- [ ] b. sarcasm.
- [ ] c. innuendo.
- [ ] d. exaggeration.

4. Freeman and Joy were
(f)
- [ ] a. lovers.
- [ ] b. married.
- [ ] c. friends.
- [ ] d. enemies.

5. Joy came from a background of
(c)
- [ ] a. politics.
- [ ] b. wealth.
- [ ] c. poverty.
- [ ] d. education.

6. Joy and others like her were victims of what
(b) might be considered
- [ ] a. a misunderstanding.
- [ ] b. Black power.
- [ ] c. recession.
- [ ] d. white backlash.

7. Joy was skillful at concealing
(f)
- [ ] a. her identity.
- [ ] b. her suspicions.
- [ ] c. her jealousy.
- [ ] d. her ambition.

8. The name "Uncle Tom" was
(h)
- [ ] a. an insult.
- [ ] b. a decoy.
- [ ] c. a contradiction.
- [ ] d. an inaccuracy.

9. At one time, Freeman had most probably been
(h)
- [ ] a. a criminal.
- [ ] b. a hustler.
- [ ] c. a double agent.
- [ ] d. a policeman.

10. The informer was
(f)
- [ ] a. Freebee.
- [ ] b. Coltrane.
- [ ] c. Joy.
- [ ] d. Dawson.

Comprehension Skills: a—isolating details; b—recalling specific facts; c—retaining concepts; d—organizing facts; e—understanding the main idea; f—drawing a conclusion; g—making a judgment; h—making an inference; i—recognizing tone; j—understanding characters; k—appreciation of literary forms.

The Spook Who Sat By the Door, II

"Anybody who gets in the way has to go — nobody counts until we're free."

Sam Greenlee

"You know the Communist party in the States is like any other white scene: a few showpiece spades in the name of integration, but whitey calling the shots."

"And, of course, a spade couldn't possibly have done this on his own?"

"Don't put me on," Dawson laughed. "The FBI detachment working on this thing say it's the most sophisticated underground in the Western Hemisphere, the creation of an expert."

"And there sure ain't no spade experts, are there, Sergeant Dawson? Expertise is a white man's monopoly—they got a patent on it. You sure are brainwashed. Well, I got news for you: it's a spade scene! A spade scene, dig. You think because you've made a career out of kissing whitey's ass, every black man is in the same bag?"

"You're not going to bug me with namecalling. You don't look so swinging on the wrong end of this gun."

"Makes you a big man, don't it? A gun, a badge and a hunting license for niggers—issued by Mr. Charlie."

"I found out a long time ago, big-time, out there in those streets, that there are the people who get their heads whipped and the people who do the whipping and it didn't take long to figure out which I was going to be."

"You're a hypocrite—all that shit about helping your people. You want it both ways, to be super-cop and have spades dig you, too. Well, you can't be a cop without betraying your people and you can't be with your people without betraying your badge." He hit Dawson in his soft spot, desperately hoping he could recruit him.

"And you think you're going to change the system, one man? There's no changing this system, not in our lifetime and maybe never and the only way to make it is get in the best spot you can find."

"I don't want to change this system, just get it off my back. I'm no integrationist. Integrate into what? Whitey's welcome to his chrome-plated shit pile. I dig being black and the only thing I don't dig about being black is white folks messing with me."

"Who appointed you the savior of soul? What makes you more sensitive than anyone else? You think nobody else feels the way you do? You think there aren't days when I want to smash every white face I see? Or are you the only black man with a sense of outrage?"

"Use your outrage, hit back. Join us, Daws! We got cats on the force, but nobody with your in. Join us."

"On the force? You don't stop at anything, do you? And you been using the Cobras, them tracks in their arms got to be phony. How could you get kids involved in a thing like this?"

"Who am I going to get involved, you? You're scared shitless you might miss a promotion, not qualify for a pension. We're a wasted generation, dehydrated by whitey. I got to those kids before whitey did; they're the only hope we have."

"How are the things you're doing any better than whitey? How are you any better?"

"Why should I be? I'll do any damn thing to be free. Yeah, I'm Uncle Tom. There ain't a damn thing nonviolent about me. Anything whitey can do to keep me on my ass, I can do double to be free and when I'm gone there are others to take my place."

"I've heard enough! Let's go."

"Sure, man, cuff me." Freeman rose, Dawson still seated, and held his hands forward for the handcuffs.

Dawson reached for the cuffs in his back pocket and, as he did, the change of his weight in the foam rubber chair threw him off-balance for a moment and his gun barrel shifted. He saw it in Freeman's eyes even before he began the kick, and with the way of an athlete Dawson compensated for his imbalance: even as he moved further into the enveloping softness of the chair, he brought his gun up and fired without aiming. Freeman's kick sent Dawson over backward with the chair, the gun spinning away, but the shot had hit Freeman a glancing blow in the side, half spinning him. Noticing that Freeman had been hit, Dawson moved for the weapon on all fours, but Freeman, recovering, kicked him again in the side, sending the gun slithering across the room on the nylon carpeting.

Dawson turned on his knees toward Freeman with his arms crossed in front of his face in a judo defense, ready to block, parry, or grasp a flailing leg; groggy, but still dangerous. Freeman faked a kick and when Dawson covered, chopped him hard on the junction of the neck with the edge of his hand. Dawson fell to all fours and another kick turned him over. Freeman, moving in, chopped him hard on either side of the neck and grasping his collar with either hand, one crossed over the other, he applied pressure until the muscles of his arms ached from the strain. He released him and knew before he searched for a pulse that Dawson was dead.

He squatted at the side of his dead companion, rocking back and forth on his heels. "Shit, Daws, shit. Why you, man, why did it have to be you? Anybody else, anybody."

Abruptly he stood and when he looked at the dead body of his friend, his face was impassive, except for one fleeting moment. He walked to the phone and dialed.

"Daddy? This is Turk. You get that stuff moved? Good. Get out to my place right away, it's Condition Red. And bring one of the big mail sacks. I got something for you to move."

He walked to the bathroom and stripped to the waist to check the wound. It did not look good and was bleeding freely. He dusted it with sulfa powder, placed a gauze compress against it and a thick towel over that. Returning to the bedroom he put on a loose sports shirt and a cardigan. He checked himself in the mirror and there was no telltale bulge. He walked to the living room and put a stack of records on the stereo and mixed a stiff drink. Then he sat down in the dark room to await the arrival of his lieutenants.

Dawson was too good a cop not to report where he was going, or check in when he could. When they found his body, Freeman's cover would be blown and probably that of the Cobras as well. The pain began to eat into him and he thought that his cover might not matter anyway. A doctor would have to treat him and there would be no first-class surgical facilities they could use if necessary. They would all have to go underground now. At least he wouldn't have to kill Joy to protect the cover.

He called a doctor he had recruited and told him to come by a half hour before curfew. The doorbell rang and he opened it to let in Daddy, Scott, Stud and Pretty Willie. He motioned to the bedroom.

"In the bedroom. Take it out and dump it somewhere."

"It's Dawson!" said Dean. They crowded around the body.

"Not Dawson?" said Stud. "He's your main man, how could you kill Dawson? It would be like me killing Daddy."

"And maybe one day you'll have to kill Daddy, or Daddy you. Yeah, I killed him because he got in the way; anybody who gets in the way has to go—nobody counts until we're free.

"Did you think we were playing games? Killing people we don't know and don't dig? Forty percent of those paratroopers out there are black; it's a badge of honor for a black man to wear those wings. They soldier and fight to earn what no man can earn: freedom.

"Dawson's one dead black generation and you might be another, but at least you won't be dying an inch at a time. No more of whitey's con man's integration games, freedom on the installment plan, interest collected daily. Freedom now! No more begging, pleading and silent suffering.

"Don't tell me who I killed or what it cost to do it; if you can't pay the dues, then get out." He paused, gazing at Dawson's body. They watched him in silence. He looked up abruptly, searching their faces in turn; he nodded in satisfaction.

"Condition Red. All attack teams in the field nationwide. Hit them everywhere you can, everywhere they're fat, smug and complacent; use his strength and cockiness. Hit him, disappear and hit him again. Hound, harass. Keep gettin' up and don't back down.

"Willie, I want you to take over the D.C. operation as soon as you can get there. Here's a phone number in Washington; call her, take her out and buy her a drink for me; she drinks Johnny Walker black label.

"All right, move out." He motioned to the body. "And take that with you." They stuffed Dawson's body in the mail sack and without a word, left the apartment, their thoughts on the fighting ahead.

They're not boys any more, Freeman thought, staring at the door of the apartment after they had left. They don't need me anymore. You grow up fast in the ghetto and I helped them grow faster than most. I wonder how many of them will be alive or free this time next year?

He poured himself a stiff drink and thought that the doctor wouldn't be of much help. Hours later he sat in the darkened living room listening to the first of the shooting, the rapid crackle of automatic weapons, the spit of rifles, the explosion of grenades. The firing grew in intensity, in counterpoint to the music, Lady Day singing "God Bless the Child."

From *The Spook Who Sat by the Door* by Sam Greenlee. Published by Richard W. Baron Publishing Co., Inc.

He sipped his drink and listened. "Say it, baby," he said aloud, "sing it like it is: 'God bless the child that's got his own. . . .' Go on, you black-ass Cobras, go get your own."

Freeman smiled and the pain didn't matter anymore. In fact, for the first time in many years, he hardly hurt at all.

Starting Time: _____	Finishing Time: _____
Reading Time: _____	Reading Rate: _____
Comprehension: _____	Vocabulary: _____

VOCABULARY: The following words have been taken from the selection you have just read. Put an *X* in the box before the best meaning or synonym for the word as used in the selection.

1. **recruit**, page 120, column 1, paragraph 8
"He hit Dawson in his soft spot, desperately hoping he could recruit him."
☐ a. recreate
☐ b. injure
☐ c. encourage
☐ d. enlist

2. **outrage**, page 120, column 2, paragraph 1
" 'Or are you the only black man with a sense of outrage?' "
☐ a. concern
☐ b. insolence
☐ c. anger
☐ d. outright

3. **dehydrated**, page 120, column 2, paragraph 4
" 'We're a wasted generation, dehydrated by whitey.' "
☐ a. destroyed
☐ b. evaporated
☐ c. hydrated
☐ d. humanized

4. **flailing**, page 121, column 1, paragraph 1
"...ready to block, parry, or grasp a flailing leg;"
☐ a. swinging
☐ b. moving
☐ c. powerful
☐ d. trailing

5. **complacent**, page 121, column 2, paragraph 6
" '...everywhere they're fat, smug and complacent;' "
☐ a. uncomfortable
☐ b. compliant
☐ c. pleasant
☐ d. self-satisfied

SELECTIONS FROM THE BLACK

SUFFIXES

Many English words consist of a base or root word to which prefixes (beginnings) and suffixes (endings) have been added. To the root word **agree** (a verb) we can add both a prefix and a suffix to get **disagreeable** (an adjective) which has an opposite meaning.

A suffix is added to the end of a word and changes the part of speech of that word. We have just seen how the suffix **able** changes **agree** from a verb to an adjective.

Two Suffixes

1. **-ic** is a Greek adjective suffix. It changes a noun like **angel** to an adjective, **angelic**.

2. **-ist** is also Greek but it is a noun suffix. It can be added to nouns and verbs; for example, **tour** and **tourist**.

In the following sentences, root words have been set in bold print. Add one of these suffixes to each root and write the new word on the line following the sentence. As you add suffixes to words, you may have to drop or change letters.

1. The moon is coated with what appears to be **volcano** dust.

   _____

2. The doctor is a **special** in heart disease.

   _____

3. There was a rule against serving **alcohol** drinks.

   _____

4. The **violin** bowed to thunderous applause.

   _____

5. That behavior is an example of his **artist** temperament.

   _____

6. In painting he would be described as a **surreal**.

   _____

7. The cross is **symbol** of Christianity.

   _____

8. She works in a laboratory assisting the **chemicals**.

   _____

9. This entire page is a **photograph** reproduction.

   _____

10. He is a **column** for the *New York Times*.

    _____

11. The illness is **chron**; it recurs from time to time.

    _____

SUMMARY SIGNALS

We have already seen some signals which appear in the text and encourage the reader to race ahead; more ideas of the same kind are coming. These, you recall, were called Forward Signals.

Another group of signals which also urge the reader forward are called Summary Signals.

Summary Signals

These are also Forward Signals but we assign them to a different classification because the function they perform is more specific. These include such words as *thus, therefore, consequently,* and *accordingly.* Not only do these signal that the thought is continuing, but they also signal a new idea—that of summary or consequence.

Summary Signals tell the reader that the author is continuing his same thought or trend but now he has a more weighty idea to introduce—an idea that summarizes what has gone before, or an idea revealing the result of earlier ideas. These signals alert the reader to this new and important idea; the reader should be aware that this is what the writer has been leading up to. Now the writer is going to pause and summarize his thoughts or show the result they have caused.

In the sentence *"Thus* it was that after years of trial and error, experimentation and failure, frustration and despair, he and his laboratory associates had isolated the deadly virus.", the word *thus* tells the reader that much has occurred to bring about this result. This is not simply more of the same—this is a thought carrying greater meaning for the reader.

In textbooks especially, summary signals identify ideas and concepts considered more important and more critical by the author.

Frequently they appear at the beginning of statements summarizing the writer's presentation.

COMPREHENSION: For each of the following statements and questions, select the option containing the most complete or most accurate answer.

1. Dawson identified Black revolution with
(c)
   - ☐ a. integration.
   - ☐ b. Communism.
   - ☐ c. gangsterism.
   - ☐ d. opportunism.

2. The exchange in Freeman's apartment serves
(f) to establish
   - ☐ a. dialogue.
   - ☐ b. rivalry.
   - ☐ c. positions.
   - ☐ d. confusion.

3. The name "Freeman" as it applies to the
(g) theme of the selection is
   - ☐ a. amusing.
   - ☐ b. common.
   - ☐ c. significant.
   - ☐ d. ethnic.

4. Sam Greenlee's style is reminiscent of the
(k) style of
   - ☐ a. Maya Angelou.
   - ☐ b. James Baldwin.
   - ☐ c. Agatha Christie.
   - ☐ d. Mickey Spillane.

5. Freeman had
(c)
   - ☐ a. a devil-may-care attitude.
   - ☐ b. a conciliatory policy.
   - ☐ c. a double identity.
   - ☐ d. a "whitey" attitude.

6. Freeman was
(f)
   - ☐ a. an anti-integrationist.
   - ☐ b. an integrationist.
   - ☐ c. a martyr.
   - ☐ d. a dope-pusher.

7. Sergeant Dawson admitted to being
(j)
   - ☐ a. an informer.
   - ☐ b. an opportunist.
   - ☐ c. a traitor.
   - ☐ d. a militant.

8. The selection is part of
(k)
   - ☐ a. a debate.
   - ☐ b. a mystery story.
   - ☐ c. an essay.
   - ☐ d. a short story.

9. Condition Red is
(c)
   - ☐ a. standard.
   - ☐ b. desperate.
   - ☐ c. hopeless.
   - ☐ d. urgent.

10. Evidence within the selection seems to indi-
(f) cate that Freeman
   - ☐ a. was convicted.
   - ☐ b. died.
   - ☐ c. betrayed the Cobras.
   - ☐ d. surrendered.

Comprehension Skills: a—isolating details; b—recalling specific facts; c—retaining concepts; d—organizing facts; e—understanding the main idea; f—drawing a conclusion; g—making a judgment; h—making an inference; i—recognizing tone; j—understanding characters; k—appreciation of literary forms.

SELECTIONS FROM THE BLACK

Black Man's Burden

"All over Africa I looked and listened, with a heart filled with hope . . . "

John Oliver Killens

Everywhere I went people called me brother. . . "Welcome, American brother." It was a good feeling for me, to be in Africa. To walk in a land for the first time in your entire life knowing within yourself that your color would not be held against you. No black man ever knows this in America.

No European-American can ever know the precise feelings I experienced in Africa. Perhaps the Jew when he sets foot in Israel, but I doubt it. No people in recorded history has known an experience similar to the African-American. In slavery our link with our past was deliberately and systematically destroyed, tribes and families separated, husbands cut off from their wives, mothers cut off from their suckling babes, our voices muted as they substituted a strange tongue for the one our mothers had given us. They taught us to despise the land from whence we came, even as they despised us in the land in which we found ourselves. And we seldom found ourselves.

In Africa one feels profoundly (against one's Western skepticism) that societies are being constructed, oriented to people rather than to things. Things are not the goal in life, but the means of achieving the pursuit of happiness. One got the feeling, a feeling one wants desperately to believe, that a new dialogue for mankind is evolving in this New World. Time and again I heard variations of that same continuous theme: "We are building a civilization oriented to man. This has been true of us historically. Our governments, our religions, our traditions, our gods are all people-oriented. You people of the West are worshipers of things. You are primarily a gadget civilization. You even think to impress us by which of you can make the biggest bomb to cause the most destruction, or which of you will make the first trip to the moon. Yet you have not figured out how to live with each other here on earth. You of the West have made great progress in technology, and we must learn from you this technology, but we will give to the world our own dialogue in human values." All over Africa I looked and listened, with a heart filled with hope and unwarped by Western disillusionment and cynicism. Did mankind dare to hope again? Could there be a body of ethics other than those four great rules of the West:

Money talks.
Everybody has a price.
Might makes right.
Do others before they can do you.

"The half ain't never been told," my grandmother used to say. I've always wanted to believe this more than anything else. If everything has already been said, let us all go to the cemetery and give ourselves up and pull the earth in after us.

Night and day along the highways of West Africa it is a common sight to see automobiles or trucks pull up alongside another stalled vehicle and men get out and gather to help until they get the crippled vehicle repaired again, or at least enough so they can make it to the nearest town. About a day and a night out of Timbuktu our mighty Land Rover bogged down axle-deep in mud forty miles south of Hombouri. A few of the indigenous population appeared from nowhere and tried to help us dig our way out but we only succeeded in digging ourselves a deeper and deeper grave.

This went on from 11 a.m. till midnight. I recall watching three naked children playing in a mud puddle at the side of the road. I remember their hairdo, one long patch down the middle of their heads from front to back. The temperature was well above one hundred degrees. I took off my shoes and put my feet in the water only to withdraw them instantly because of the scalding heat. I watched the children at play in all their unclothed innocence and was moved deeply by their naked poverty. They had nothing, and then suddenly I realized that they had everything. They had their country. They had human dignity. My children back in the States had far more creature comforts but they had never had a country, they were forever aliens in their own, their native land. One of those naked boys might one day be the President of the République du Mali. There was no position in their country to which they could not one day aspire. My heart filled up and overflowed. I wanted to put my arms around them and tell them that the world was theirs in a way it had never been before. At that moment they were the

John Oliver Killens was born in Macon, Georgia, in 1916 and is a resident of Brooklyn. During World War II for three years he was a member of an amphibian unit in the South Pacific. He has written two novels, *Youngblood* and *And Then We Heard the Thunder*; a book of essays, *Black Man's Burden* and a motion picture, *Odds Against Tomorrow,* which starred Harry Belafonte. He is a teaching fellow in creative writing at Fisk University and chairman of the Workshop of the Harlem Writers Guild.

most beautiful children who ever existed in all the centuries of mankind's sojourn on this lonesome planet. They were the future. They were the proof that man could have a future. I thought once more of my own children and incorrigible optimist that I am I knew realistically that without fundamental changes in their own country they could never achieve the freedom of spirit and self-confidence that these naked black kids possessed. Baked black beneath a semi-desert sun, they knew their beauty without question, saw it reflected in the puddles of water and took their dignity for granted because they lived in a country where they were in style. They were the country. They lived in a land where their color was never held against them. Their color was the land and the land was their color.

I remembered what Dorothy Dandridge had told me when she returned from Europe after having worked on a film with men from Senegal. "I have brand-new values for what is beautiful, John. Those Sengalese men with their tribal scars had a look in their eyes you do not find in the eyes of American Negroes. In all their majestic blackness, they knew who they were and they were proud of who they were. It was an experience I shall never forget."

I knew what she meant. I knew the hangdog look that even the most militant among us often carry around. I know the quick laughter, often to hide the pain and anguish gnawing away at our insides. And mostly because we had to contribute to our own castration. It was expected of us. It was traditional. It was the American Way of Life. We had to give that happy-go-lucky appearance because "that's why darkies were born," according to the script. Let the black man have humility, that greatest of all virtues residing in the soul and bosom of every black man, and let him not deny it. Every American boy-child of a black woman who lives to reach the age of manhood has done a soft-shoe routine for Mister Charlie at least one little old time. It is one of the vestiges of slavery. Psychologically old Massa couldn't live without his grinning, humble darkies. Most white folk aren't ready yet for the black man who tells it like it is.

No other vehicle passed our way all that day and far into the night. It was the rainy season and Malians had sense enough to stay at home. About

midnight two sets of headlights appeared on the black horizon coming toward us. When the truck reached us they stopped, and the men jumped down and had us out of our predicament within half an hour. One of the men, a Tuareg, told us that it was against the law in Mali to pass another vehicle in trouble on the road. I thought to myself, "In America if you saw a car stalled at night by the side of the road and somebody trying to wave you down, the first thing that would cross your mind would be that somebody was trying to rob you. And nine times out of ten, somebody *would* be trying to rob you!"

Was it possible in this the mid-twentieth-century world for Africa and Asia to accept the techniques of the West without absorbing Western values in the process? Could one realistically separate form from content, accepting one while rejecting the other? Or are they one and indivisible?

It is time for Americans, and particularly Negro Americans, to understand that so long as this nation's *raison d'etre* is "free enterprise" rather than "free people" there will be the Haves and the Have-Nots, poverty in the midst of debaucheries of wealth, as newspaper headlines announce increasing unemployment while reporting Long Island matrons being burglarized of a quarter of a million dollars' worth of jewelry. So long as a society evaluates itself on the basis of how many things it can produce and at how great a profit rather than how many citizens can achieve humanity, the White Problem and the Black Man's Burden will be forever with us. In almost every independent country in Africa, people are building what they call Pan-African Socialism, a socialism not of foreign import but based on their own indigenous frame of reference. If socialism is a dirty word to many of my countrymen, why call it socialism? If it conjures up Russian bogeymen, forget it. Call it "Africanism," or "true democracy," if the words taste better in your mouth.

We in America need to reconstruct our society so that people take precedence over poverty, and all men—white, black, brown, yellow—are masters, and only things are slaves.

Starting Time: _____	Finishing Time: _____
Reading Time: _____	Reading Rate: _____
Comprehension: _____	Vocabulary: _____

SELECTIONS FROM THE BLACK

VOCABULARY: The following words have been taken from the selection you have just read. Put an *X* in the box before the best meaning or synonym for the word as used in the selection.

1. **ethics**, page 125, column 2, line 1
   "...a body of ethics other than those..."
   □ a. motives
   □ b. moral principles
   □ c. values
   □ d. logical precepts

2. **indigenous**, page 125, column 2, line 20
   "A few of the indigenous population..."
   □ a. native
   □ b. foreign
   □ c. village dwellers
   □ d. industrious

3. **incorrigible**, page 126, column 1, paragraph 1
   "...incorrigible optimist that I am..."
   □ a. bad beyond reform
   □ b. uncontrollable
   □ c. not easily swayed
   □ d. uncorruptible

4. **vestiges**, page 126, column 1, paragraph 3
   "...one of the vestiges of slavery."
   □ a. traces
   □ b. tokens
   □ c. shames
   □ d. hints

5. **debaucheries**, page 126, column 2, paragraph 3
   "...in the midst of debaucheries of wealth,"
   □ a. indulgences
   □ b. seductions
   □ c. excesses
   □ d. pleasures

CONTEXTUAL AIDS: MOOD AND SETTING

Studies of good readers show that they are aware of the context of what they are reading. This means that they are anticipating what is coming next by what has gone before.

The many ways in which context functions to help the reader recognize words are called contextual aids.

Contextual Aid 7. Words can be understood through the setting and mood of the context. The reader's understanding of the impression created by the author can help him understand an unfamiliar word. In the example, **It was dark and gloomy; _____ was falling,** the reader guesses that the missing word is **rain,** the element that would add to the mood of the context.

The following sentences contain nonsense words which can be recognized from the mood and setting of the sentence. Underline the nonsense word and write the correct word on the line following each sentence. The first one has been done for you.

1. It was cold and bleak; nerf was everywhere.

   _____ *snow* _____

2. The kitchen smelled of delicious fragrances as Mother was banting for the holidays.

   _____

3. Saddened by his loss, the little boy nulled.

   _____

4. Strapped on their couches, the piltersoms hurtled through space on their journey to the moon.

   _____

5. The jury was quiet as the drurl ascended to the bench.

   _____

6. The climbers gazed up the plantic before starting to ascend.

   _____

7. The house was consumed by flames before the sendents arrived.

   _____

8. With a can of worms and a pole on his shoulder, the boy went washling.

   _____

9. He made music by sitting at the drampert and banging on the keys in random fashion.

   _____

10. Mounted on his horse and covered with armor, the blodl rode out to do battle.

    _____

TERMINAL SIGNALS

We have been looking at two types of signals which urge the reader forward, words which signal the continuance of the same thoughts and ideas.

The second of these signals indicated the appearance of a more weighty or important thought—one brought about as a result or a consequence of the foregoing ideas. These, you recall, we labeled Summary Signals. Still another type of Forward Signal exists and it performs an even more critical function. This last signal is called the Terminal Signal.

Terminal Signals

As the label suggests, Terminal Signals indicate to the reader that the end is here—the author is concluding his remarks. They announce that the writer has developed all of the ideas in his presentation and now he is about to state the final step, sum up, or draw the conclusion. Some Terminal Signals are *as a result, finally,* and *in conclusion.* These signal that the thought that has been continuing is now terminated. What follows will be new—not more of the same.

A major distinction between these and Summary Signals is this finality. Summary Signals indicate a pause in the forward trend while the writer gathers his thoughts and tells the reader where he stands. But this is not all; the reader still expects more on the subject. The author has reached a summary point, but not the conclusion.

Observe the following use of the Terminal Signal:

> Once the police patrols had been doubled and the aid of the occupants enlisted, the catburglar was caught. *As a result,* this burglar's days of catting are all over.

Notice how this is obviously the end of the account. The writer has said all he intends to on the subject and his signal indicates this to the reader.

To the textbook reader the Terminal Signal may present one of the major points of the entire lesson or chapter.

COMPREHENSION: For each of the following statements and questions, select the option containing the most complete or most accurate answer.

1. Africans
(e)
- [ ] a. despise the technology of the West and refuse to implement it.
- [ ] b. are impressed with Western gadgetry and give it first priority.
- [ ] c. pursue human values to the exclusion of material comforts.
- [ ] d. acknowledge Western technology but place human values first.

2. The tone of the selection is
(i)
- [ ] a. reminiscent and speculative.
- [ ] b. exasperating and condemnatory.
- [ ] c. pleasant and unassuming.
- [ ] d. critical and hopeful.

3. The author concludes, after observing Africans at close hand, that the West is overly pre-occupied with
(c)
- [ ] a. tradition.
- [ ] b. civilization.
- [ ] c. materialism.
- [ ] d. cynicism.

4. John Killens is very much concerned with
(h)
- [ ] a. free enterprise.
- [ ] b. socialism.
- [ ] c. Pan-Africanism.
- [ ] d. human values.

5. The following: a) "mothers cut off from their suckling babes," b) "our voices muted as they substituted a strange tongue," are examples of
(k)
- [ ] a. imagery.
- [ ] b. personification.
- [ ] c. comparison.
- [ ] d. simile.

6. Killens' reaction to the naked African children was
(i)
- [ ] a. pitiful.
- [ ] b. despairing.
- [ ] c. embarrassing.
- [ ] d. tender.

7. The African road incident might suggest to Killens which of the following?
(g)
- [ ] a. We must all hang together, or assuredly we shall all hang separately.
- [ ] b. That action is the best which procures the greatest happiness for the greatest numbers.
- [ ] c. If a house be divided against itself, that house cannot stand.
- [ ] d. There is no structural organization of society which can bring about the coming of the Kingdom of God on earth, since all systems can be perverted by the selfishness of man.

8. According to Dorothy Dandridge, the African as opposed to the Black American has
(h)
- [ ] a. identity.
- [ ] b. prosperity.
- [ ] c. education.
- [ ] d. opportunity.

9. Killens believes that every Black American at least once in his life is
(c)
- [ ] a. a criminal.
- [ ] b. a psychotic.
- [ ] c. a neurotic.
- [ ] d. an Uncle Tom.

10. Another title for this selection could be
(e)
- [ ] a. The Rape of a Race.
- [ ] b. Africa for Africans.
- [ ] c. Everybody Has a Price.
- [ ] d. Return to Africa.

> Comprehension Skills: a—isolating details; b—recalling specific facts; c—retaining concepts; d—organizing facts; e—understanding the main idea; f—drawing a conclusion; g—making a judgment; h—making an inference; i—recognizing tone; j—understanding characters; k—appreciation of literary forms.

The Revolt of the Black Athlete

There is no such thing as a "free" ride. A black athlete pays dearly.

Harry Edwards

Profit, Property, and the
Black Amateur Athletic Machine

Once he is on campus, a black athlete does in fact become part of the big team, and an important part. As the head basketball coach at San Jose State College, Dan Glines, once emphatically stated, "Without the black athlete, you don't have a chance in this game. You don't draw fans, and you don't win." But a black athlete also finds that his equals are not his white teammates, but the basketballs, baseballs, jockey straps, and other forms of property and equipment—all of which, like him, are important and vital to sports. Like a piece of equipment, the black athlete is used. The old cliché about "You give us your athletic ability, we give you a free education" is a bare-faced lie, concocted by the white sports establishment to hoodwink athletes, white as well as black.

First of all, there is no such thing as a "free" ride. A black athlete pays dearly with his blood, sweat, tears, and ultimately with some portion of his manhood, for the questionable right to represent his school on the athletic field. Second, the white athletic establishments on the various college campuses frequently fail to live up to even the most rudimentary responsibilities implied in their half of the agreement. As we have seen, the educational experiences of most black athletes on white college campuses would insult the intellectual aspirations of an idiot. At one large California school, a black athlete merely had to pass out the basketballs and volley balls for a coach who taught two "techniques of teaching" athletics courses to get four units of credit toward the twelve he needed to maintain his athletic eligibility. None of the four units counted toward his degree requirements. Few schools provide the tutors so often promised to black athletes prior to their enrollments. Usually the coach, rather than supplying tutors, simply obtains copies of tests for his black athletes. (This also happens upon occasion with white athletes, but not very frequently. Sometimes it is not even necessary for a coach to get a test for his academically vulnerable white athletes, because they may have already secured the test from the files of their fraternity house.) And if he is injured or if he fails to live up to the coach's expectations, a black athlete may be required to work at various campus jobs to "help balance things out."

Gradually, most black college athletes begin to realize that his white employers, his teammates, even his fellow students, in spite of the cheers and adulations they shower upon him, regard him as something akin to a super animal, but an animal nevertheless. He is expected to run faster, jump higher, dribble better, pass fancier, and play longer in general than any of his white teammates. The black halfback in football who has only average speed does not play. The black basketball player who cannot jump, dribble, run, *and* shoot does not play. A black athlete on a white campus cannot afford to make mistakes or perform occasionally at a mediocre level. If he does, he does not play. He is expected to be tireless. If he slows up, it is because he is not in shape. He is always supposed to go at top speed and if he doesn't, he has let the entire Negro race down. He is expected to be better in general than his white teammates. In fact, he has to be to play at all.

A common practice on many white college campuses is to "stack" black players in one position or another in order to limit the number who actually make the team. It is a *de facto* quota system. As we mentioned, only the top black athletes are offered grants-in-aid to the big-name schools from the outset. This situation, combined with the public pressures on black high school stars to go to big schools and the fact that white players do not have to be, nor are they expected to be, as good as black athletes, means that theoretically most of the positions on predominantly white college athletic teams could in fact be manned by black players. So, the black players are stacked at one position or another—such as halfback or end in football, or center or guard in basketball—and left to fight among themselves for the positions on the team that are open to them. The results are usually the same. A few blacks make the team, usually in first-string positions. Other blacks with athletic abilities far and above those of many of the whites who make the team are summarily dismissed or told that they can stay on the team but only if they agree to a cut in their financial support or consent to give it up altogether.

Other techniques for maintaining the quota system on predominantly white teams are equally as simple, and as effective. At most white schools, certain positions are reserved exclusively for whites. Take the position of quarterback. You could count the number of quarterbacks who have played intercollegiate football for predominantly white colleges without taking off your shoes — Ron Burton at Colgate, Jimmy Raye at Michigan State, Sandy Stevens at Minnesota, Wilburn Hollis at Iowa, and a few others. Many coaches and athletic establishment members feel that blacks lack the necessary intellectual equipment to become quarterbacks, that they will be unable to remember plays or formations and pick apart a defense, that running things on the field would be "too much for the coon's mustard-seed brain to handle," as one trainer stated to another during a football game at a large Mid-western university in 1966.

If, then, so many white college coaches, white athletes, and white students in general so deplore and are repulsed by the presence of black athletes, why are they recruited? The answer is obvious. We have already alluded to it. One has only to read the minutes of the congressional hearings on the dispute between the National Collegiate Athletic Association and the Amateur Athletic Union to understand that amateur athletics in America is big business. One element in the dispute between the N.C.A.A. and the A.A.U. centers around the control of ten million dollars presently held in banks and investment capital by the A.A.U. The N.C.A.A. maintains that a sizable proportion of these funds was put there by college athletes affiliated with the N.C.A.A. and that therefore the N.C.A.A. should have a cut of the booty. Individual schools also fare handsomely from amateur athletics. Athletic receipts have provided funds for constructing many new buildings on many college campuses throughout the country. A player such as O. J. Simpson is worth approximately three million dollars in gate receipts and television rights to the University of Southern California. Much the same can be said of Lew Alcindor at the University of California at Los Angeles. Every white coach who recruits a black athlete hopes that he has uncovered a potential O. J. Simpson or Lew Alcindor, because that would mean money for his school and prestige, and money, for him. And what do the black athletes receive in return? Most often, with few exceptions, their walking papers as soon as their eligibility is up. They join the ranks of has-beens, who never really were.

Why then do black athletes go to white schools, if they find nothing but humiliation or at best toleration from the time of their recruitment until they remove their uniforms for the last time? The answers to this question are as varied as the dreams and hopes of all black athletes who yearly leave the ghettos and poverty to attend predominantly white schools. Perhaps a more pertinent question would be, Why do they stay? Black athletes stay on racist white college campuses because of a driving obsession to prove themselves and because, in the black community itself, a heavy stigma attaches to the black athlete who goes to a big-name school and "fails to make the grade." If he fails academically, he is ridiculed; but if he quits, he is despised. For he has not taken advantage of "the chance that his parents didn't have." He has failed those who had faith in him. He has added validity to the contention held by whites that black people are lazy, ignorant, and quit when the going gets rough. In essence then, he is despised because he has failed to prove himself to whites. He has failed to demonstrate unequivocally that he can take it. A black athlete himself may feel guilty even about the thought of quitting. But what he doesn't realize is that he can never prove himself in the eyes of white racists—not, at any rate, as a man or even as a human being. From their perspective he is, and will always be, a nigger. From their perspective the only difference between the black man shining shoes in the ghetto and the champion black sprinter is that the shoe shine man is a nigger, while the sprinter is a fast nigger.

The black athlete on the white-dominated college campus, then, is typically exploited, abused, dehumanized, and cast aside in much the same manner as a worn basketball. His lot from that point on does not differ greatly from that of any other Afro-American. His life is riddled with insults, humiliations, and all other manner of degrading experiences. The coach will no longer call a racist landlord and request that he rent to the former black athlete because he is a "good Negro." Few white coaches work to get black athletes respectable summer jobs or their wives full-time jobs during their eligibility; one can imagine what the efforts amount to after the athletes' eligibility has expired. Then the athlete is finally and desperately on his own. Then, and only then, do most of them realize the degree to which they have been exploited for four long years. As a result, some simply give up on the society and join the armed forces. Others attempt to cling to the one commodity that they have been able to peddle, however cheaply—their athletic abilities. These pathetic, brooding, black figures can be seen playing in hunch games and city league games in any college town. And then, when they are invited, there is always the periodic return to the old college campus to play against the new recruits and relive some of the old excitement. These former athletes seldom tell new black recruits the truth about the "big team." They avoid the issue partly because they do not wish to face humiliating questions about why they themselves stayed on for four years in the face of such conditions. Partly, it is because they want the new young recruits to look up to them as heroes, as black men who had proven themselves in athletic competition where, as they say, each man is rated according to his courage, his ability, and his winning record. But most of all, the former black athlete does not tell the new black recruit the truth because, at a time when he is trying to salvage and preserve whatever masculinity he has left, he also wants to maintain as much as possible the fantastic delusion that in some way his four college years had been everything that he had wanted them to be. For him, the future looks dismal and hostile and the present is a farce. The only phase of his life that he can control is the past, and this he attempts to do through deluding himself, by rationalizing, and by lying to the new black recruits at his alma mater.

Starting Time: _____	Finishing Time: _____
Reading Time: _____	Reading Rate: _____
Comprehension: _____	Vocabulary: _____

VOCABULARY: The following words have been taken from the selection you have just read. Put an *X* in the box before the best meaning or synonym for the word as used in the selection.

1. **rudimentary**, page 130, column 1, paragraph 2
   "...even the most rudimentary responsibilities..."
   ☐ a. undeveloped
   ☐ b. imperfect
   ☐ c. fundamental
   ☐ d. advanced

2. **secured**, page 130, column 1, last line
   "...have already secured the test..."
   ☐ a. guarded
   ☐ b. obtained
   ☐ c. locked up
   ☐ d. protected

3. **summarily**, page 130, column 2, last line
   "...are summarily dismissed..."
   ☐ a. promptly
   ☐ b. briefly
   ☐ c. comprehensively
   ☐ d. concisely

4. **stigma**, page 131, column 2, paragraph 1
   "...a heavy stigma attaches to the..."
   ☐ a. mental state
   ☐ b. disease
   ☐ c. sign of defeat
   ☐ d. mark of disgrace

5. **unequivocally**, page 131, column 2, paragraph 1
   "...to demonstrate unequivocally..."
   ☐ a. reasonably
   ☐ b. forcefully
   ☐ c. disputedly
   ☐ d. conclusively

SELECTIONS FROM THE BLACK

SYLLABICATION

Knowing how to reduce words to their syllables aids both reading and spelling. Frequently a long word can be recognized and understood if pronounced by syllables. And knowledge of syllabication (frequently spelled *syllabification)* contributes to accuracy in spelling.

There are rules or generalizations which we can follow when dividing words. One such rule tells us that **ed** added to a word which ends in **d** or **t** becomes a separate syllable, like **wait** and **wait-ed.** When **ed** is added to other words, the words remain one syllable, like **call** and **called.**

The following sentences contain similar words. If according to the rule above, **ed** is a separate syllable, write the word on the line following each sentence, separating the syllables. If the **ed** word in a sentence remains a one-syllable word, write nothing on the line.

1. The girl sighed with relief at the good news.

    _____

2. A ship was sighted on the horizon, many miles away.

    _____

3. The committee asked for a vote on the matter.

    _____

4. He boasted that he wouldn't be caught, but he was.

    _____

5. The cars bumped at the intersection, causing minor damage.

    _____

6. The candidate campaigned vigorously for reelection.

    _____

7. The appointment was confirmed by congress.

    _____

8. The fire was doused with water, extinguishing the flames.

    _____

9. Water flowed from the pipe, flooding the basement.

    _____

10. The newspaper hinted at his guilt, preventing a fair trial.

    _____

11. He slouched, hoping he wouldn't be seen.

    _____

12. Many drowned before the rescue ship came.

    _____

COUNTER SIGNALS

We have been looking at Forward Signals—those that signal the reader that the thought is continuing, that more of the same is coming.

The final signal we will examine is different in that it signals a turnaround in the thought. We call this type a Counter Signal.

Counter Signals

These turn the thought sharply in a different direction. They tell the reader that the writer has a countering idea to present and we should be alert for it.

Common Counter Signals are *but, yet, nevertheless, otherwise, although, despite, in spite of, not, on the contrary, however.* These are all used to introduce an idea not only different from what has gone before, but also one that leads the reader in a new direction.

By far the most common of these adversative words is *but.* In the words of Samuel Daniel, the English poet, "Oh, now comes that bitter word—*but,* which makes all nothing that was said before, that smooths and wounds, that strikes and dashes more than flat denial, or a plain disgrace."

Most of us can testify to the power of the word. At one time or another we've all overlooked it and suffered the consequences. It is a little word, but it's packed with significance. Don't pass over it in your reading—check to see how it affects the thought of the passage.

When you come upon any of these Counter Signals, prepare yourself. They tell you that the thought is not going forward any longer, it has stopped.

In textbooks especially, be alert for Counter Signals. The author has come to a turn in the road and is about to go in a different direction.

COMPREHENSION: For each of the following statements and questions, select the option containing the most complete or most accurate answer.

1. The tone of the selection is
(i)
   □ a. argumentative.
   □ b. impassioned.
   □ c. restrained.
   □ d. acquiescent.

2. The work required of the Black athlete to pass
(g) the course in "techniques of teaching" athletic courses was
   □ a. adequate.
   □ b. undemanding.
   □ c. belittling.
   □ d. annoying.

3. Most colleges recruit Black athletes because
(c)
   □ a. the colleges want to appear integrated.
   □ b. Black athletes excel in ability.
   □ c. the colleges are pressured by alumni groups.
   □ d. federally-supported colleges must maintain a black-white ratio.

4. The scarcity of Black quarterbacks in inter-
(c) collegiate football reflects
   □ a. the biased reasoning of some coaches.
   □ b. the preference Black athletes have for line positions.
   □ c. the inferior academic preparation of many Black athletes.
   □ d. superior white competition.

5. De facto segregation practiced by some col-
(b) lege coaches takes the form of
   □ a. restricting the number of positions open to Blacks.
   □ b. promoting unhealthy rivalries between Blacks and whites.
   □ c. denying Black athletes membership to fraternities.
   □ d. demanding more from white athletes.

6. According to Edwards, Black athletes can do
(f) something about the exploitation to which they are subjected by
   □ a. demonstrating their athletic superiority and making themselves indispensable.
   □ b. uniting and bargaining from a position of strength.
   □ c. staging demonstrations to expose the colleges' racist policies.
   □ d. none of the above.

7. Former Black athletes seldom present a com-
(c) plete picture of the significance of athletic scholarships to Black recruits because
   □ a. the young recruits might be instrumental in changing the system.
   □ b. parting with their illusions might shatter their self-image.
   □ c. they have a sense of responsibility to their alma maters.
   □ d. they enjoy the recognition and admiration of the young students.

8. The Black athlete generally realizes that he
(d) has been exploited when
   □ a. he is abused by a racist landlord.
   □ b. he decides to join the armed forces.
   □ c. his eligibility has expired.
   □ d. he is reduced to playing for city league teams.

9. Some readers may disagree with Edwards'
(g) position concerning Black athletes. They might argue that
   □ a. the unfair treatment given to Black athletes is also given to white athletes who have similar financial problems.
   □ b. not being an athlete, Edwards is not in a position to make a judgment.
   □ c. Edwards has overlooked the basic, human aspirations of athletes, Black or white.
   □ d. the conditions described by Edwards are found in very few colleges and universities.

10. Which of the following points does the author
(e) make?
   □ a The Black athlete's college experience opens the door to professional sports.
   □ b. The well-conditioned Black athlete is a profitable asset to a college.
   □ c. Promising Black athletes should not apply to predominantly white colleges.
   □ d. Black athletes should swallow their pride and exploit their situation for personal gain.

Comprehension Skills: a—isolating details; b—recalling specific facts; c—retaining concepts; d—organizing facts; e—understanding the main idea; f—drawing a conclusion; g—making a judgment; h—making an inference; i—recognizing tone; j—understanding characters; k—appreciation of literary forms.

What to the Slaves Is the Fourth of July?

An Independence Day Address Delivered in Rochester, New York, on July 4, 1852

Frederick Douglass

Fellow Citizens: Pardon me, and allow me to ask, why am I called upon to speak here today? What have I or those I represent to do with your national independence? Are the great principles of political freedom and of natural justice, embodied in that Declaration of Independence, extended to us? And am I, therefore, called upon to bring our humble offering to the national altar, and to confess the benefits, and express devout gratitude for the blessings resulting from your independence to us?

Would to God, both for your sakes and ours, that an affirmative answer could be truthfully returned to these questions. Then would my task be light, and my burden easy and delightful. For who is there so cold that a nation's sympathy could not warm him? Who so obdurate and dead to the claims of gratitude, that would not thankfully acknowledge such priceless benefits? Who so stolid and selfish that would not give his voice to swell the halleluiahs of a nation's jubilee, when the chains of servitude had been torn from his limbs? I am not that man. . . .

I am not included within the pale of this glorious anniversary! Your high independence only reveals the immeasurable distance between us. The blessings in which you this day rejoice are not enjoyed in common. The rich inheritance of justice, liberty, prosperity, and independence bequeathed by your fathers is shared by you, not by me. The sunlight that brought life and healing to you has brought stripes and death to me. This Fourth of July is *yours,* not *mine. You* may rejoice, *I* must mourn. To drag a man in fetters into the grand illuminated temple of liberty, and call upon him to join you in joyous anthems, were inhuman mockery and sacrilegious irony. Do you mean, citizens, to mock me, by asking me to speak today? . . .

Fellow citizens, above your national, tumultuous joy, I hear the mournful wail of millions, whose chains, heavy and grievous yesterday, are today rendered more intolerable by the jubilant shouts that reach them. If I do forget, if I do not remember those bleeding children of sorrow this day, "may my right hand forget her cunning, and may my tongue cleave to the roof of my mouth!" To forget them, to pass lightly over their wrongs, and to chime in with the popular theme, would be treason, most scandalous and shocking, and would make me a reproach before God and the world. My subject, then, fellow citizens, is "American Slavery." I shall see this day and its popular characteristics from the slave's point of view. Standing here, identified with the American bondman, making his wrongs mine, I do not hesitate to declare, with all my soul, that the character and conduct of this nation never looked blacker to me than on this Fourth of July. Whether we turn to the declarations of the past, or to the professions of the present, the conduct of the nation seems equally hideous and revolting. America is false to the past, false to the present, and solemnly binds herself to be false to the future. Standing with God and the crushed and bleeding slave on this occasion, I will, in the name of humanity, which is outraged, in the name of liberty, which is fettered, in the name of the Constitution and the Bible, which are disregarded and trampled upon, dare to call in question and to denounce, with all the emphasis I can command, everything that serves to perpetuate slavery — the great sin and shame of America! "I will not equivocate; I will not excuse;" I will use the severest language I can command, and yet not one word shall escape me that any man, whose judgment is not blinded by prejudice, or who is not at heart a slave-holder, shall not confess to be right and just.

But I fancy I hear some of my audience say it is just in this circumstance that you and your brother Abolitionists fail to make a favorable impression on the public mind. Would you argue more and denounce less, would you persuade more and rebuke less, your cause would be much more likely to succeed. But, I submit, where all is plain there is nothing to be argued. What point in the antislavery creed would you have me argue? On what branch of the subject do the people of this country need light? Must I undertake to prove that the slave is a man? That point is conceded already. Nobody doubts it. The slaveholders themselves acknowledge it in the enactment of laws for their government.

In 1817 in Talbot County, Maryland, Frederick Douglass was born of a slave mother and white father. He was to become the best-known abolitionist in the history of slavery in the United States.

He was raised by his grandparents until the age of eight, then sent to live in the home of Hugh Auld where his struggles to learn to read and write began. By the time he was seventeen he had to be sent to a slave breaker who specialized in cracking the spirit of hard-to-manage slaves. Although he was whipped and beaten daily, Douglass' spirit was never broken and he continued to fight back.

Eventually he was apprenticed to a shipyard to learn the trade of caulker. Armed with seaman's papers supplied him by a free Black, he escaped via the Underground Railroad to New Bedford, Massachusetts.

They acknowledge it when they punish disobedience on the part of the slave. There are seventy-two crimes in the State of Virginia, which, if committed by a black man (no matter how ignorant he be), subject him to the punishment of death; while only two of these same crimes will subject a white man to like punishment. What is this but the acknowledgment that the slave is a moral, intellectual, and responsible being? The manhood of the slave is conceded. It is admitted in the fact that Southern statute-books are covered with enactments, forbidding, under severe fines and penalties, the teaching of the slave to read and write. When you can point to any such laws in reference to the beasts of the field, then I may consent to argue the manhood of the slave. When the dogs in your streets, when the fowls of the air, when the cattle on your hills, when the fish of the sea, and the reptiles that crawl, shall be unable to distinguish the slave from a brute, then I will argue with you that the slave is a man!

For the present it is enough to affirm the equal manhood of the Negro race. Is it not astonishing that, while we are plowing, planting, and reaping, using all kinds of mechanical tools, erecting houses, constructing bridges, building ships, working in metals of brass, iron, copper, silver, and gold; that while we are reading, writing, and cyphering, acting as clerks, merchants, and secretaries, having among us lawyers, doctors, ministers, poets, authors, editors, orators, and teachers; that while we are engaged in all the enterprises common to other men — digging gold in California, capturing the whale in the Pacific, feeding sheep and cattle on the hillside, living, moving, acting, thinking, planning, living in families as husbands, wives, and children, and above all, confessing and worshipping the Christian God, and looking hopefully for life and immortality beyond the grave — we are called upon to prove that we are men?

Would you have me argue that man is entitled to liberty? That he is the rightful owner of his own body? You have already declared it. Must I argue the wrongfulness of slavery? Is that a question for republicans? Is it to be settled by the rules of logic and argumentation, as a matter beset with great difficulty, involving a doubtful application of the principle of justice, hard to understand? How should I look today in the presence of Americans, dividing and subdividing a discourse, to show that men have a natural right to freedom, speaking of it relatively and positively, negatively and affirmatively? To do so would be to make myself ridiculous, and to offer an insult to your understanding. There is not a man beneath the canopy of heaven who does not know that slavery is wrong *for him.*

What! Am I to argue that it is wrong to make men brutes, to rob them of their liberty, to work them without wages, to keep them ignorant of their relations to their fellow men, to beat them with sticks, to flay their flesh with the lash, to load their limbs with irons, to hunt them with dogs, to sell them at auction, to sunder their families, to knock out their teeth, to burn their flesh, to starve them into obedience and submission to their masters? Must I argue that a system thus marked with blood and stained with pollution is wrong? No; I will not. I have better employment for my time and strength than such arguments would imply.

What, then, remains to be argued? Is it that slavery is not divine; that God did not establish it; that our doctors of divinity are mistaken? There is blasphemy in the thought. That which is inhuman cannot be divine. Who can reason on such a proposition? They that can, may; I cannot. The time for such argument is past.

From Frederick Douglass' Independence Day Address, 1852.

SELECTIONS FROM THE BLACK

At a time like this, scorching irony, not convincing argument, is needed. O! had I the ability, and could I reach the nation's ear, I would today pour out a fiery stream of biting ridicule, blasting reproach, withering sarcasm, and stern rebuke. For it is not light that is needed, but fire; it is not the gentle shower, but thunder. We need the storm, the whirlwind, and the earthquake. The feeling of the nation must be quickened; the conscience of the nation must be exposed; and its crimes against God and man must be denounced.

What to the American slave is your Fourth of July? I answer a day that reveals to him more than all other days of the year, the gross injustice and cruelty to which he is the constant victim. To him your celebration is a sham; your boasted liberty an unholy license; your national greatness, swelling vanity; your sounds of rejoicing are empty and heartless; your denunciation of tyrants, brass-fronted impudence; your shouts of liberty and equality, hollow mockery; your prayers and hymns, your sermons and thanksgivings, with all your religious parade and solemnity, are to him mere bombast, fraud, deception, impiety, and hypocrisy — a thin veil to cover up crimes which would disgrace a nation of savages. There is not a nation of the earth guilty of practices more shocking and bloody than are the people of these United States at this very hour.

Go where you may, search where you will, roam through all the monarchies and despotisms of the Old World, travel through South America, search out every abuse and when you have found the last, lay your facts by the side of the everyday practices of this nation, and you will say with me that, for revolting barbarity and shameless hypocrisy America reigns without a rival.

Starting Time: _____   Finishing Time: _____

Reading Time: _____   Reading Rate: _____

Comprehension: _____   Vocabulary: _____

VOCABULARY: The following words have been taken from the selection you have just read. Put an *X* in the box before the best meaning or synonym for the word as used in the selection.

1. **perpetuate**, page 135, column 2, paragraph 1
"...everything that serves to perpetuate slavery—the great sin..."
☐ a. perpetrate
☐ b. discontinue
☐ c. vindicate
☐ d. continue

2. **equivocate**, page 135, column 2, paragraph 1
" 'I will not equivocate;' "
☐ a. hedge
☐ b. accuse
☐ c. lie
☐ d. equalize

3. **conceded**, page 135, column 2, paragraph 2
"That point is conceded already."
☐ a. withdrawn
☐ b. acknowledged
☐ c. denied
☐ d. confessed

4. **responsible**, page 136, column 1, paragraph 1
"...a moral, intellectual, and responsible being?"
☐ a. accountable
☐ b. unreliable
☐ c. competent
☐ d. responsive

5. **sham**, page 137, column 1, paragraph 2
"...your celebration is a sham;"
☐ a. shame
☐ b. pretense
☐ c. counterfeit
☐ d. imitation

ROOTS

Many English words consist of a base or root word to which prefixes (beginnings) and suffixes (endings) have been added. To the root word **agree** (a verb) we can add both a prefix and a suffix to get **disagreeable** (an adjective) which has an opposite meaning.

Roots are Latin and Greek stems on which our English words are based. For example, **bio** (life) is a Greek root on which our word **biology** (the study of plant and animal life) is built.

Two Roots

1. **-grat** is a Latin root which means **please**, **favor** or **thanks**. When we are thankful we express our **gratitude**.

2. **-mal** is also from Latin and it means **bad**, **evil** or **ill**. A **malady** is an illness.

In the following sentences, these two roots have been left out. Space has been left indicating where the root belongs. Add one of these two roots and write the word on the line following each sentence.

1. He's an **in—e** if he doesn't appreciate all you've done.

_____

2. The destruction was **—icious**, obviously done intentionally.

_____

3. Leave the waiter a tip or **—uity** to thank him.

_____

4. The tumor was **—ignant**; it was very likely to cause death.

_____

5. I am tremendously **—ified** by your response.

_____

6. In spite of his kind words, there was **—ice** in his heart.

_____

7. We **con—ulated** the boy who won the race.

_____

8. His reputation has been **—igned** by vicious slander.

_____

9. His services were given **—is**, without charge or payment.

_____

10. The administration termed the rebellious students **—contents**.

_____

11. Poorly balanced diets lead to **—nutrition**.

_____

PARAGRAPHS OF INTRODUCTION

The textbook writer works through paragraphs. The effectiveness with which he communicates with his reader depends on how well and how carefully he has structured his paragraphs.

In each chapter or article, the writer begins with an introductory paragraph. Like a speaker the writer offers prefacing remarks to open his discussion of a particular topic or subject.

We have all heard the speaker who tells an anecdote or two to "warm up" his listeners before he gets into his talk. The writer has a much more difficult task — he is not face to face with his listeners, he must do more than tell an amusing story to get his readers ready for his presentation. Recognizing this limitation of communication through the printed page, writers strive to create an effective opening with which to introduce their subject to the reader.

We call the opening the paragraph of introduction — used as a kind of announcement of what is to follow. Frequently the writer will state the purpose he hopes to accomplish in the following paragraphs; he may offer a brief outline of the major concepts he intends to discuss; he may merely mention one or two of the ideas the reader can expect later in the chapter.

Obviously paragraphs of introduction are packed with significance. Because they offer such a preview of what is to come, it is one of the only two paragraphs read when previewing.

In magazine articles and similar leisure reading publications, the paragraph of introduction has a special function to perform — it's used frequently as bait to lure the reader into the account. The feature writer knows that he has to capture the reader's interest and attention with just a few words. The reader can expect any kind of interest-compelling device to be employed for this purpose — it is the skilled writer at his best.

COMPREHENSION: For each of the following statements and questions, select the option containing the most complete or most accurate answer.

1. Throughout his speech, the author relies heavily on questions. They are
(k)
- [ ] a. rhetorical.
- [ ] b. direct.
- [ ] c. inquisitive.
- [ ] d. declarative.

2. Viewed in the light of Douglass' speech, the Fourth of July celebrations can be considered
(e)
- [ ] a. appropriate.
- [ ] b. hypocritical.
- [ ] c. patriotic.
- [ ] d. artificial.

3. The author's intellectualism and unique writing style is reminiscent of which modern Black American?
(g)
- [ ] a. Malcolm X
- [ ] b. Richard Wright
- [ ] c. H. Rap Brown
- [ ] d. Martin Luther King, Jr.

4. The tone of the speech is one of
(i)
- [ ] a. searching inquiry.
- [ ] b. violent militancy.
- [ ] c. gauche inappropriateness.
- [ ] d. scathing indictment.

5. Considering the occasion and the content of the speech, the careful reader can infer that
(h)
- [ ] a. Douglass had been invited to speak by white liberals.
- [ ] b. Douglass was attempting to incite his audience to rebellion.
- [ ] c. Douglass was frequently interrupted by hecklers.
- [ ] d the audience was primarily Black.

6. To Frederick Douglass, the gay, noisy Fourth of July celebrations
(f)
- [ ] a. suggested hope for his oppressed race.
- [ ] b. made him fear a violent slave uprising.
- [ ] c. filled him with doubt and concern.
- [ ] d. were cruel reminders of inhuman injustice.

7. America's record during her involvement with slavery indicates that she will
(h)
- [ ] a. be helpless in easing the tensions of the present.
- [ ] b. fight integration with every legal weapon at her disposal.
- [ ] c. attempt to right the wrongs of the past.
- [ ] d. attempt to revert to the past.

8. The attitude of the slave owner toward his slaves was contradictory because he
(c)
- [ ] a. held them accountable for their actions.
- [ ] b. permitted them to hold church meetings.
- [ ] c. destroyed the unity of the Black family.
- [ ] d. encouraged them to work for their freedom.

9. To awaken America from her lethargy and open her eyes to reality, convincing arguments will not suffice. America needs
(b)
- [ ] a. violent and bloody revolution.
- [ ] b. scorching irony.
- [ ] c. enlightened reasoning.
- [ ] d. vigorous rhetoric.

10. Generally, the slave owners viewed their slaves in no better light than they did their animals because
(h)
- [ ] a. they sought a moral justification for slavery.
- [ ] b. they were morally justified as slave owners.
- [ ] c. the American Constitution denied the slaves their human rights.
- [ ] d. the slaves offered no resistance to their white masters.

Comprehension Skills: a—isolating details; b—recalling specific facts; c—retaining concepts; d—organizing facts; e—understanding the main idea; f—drawing a conclusion; g—making a judgment; h—making an inference; i—recognizing tone; j—understanding characters; k—appreciation of literary forms.

Black Rage

When the servile men and women stand up, we had all better duck.

William H. Grier
Price M. Cobbs

Depression and grief are hatred turned on the self. It is instructive to pursue the relevance of this truth to the condition of black Americans.

Black people have shown a genius for surviving under the most deadly circumstances. They have survived because of their close attention to reality. A black dreamer would have a short life in Mississippi. They are of necessity bound to reality, chained to the facts of the times; historically the penalty for misjudging a situation involving white men has been death. The preoccupation with religion has been a willing adoption of fantasy to prod an otherwise reluctant mind to face another day.

We will even play tricks on ourselves if it helps us stay alive.

The psychological devices used to survive are reminiscent of the years of slavery, and it is no coincidence. The same devices are used because black men face the same danger now as then.

The grief and depression caused by the condition of black men in America is an unpopular reality to the sufferers. They would rather see themselves in a more heroic posture and chide a disconsolate brother. They would like to point to their achievements (which in fact have been staggering); they would rather point to virtue (which has been shown in magnificent form by some blacks); they would point to bravery, fidelity, prudence, brilliance, creativity, all of which dark men have shown in abundance. But the overriding experience of the black American has been grief and sorrow and no man can change that fact.

His grief has been realistic and appropriate. What people have so earned a period of mourning?

We want to emphasize yet again the depth of the grief for slain sons and ravished daughters, how deep and lingering it is.

If the depth of this sorrow is felt, we can then consider what can be made of this emotion.

As grief lifts and the sufferer moves toward health, the hatred he had turned on himself is redirected toward his tormentors, and the fury of his attack on the one who caused him pain is in direct proportion to the depth of his grief. When the mourner lashes out in anger, it is a relief to those who love him, for they know he has now returned to health.

Observe that the amount of rage the oppressed turns on his tormentor is a direct function of the depth of his grief, and consider the intensity of black men's grief.

Slip for a moment into the soul of a black girl whose womanhood is blighted, not because she is ugly, but because she is black and by definition all blacks are ugly.

Become for a moment a black citizen of Birmingham, Alabama, and try to understand his grief and dismay when innocent children are slain while they worship, for no other reason than that they are black.

Imagine how an impoverished mother feels as she watches the light of creativity snuffed out in her children by schools that dull the mind and environs that rot the soul.

For a moment make yourself the black father whose son went innocently to war and there was slain—for whom, for what?

For a moment be any black person, anywhere, and you will feel the waves of hopelessness that engulfed black men and women when Martin Luther King was murdered. All black people understood the tide of anarchy that followed his death.

It is the transformation of *this* quantum of grief into aggression of which we now speak. As a sapling bent low stores energy for a violent backswing, blacks bent double by oppression have stored energy that will be released in the form of rage—black rage, apocalyptic and final.

White Americans have developed a high skill in the art of misunderstanding black people. It must have seemed to slaveholders that slavery would last through all eternity, for surely their misunderstanding of black bondsmen suggested it. If the slaves were eventually to be released from bondage, what could be the purpose of creating the fiction of their subhumanity?

It must have seemed to white men during the period 1865 to 1945 that black men would always be a passive, compliant lot. If not, why would they

William H. Grier, M. D., was graduated from the University of Michigan Medical School and took his residency in psychiatry at the Menninger Clinic.

In addition to their private practice in the city of San Francisco, both Dr. Grier and Dr. Cobbs are Assistant Professors of Psychiatry at the San Francisco Medical Center, University of California.

Price M. Cobbs, M.D., is a graduate of the Meharry Medical College and attended Langley Porter Neuropsychiatric Institute in San Francisco.

have stoked the flames of hatred with such deliberately barbarous treatment?

White Americans today deal with "racial incidents" from summer to summer as if such minor turbulence will always remain minor and one need only keep the blacks busy till fall to have made it through another troubled season.

Today it is the young men who are fighting the battles, and, for now, their elders, though they have given their approval, have not joined in. The time seems near, however, for the full range of the black masses to put down the broom and buckle on the sword. And it grows nearer day by day. Now we see skirmishes, sputtering erratically, evidence if you will that the young men are in a warlike mood. But evidence as well that the elders are watching closely and may soon join the battle.

Even these minor flurries have alarmed the country and have resulted in a spate of generally senseless programs designed to give *temporary summer jobs!!* More interesting in its long-range prospects has been the apparent eagerness to draft black men for military service. If in fact this is a deliberate design to place black men in uniform in order to get them off the street, it may be the most curious "instant cure" for a serious disease this nation has yet attempted. Young black men are learning the most modern techniques for killing —techniques that may be used against *any* enemy.

But it is all speculation. The issue finally rests with the black masses. When the servile men and women stand up, we had all better duck.

We should ask what is likely to galvanize the masses into aggression against the whites.

Will it be some grotesque atrocity against black people that at last causes one-tenth of the nation to rise up in indignation and crush the monstrosity?

Will it be the example of black people outside the United States who have gained dignity through their own liberation movement?

Will it be by the heroic action of a small group of blacks which by its wisdom and courage commands action in a way that cannot be denied?

Or will it be by blacks, finally and in an unpredictable way, simply getting fed up with the bumbling stupid racism of this country? Fired not so much by any one incident as by the gradual accretion of stupidity into fixtures of national policy.

All are possible, or any one, or something yet unthought. It seems certain only that on the course the nation now is headed it will happen.

One might consider the possibility that, if the national direction remains unchanged, such a conflagration simply might *not* come about. Might not black people remain where they are, as they did for a hundred years during slavery?

Such seems truly inconceivable. Not because blacks are so naturally warlike or rebellious, but because they are filled with such grief, such sorrow, such bitterness, and such hatred. It seems now delicately poised, not yet risen to the flash point, but rising rapidly nonetheless. No matter what repressive measures are invoked against the blacks, they will never swallow their rage and go back to blind hopelessness.

If existing oppressions and humiliating disenfranchisements are to be lifted, they will have to be lifted most speedily, or catastrophe will follow.

For there are no more psychological tricks blacks can play upon themselves to make it possible to exist in dreadful circumstances. No more lies can they tell themselves. No more dreams to fix on. No more opiates to dull the pain. No more patience. No more thought. No more reason. Only a welling tide risen out of all those terrible years of grief, now a tidal wave of fury and rage, and all black, black as night.

Starting Time: _____   Finishing Time: _____

Reading Time: _____   Reading Rate: _____

Comprehension: _____   Vocabulary: _____

From Chapter X of *Black Rage* by William H. Grier and Price M. Cobbs. ©1968 by William H. Grier and Price M. Cobbs, Basic Books, Inc., Publishers, New York.

VOCABULARY: The following words have been taken from the selection you have just read. Put an *X* in the box before the best meaning or synonym for the word as used in the selection.

1. **relevance,** page 93, column 1, paragraph 1
"It is instructive to pursue the relevance of this truth..."
☐ a. accuracy
☐ b. pertinence
☐ c. reliability
☐ d. reluctance

2. **environs,** page 93, column 2, paragraph 5
"...by schools that dull the mind and environs that rot the soul."
☐ a. disappointments
☐ b. subjects
☐ c. surroundings
☐ d. resentments

3. **erratically,** page 94, column 1, paragraph 3
"Now we see skirmishes, sputtering erratically,"
☐ a. indiscriminately
☐ b. unpredictably
☐ c. irrationally
☐ d. in error

4. **design,** page 94, column 1, paragraph 4
"If in fact this is a deliberate design to place black men in uniform..."
☐ a. desire
☐ b. pattern
☐ c. purpose
☐ d. scheme

5. **opiates,** page 94, column 2, last paragraph
"No more opiates to dull the pain."
☐ a. stimulants
☐ b. drugs
☐ c. opinions
☐ d. opium

PREFIXES

Many English words consist of a base or root word to which prefixes (beginnings) and suffixes (endings) have been added. To the root word **agree** (a verb) we can add both a prefix and a suffix to get **disagreeable** (an adjective) which has an opposite meaning.

A prefix is added to the beginning of a word and causes a change in the meaning of that word. We have just seen how the prefix **dis** reverses the meaning of **agree**. Most of the prefixes we will be examining in this book will come from Latin.

Two Prefixes

1. **bi-** is a Latin prefix which means **two**. The adjective **bilingual** describes someone who speaks two languages.

2. **syn-** is from the Greek and it means **with** or **together with**. In the verb **synchronize**, we cause our watches to move together, to keep the same time. Sometimes this prefix is spelled **sym**, as in **symphony**, describing an orchestra whose members play in harmony.

In the following sentences the words in bold print need prefixes. Add one of these two prefixes to each word and write your word.

1. A **partisan** committee consists of members from both political parties.

   _____

2. A condition accompanying a disease is called a **ptom**.

   _____

3. A person commits **gamy** by marrying again without divorce.

   _____

4. Several symptoms occurring together constitute a **drome**.

   _____

5. A two-wheeled self-propelled vehicle is a **cycle**.

   _____

6. A paper issued every two weeks is referred to as a **monthly**.

   _____

7. A summary, putting all the facts together, is called a **opsis**.

   _____

8. A **onym** is a word with nearly the same meaning as another.

   _____

9. **Thesis** refers to putting parts together so as to form a whole.

   _____

10. Draw a line which **sects** that angle.

   _____

PARAGRAPHS OF DEFINITION

We have seen how authors use their paragraphs of introduction to "kick off" the article or chapter, to introduce the reader to the subject or topic.

The next paragraph we are going to examine is the one used to define or explain an idea or concept that is new to the reader.

Fortunately paragraphs of definition are easily recognizable. Frequently, the word, phrase, or concept being defined is shown in italics—this tells the reader that the word or words in italics are being studied and analyzed. Certain key words appear regularly in these paragraphs, words authors use when defining. Look for phrases like "We can define this as..." or "When we say ____, we mean that..." or "This simply means..." and similar phrases, often including the word "define."

It is essential that the reader recognize these paragraphs because what is defined is important to know and understand. The reader can be certain that much of what is to follow may hinge on his understanding of the new word or concept.

Students should study carefully each word of the definition because every word is loaded with essential information. The reason for this is that definitions are by nature precisely constructed. The words have been carefully selected to convey the exact meaning that the concept demands. The greatest mistake a student can make is to hurry past a definition. Look at the contribution of each word to the total meaning.

Question the author: "What exactly does this word add to the meaning? How would the definition change with this word left out?" The wise student always pauses and rereads definitions, at least once. No other single paragraph may be so essential to comprehension of the chapter.

Paragraphs of definition appear often in textbooks. Consequently they are of extreme value to the student.

COMPREHENSION: For each of the following statements and questions, select the option containing the most complete or most accurate answer.

1. The selection portrays the Black man as
(f)
   □ a. naturally warlike and rebellious.
   □ b. uncertain of his destiny.
   □ c. the symbol of suffering humanity.
   □ d. a victim of his own limitations.

2. Historically, the Black people's approach to
(b) life was
   □ a. prideful.
   □ b. realistic.
   □ c. fanciful.
   □ d. carefree.

3. Following the assassination of Martin Luther
(b) King, Jr., Blacks were engulfed by a feeling of
   □ a. bewilderment.
   □ b. frustration.
   □ c. anxiety.
   □ d. hopelessness.

4. The quotation "As a sapling bent low stores
(k) energy for a violent backswing, Blacks ..."
   contains a figure of speech known as
   □ a. a metaphor.
   □ b. an onomatopoeia.
   □ c. a simile.
   □ d. an alliteration.

5. The authors suggest that white Americans are
(c)
   □ a. insensitive.
   □ b. ingenious.
   □ c. organized.
   □ d. productive.

6. The selection suggests that Blacks will no
(c) longer
   □ a. accept stop-gap summer jobs.
   □ b. accept their condition.
   □ c. be disturbed by the oppressor.
   □ d. be filled with grief and sorrow.

7. The authors predict that
(c)
   □ a. the final outcome in the struggle for equality will be determined by Black youths.
   □ b. Black elders will limit their involvement to encouragement.
   □ c. Black youths will follow the example of their elders.
   □ d. Black elders will become active participants in the struggle for equality.

8. The expression "psychological tricks" refers to
(c)
   □ a. a tidal wave of fury.
   □ b. blind hopelessness.
   □ c. a form of escapism.
   □ d. mental imbalance.

9. Given that the French Revolution was inspired
(g) by the American Revolution, the Black revolution could be inspired by
   □ a. Black American youth.
   □ b. African nationalism.
   □ c. foreign agitators.
   □ d. militant Black leaders.

10. Considered in its totality, the selection sug-
(e) gests that
   □ a. the establishment will take the initiative to avoid violence.
   □ b. Blacks will adjust their demands to the changing times.
   □ c. only violence will goad the establishment from its lethargy.
   □ d. the establishment will modify its approach to meet Black demands.

Comprehension Skills: a—isolating details; b—recalling specific facts; c—retaining concepts; d—organizing facts; e—understanding the main idea; f—drawing a conclusion; g—making a judgment; h—making an inference; i—recognizing tone; j—understanding characters; k—appreciation of literary forms.

Negro Firsts in Sports

Talents Required by the Root Sports of Africans Have Carried over to "American Games"

A. S. "Doc" Young

There is no direct line of recorded sports between the pre-slavery days of African life and Americans of African descent. To be sure, the Africans who were to become American slaves had their sports, among them: horse racing, at which they were skillful; canoe racing, archery, sports involving the throwing of stones, fruit games (something like lawn bowling, with native fruits used as "balls"), foot racing, acrobatics, wrestling and stick fights. Talents required by these root sports of Africans have been carried over, in an easy, smooth adaptation, to "American games."

In general, the early years refer to that period of time extending from Bill Richmond to Joe Louis, encompassing primarily Negro participation in boxing, horse racing, baseball, football, basketball, track and field. It is most probable that some of the early American settlers' interest in sports rubbed off on Negro slaves. If so, the records are obscure. The unearthing of any such records is virtually impossible because: (1) no great effort was ever made to record slave achievements in this field; (2) the meticulous coverage of sports is a fairly recent development.

Racial prejudice operated during the early years. But even in the days of slavery its operations were inconsistent. Beginning with Bill Richmond, boxing has been fairly well open to Negroes, though heavyweight champion John L. Sullivan drew the color line. Negroes were prominent in racing in the nineteenth century; but they are seldom to be seen as stars in this sport today. Negroes played baseball during the Civil War, if not earlier. Only three years after the first American professional team, the Cincinnati Red Stockings, was organized (1869), a Negro, Bud Fowler, was known to star with an integrated club in Pennsylvania (Newcastle). Moreover, Moses Fleetwood Walker, a Negro graduate of Ohio's Oberlin College, caught barehanded for the Toledo club of the then major league American Association in 1884. Other Negroes were also prominent in the early integrated phase of the game. Yet in 1888, the doors were slammed shut and Adrian Constanstine (Cap) Anson, a major league immortal, was the chief slammer. This was not, however, baseball's first instance of "approved discrimination" against Negro players. During its convention of 1867, the National Association of Base Ball Players (amateur) approved a resolution which declared:

"It is not presumed by your (nominating) committee that any clubs who have applied are composed of persons of color, or any portion of them; and the recommendations of your committee in this report are based upon this view, and they unanimously report against the admission of any club which may be composed of one or more colored persons." The explanation of this "presumption" followed: "If colored clubs were admitted, there would be in all probability some division of feeling, whereas, by excluding them no injury could result to anybody and the possibility of any rupture being created on political grounds would be avoided." This was a *written law*. During the years 1888 to 1945, known Negroes were barred, the claim is, by an *unwritten law,* which an oldtime major league star once described to me as being "a *gentlemen's* agreement."

Most of America's mass-appeal sports originated elsewhere. Basketball, is a notable exception. Even baseball, the "National Pastime," is a derivative of, an improvement on, somewhat similar games played in the old countries. Negroes originated boxing as a professional sport in the United States. But the sport itself harks back to Mesopotamia, in ancient Asia, where it existed centuries before ancient Greece and ancient Rome. Boxing reached its peak of brutality around 900 B.C., when men fought to the death. They sat on flat stones, facing each other, and with lethally armed fists, they pummelled each other until one or the other, if not both, dropped dead. A remarkable man named Theagenes, skilled in the vital art of landing the first blow, won more than fourteen hundred of these bloody battles, assuredly earning for himself a rating as the greatest killer in sports history. St. Bernardine, the priest, was a boxing promoter. That is, he encouraged boxing among his parishioners in A.D. 1201. He felt that boxing was a safer form of combat than certain other forms for which they displayed a distinct penchant. In the seventeenth century, boxing became popular in England. The basic refinements of the sport must be credited to the British. Their James Figg was the world's first heavyweight champion (1719). An all-around athlete, Figg discarded wrestling as a part of boxing; he concentrated, instead, on the object of beating his opponent solely with bare-knuckle fists. Figg, recognized as heavyweight champion from 1719 until 1730, when he retired "undefeated," was a teacher as well as a fighter. He established a school called "Figg's Academy of Boxing," later renamed "Figg's Amphitheatre." Many of Figg's pupils themselves opened schools and the popularity of boxing grew. However, Figg's rules fell considerably short of what boxing observers considered to be the optimum even then. For one, Figg's way of it was for boxers to fight each other, *sans rest periods,* until one or the other was a definite winner. In 1743, Jack Broughton, both a fighter and a student of fighting, decided to institute certain "radical changes" for the purpose of lessening "the brutality of pugilism." Broughton's rules principally established a set area for fighting, created certain time limits and a fine piece of humanizing: "No person is to hit his adversary when he is down, or seize him by the hair, the breeches or any part below the waist..." In 1838, Broughton's rules were elaborated as "London Prize Ring Rules." Additional improvements in the conduct of boxing were wrought through the "Revised London Prize Ring Rules," which remained the authority for conduct of bare knuckle fighting from the middle of the eighteenth century until the last bare knuckle championship between John L. Sullivan and Jake Kilrain on July 8, 1889. Yet there were observers who believed, just as there are those who believe so today, that boxing was still "too barbarous." The Marquis of Queensbury responded to this charge by composing his famous set of rules in 1865. His rules provided for the use of gloved fists instead of bare fists (he was not, however, the originator of the idea; two English boxers fought with padded gloves in Paris on October 8, 1818). Other facets of the Marquis of Queensbury rules included prohibition of wrestling and hugging, allowance of ten seconds for a fallen man to rise without assistance and continue fighting, establishment of the three-minute round with one-minute rest periods. In fact, boxing as it is ruled today can be attributed largely to the Marquis. Proof of the fact that his basic intent was to improve the game instead of change it all around can be found here: after writing eleven rules of his own (the 11th: "No shoes or boots with springs allowed), the Marquis concluded in Rule 12: "The contest in all other respects to be governed by revised rules of the London Prize Ring."

England gave the American Negro his first opportunity to box as a free man and as a professional. Bill Richmond, born on August 5, 1763, in Staten Island, New York, was the first *American* to gain fame as a professional fighter, and he was the first *American* professional to fight on foreign soil. A light heavyweight by current standards, he stood five feet nine inches tall and weighed 175 pounds. He was taken to England in 1777 by General Earl Percy, a commander of British forces then occupying New York. Richmond had engaged in, and won, several bouts with British soldiers privately sponsored by General Percy for the amusement of his friends. In England, General Percy matched Richmond with one George Moore and Richmond knocked him out in twenty-five minutes. Successively, Richmond then fought Paddy Green and Frank Mayers, winning both bouts. In his fourth fight, on January 23, 1804, Richmond was knocked out by George Maddox in the third round at Wimbledon, which is more famous now for tennis than it is for boxing. Richmond reversed this loss in a terrific battle on August 9, 1809, winning in fifty-two minutes. One of Richmond's most important fights pitted him against Tom Cribb, then a title aspirant, on October 8, 1805. Cribb won in an hour and a half. Between his arrival in England and his official retirement at age fifty-four on August 11, 1815, Richmond won twelve bouts and lost two. On November 12, 1818, Richmond fought an "impromptu" bout with Jack Carter, kayoed him in three rounds, and never, as far as is known, fought again. He died on December 29, 1829, at the age of sixty-six. The records show that while Richmond fought his *fourth* bout in England in 1804, having previously fought in America, the Caucasians Jacob Hyer and Tom Beasley fought the first "recognized" American bout in 1816. Winning, Hyer declared himself champion. But he fought no more and the "title" was vacant for twenty-five years, until 1841, when son Tom Hyer claimed the crown.

In a manner of speaking, Bill Richmond was the "first Joe Louis," and several others among the early-day Negro fighters, notably George Dixon and Peter Jackson, fit this same mold. Richmond was a skilled cabinet-maker. Lord Camelford, a nobleman and a sports fan, was attracted to Richmond by the latter's fine physique and ability to fight. Lord Camelford hired Richmond as a valet. Subsequently, as Richmond's fighting fame spread, he became a favorite with all classes of Englishmen. He opened a hotel in Haymarket and drew extensive patronage from nobility and others. Richmond

From *Negro Firsts in Sports* by A.S. "Doc" Young. Used with permission of Johnson Publishing Co., Inc.

SELECTIONS FROM THE BLACK

was a man of impeccable personal habits, a master of self-control, highly intelligent and civil at all times. An early writer said: "Richmond may be pointed to as one of the men who never lost sight of the situation in which he was placed in society. In the elevation of the moment, he always bore in mind that, however the Corinthian fancier may connect himself with milling, there are times when he has a different character to support and must not be intruded upon. Would that many of our white-faced boxers would take a hint on this point from Bill Richmond, the Black." There are two ways of appraising this "high praise." Surely, when this tribute was paid Richmond, the intention was to honor him in the *highest*. Yet the final words, as pure of sound as they are, contain an inference which, in the context of modern thinking, especially among Negroes, is disturbing. Similar words were spoken in November, 1927, by ex-heavyweight champion Gene Tunney who, in paying tribute to the lately deceased Tiger Flowers, said: "When I think of Flowers, Kipling's line on Gunga Din keeps running in my ears: '*He was white, clean white, inside.*' That's my tribute to a great fighter and a real man!" Indubitably, Tunney was sincere. *Yet the inference was* (is) *devastating!* This is indeed praise, but it is left-handed. The words are not *sporting* enough to omit the matter of race or to still the deep-down belief in racial superiority. Richmond and Flowers were, in other words, *exceptional Negroes*, too bad, in a way, they weren't white! Hundreds of times, this type of praise has been ladled out to Negro athletes, as well as other Negroes, on the discriminatory basis that they were "a credit to their race." Only in recent years has it become something of a habit for Caucasians to pay tribute to Negroes, such as Joe Louis, for being *credits to the human race*.

VOCABULARY: The following words have been taken from the selection you have just read. Put an *X* in the box before the best meaning or synonym for the word as used in the selection.

1. **pummelled**, page 145, column 2, paragraph 3
"...they pummelled each other until one or the other, if not both, dropped dead."
☐ a. threatened
☐ b. pumiced
☐ c. fought
☐ d. thrashed

2. **penchant**, page 145, column 2, paragraph 3
"...for which they displayed a distinct penchant."
☐ a. pendant
☐ b. strong inclination
☐ c. aversion
☐ d. mild interest

3. **impromptu**, page 146, column 2, line 31
"...Richmond fought an 'impromptu' bout with Jack Carter,"
☐ a. unimportant
☐ b. significant
☐ c. hastily arranged
☐ d. short-lived

4. **impeccable**, page 147, column 1, line 1
"Richmond was a man of impeccable personal habits,"
☐ a. irreproachable
☐ b. respectable
☐ c. presentable
☐ d. eccentric

5. **Indubitably**, page 147, column 2, line 1
"Indubitably, Tunney was sincere."
☐ a. industriously
☐ b. unquestionably
☐ c. conditionally
☐ d. apparently

CONTEXTUAL AIDS: ASSOCIATION

Studies of good readers show that they are aware of the context of what they are reading. This means that they are anticipating what is coming next by what has gone before.

The many ways in which context functions to help the reader recognize words are called contextual aids.

Contextual Aid 8. Certain words bring associations to the mind of the reader, which in turn serve as an aid in understanding an unfamiliar word. In the example, **The symphony was _____ for the first time by the orchestra**, the reader can guess that the missing word is **played** because this is what we associate with **symphony** and **orchestra**.

In the following sentences association clues have been provided to help you interpret nonsense words. Underline the nonsense word and write the correct word on the line.

1. Take the clothes out of the washer and put them in the fanda.

   _____

2. The hungry animals continued their search for groll.

   _____

3. When a good drane arises, the sailboats start to move.

   _____

4. A house is not a wast until it's lived in.

   _____

5. The amlnat stood by the easel with his brush in hand.

   _____

6. After the jury came back in, their sumptil was read.

   _____

7. We saw hundreds of school children playing bunds in the huge schoolyard.

   _____

8. The flight captain warmed up the engines before maldering to the airport runway.

   _____

9. He turned the pages rapidly as he skimmed through the hamp.

   _____

10. Unwrapping it greedily, the child stuffed the pelmp into his mouth.

    _____

11. The secretary fed paper in the machine and began hamping the letter which had been dictated.

    _____

PARAGRAPHS OF ILLUSTRATION

As the name suggests, paragraphs of illustration present examples, illustrations, stories, anecdotes, and so on. They are used by the author to illustrate, clarify, demonstrate, or amplify some idea or concept for the reader. Authors use many paragraphs of illustration to help the reader understand the subject.

These paragraphs are also easy to recognize and identify because of the use of key words and phrases like "For example," "An illustration of this," "By way of illustration," and so on. These and similar phrases tell the reader that an example or illustrative story is coming up.

Surprisingly, half a chapter, lesson or article may be composed of paragraphs of illustration. Unlike lecturers who are face-to-face with their students, the author is confined by the limitations of print. He cannot see his students; he cannot tell how effectively his ideas are coming across. Because the author has no way of knowing, he must use more illustrations than he would when speaking. He cannot take a chance; he must ensure that everyone will get the point.

The writer, too, cannot be questioned over a misunderstood concept; he has no way to pause and clarify. He must make certain the first time that the student gets it—there are no second chances. For all of these reasons, we can see why much of what we read is illustrative, even in textbooks.

Selective readers are flexible in their approach. This means that while they may pause over paragraphs of definition, they often speed past paragraphs of illustration. After all, if you understand the point being illustrated, it is not necessary to linger over additional paragraphs illustrating this same point. You can move on to the place where something new is being presented.

SELECTIONS FROM THE BLACK

COMPREHENSION: For each of the following statements and questions, select the option containing the most complete or most accurate answer.

1. Sports coverage
(b)
   - ☐ a. is an outgrowth of American technology.
   - ☐ b. was initiated by early settlers.
   - ☐ c. is a relatively new development.
   - ☐ d. has always neglected Blacks.

2. The famous boxer John L. Sullivan
(h)
   - ☐ a. lost his title to a Black.
   - ☐ b. won his title from Bill Richmond.
   - ☐ c. never boxed with Blacks.
   - ☐ d. was idolized by many Blacks.

3. Basketball originated in
(a)
   - ☐ a. Africa.
   - ☐ b. Mesopotamia.
   - ☐ c. Rome.
   - ☐ d. America.

4. Professional basketball
(b)
   - ☐ a. had admitted Blacks since the Bud Fowler days.
   - ☐ b. restricted Blacks to the member clubs of the National Association of Base Ball Players.
   - ☐ c. barred Blacks from 1888 to 1945.
   - ☐ d. was the first sport to integrate.

5. Which of the following was not involved in
(d) boxing?
   - ☐ a. St. Bernardine
   - ☐ b. James Figg
   - ☐ c. Moses Walker
   - ☐ d. Theagenes

6. Today's boxing rules can be largely attributed
(a) to
   - ☐ a. the Marquis of Queensbury.
   - ☐ b. Jack Broughton.
   - ☐ c. James Figg.
   - ☐ d. St. Bernardine.

7. The first American to box professionally in a
(a) foreign country was
   - ☐ a. Bill Richmond.
   - ☐ b. Gene Tunney.
   - ☐ c. George Dixon.
   - ☐ d. John L. Sullivan.

8. Tunney complimented Flowers by comparing
(h) him to Gunga Din: "He was white, clean white, inside." The inference is
   - ☐ a. unfair.
   - ☐ b. sportsmanlike.
   - ☐ c. complimentary.
   - ☐ d. racist.

9. Which of the following best describes the
(g) author's attitude toward Flowers and Richmond?
   - ☐ a. They were exceptional Blacks.
   - ☐ b. They were exceptional people.
   - ☐ c. They were likeable athletes.
   - ☐ d. They were experienced athletes.

10. The selection ends on a note of
(i)
   - ☐ a. despair.
   - ☐ b. hope.
   - ☐ c. anger.
   - ☐ d. pride.

Comprehension Skills: a—isolating details; b—recalling specific facts; c—retaining concepts; d—organizing facts; e—understanding the main idea; f—drawing a conclusion; g—making a judgment; h—making an inference; i—recognizing tone; j—understanding characters; k—appreciation of literary forms.

The Bench

Suddenly it dawned upon him. Here was his challenge! The bench.

Richard Rive

"We form an integral part of a complex society, a society in which a vast proportion of the population is denied the very basic right of existence, a society that condemns a man to an inferior position because he has the misfortune to be born black, a society that can only retain its precarious social and economic position at the expense of an enormous oppressed mass!"

The speaker paused for a moment and sipped some water from a glass. Karlie's eyes shone as he listened. Those were great words, he thought, great words and true. Karlie sweated. The hot November sun beat down on the gathering. The trees on the Grand Parade in Johannesburg afforded very little shelter and his handkerchief was already soaked where he had placed it between his neck and his shirt collar. Karlie stared around him at the sea of faces. Every shade of color was represented, from shiny ebony to the one or two whites in the crowd. Karlie stared at the two detectives who were busily making shorthand notes of the speeches, then turned to stare back at the speaker.

"It is up to us to challenge the right of any group who willfully and deliberately condemn a fellow group to a servile position. We must challenge the right of any people who see fit to segregate human beings solely on grounds of pigmentation. Your children are denied the rights which are theirs by birth. They are segregated educationally, socially, economically . . ."

Ah, thought Karlie, that man knows what he is speaking about. He says I am as good as any other man, even a white man. That needs much thinking. I wonder if he means I have the right to go to any bioscope [movie], or eat in any restaurant, or that my children can go to a white school. These are dangerous ideas and need much thinking. I wonder what Ou Klaas would say to this. Ou Klaas said that God made the white man and the black man separately, and the one must always be 'baas' [boss] and the other 'jong' [young man]. But this man says different things and somehow they ring true.

Karlie's brow was knitted as he thought. On the platform were many speakers, both white and black, and they were behaving as if there were no differences of color among them. There was a white woman in a blue dress offering Nixeli a cigarette. That never could have happened at Bietjiesvlei. Old Lategan at the store there would have fainted if his Annatjie had offered Witbooi a cigarette. And Annatjie wore no such pretty dress.

These were new things and he, Karlie, had to be careful before he accepted them. But why shouldn't he accept them? He was not a colored man any more, he was a human being. The last speaker had said so. He remembered seeing pictures in the newspapers of people who defied laws which relegated them to a particular class, and those people were smiling as they went to prison. This was a queer world.

The speaker continued and Karlie listened intently. He spoke slowly, and his speech was obviously carefully prepared. This is a great man, thought Karlie.

The last speaker was the white lady in the blue dress, who asked them to challenge any discriminatory laws or measures in their own way. Why should she speak like that? She could go to the best bioscopes and swim at the best beaches. Why she was even more beautiful than Annatjie Lategan. They had warned him in Bietjiesvlei about coming to the city. He had seen the skollies [young hoodlums] in District Six and he knew what to expect there. Hanover Street held no terrors for him. But no one had told him about this. This was new, this set one's mind thinking, yet he felt it was true. She had said one should challenge. He, Karlie, would astound old Lategan and Van Wyk at the Dairy Farm. They could do what they liked to him after that. He would smile like those people in the newspapers.

The meeting was almost over when Karlie threaded his way through the crowd. The words of the speakers were still milling through his head. It could never happen in Bietjiesvlei. Or could it? The sudden screech of a car pulling to a stop whirled him back to his senses. A white head was thrust angrily through the window.

"Look where you're going, you black. . .!"

Karlie stared dazedly at him. Surely this white man never heard what the speakers had said. He could never have seen the white woman offering Nixeli a cigarette. He could never imagine the white lady shouting those words at him. It would be best to catch a train and think these words over.

He saw the station in a new light. Here was a mass of human beings, black, white and some brown like himself. Here they mixed with one another, yet each mistrusted the other with an unnatural fear, each treated the other with suspicion, moved in a narrow, haunted pattern of its own. One must challenge these things the speaker had said . . . in one's own way. Yet how in one's own way? How was one to challenge? Suddenly it dawned upon him. Here was his challenge! *The bench.* The railway bench with "Europeans Only" neatly painted on it in white. For one moment it symbolized all the misery of the plural South African society.

Here was his challenge to the rights of a man. Here it stood. A perfectly ordinary wooden railway bench, like thousands of others in South Africa. His challenge. That bench now had concentrated in it all the evils of a system he could not understand and he felt a victim of. It was the obstacle between himself and humanity. If he sat on it, he was a man. If he was afraid he denied himself membership as a human being in a human society. He almost had visions of righting this pernicious system, if he only sat down on that bench. Here was his chance. He, Karlie, would challenge.

He seemed perfectly calm when he sat down on the bench, but inside his heart was thumping wildly. Two conflicting ideas now throbbed through him. The one said, "I have no right to sit on this bench." The other was the voice of a new religion and said, "Why have I no right to sit on this bench?" The one voice spoke of the past, of the servile position he had occupied on the farm, of his father, and his father's father who were born black, lived like blacks, and died like mules. The other voice spoke of new horizons and said, "Karlie, you are a man. You have dared what your father's father would not have dared. You will die like a man."

Karlie took out a cigarette and smoked. Nobody seemed to notice his sitting there. This was an anticlimax. The world still pursued its monotonous way. No voice had shouted, "Karlie has conquered!" He was a normal human being sitting on a bench in a busy station, smoking a cigarette. Or was this his victory: the fact that he was a normal human being? A well-dressed white woman walked down the platform. Would she sit on the bench? Karlie wondered. And then that gnawing voice, "You should stand and let the white woman sit!" Karlie narrowed his eyes and gripped tighter at his cigarette. She swept past him without the slightest twitch of an eyelid and continued walking down the platform. Was she afraid to challenge—to challenge his right to be a human being? Karlie now felt tired. A third conflicting idea was now creeping in, a compensatory idea which said, "You sit on this bench because you are tired; you are tired therefore you sit." He would not move because he was tired, or was it because he wanted to sit where he liked?

People were now pouring out of a train that had pulled into the station. There were so many people pushing and jostling one another that nobody noticed him. This was his train. It would be easy to step into the train and ride off home, but that would be giving in, suffering defeat, refusing the challenge, in fact admitting that he was not a human being. He sat on. Lazily he blew the cigarette smoke into the air, thinking . . . His mind was away from the meeting and the bench: he was thinking of Bietjiesvlei and Ou Klaas, how he had insisted that Karlie should come to Cape Town. Ou Klaas would suck on his pipe and look so quizzically at one. He was wise and knew much. He had said one must go to Cape Town and learn the ways of the world. He would spit and wink slyly when he spoke of District Six and the women he knew in Hanover Street. Ou Klaas knew everything. He said God made us white or black and we must therefore keep our places.

"Get off this seat!"

Karlie did not hear the gruff voice. Ou Klaas would be on the land now waiting for his tot of cheap wine.

"I said get off the bench, you swine!" Karlie suddenly whipped back to reality. For a moment he was going to jump up, then he remembered who he was and why he was sitting there. He suddenly felt very tired. He looked up slowly into a very red face that stared down at him.

"Get up!" it said. "There are benches down there for you."

Karlie looked up, and said nothing. He stared into a pair of sharp, gray, cold eyes.

"Can't you hear me speaking to you? You black swine!"

Slowly and deliberately Karlie puffed at the cigarette. This was his test. They both stared at each other, challenged with the eyes, like two boxers, each knowing that they must eventually trade blows yet each afraid to strike first.

"The Bench" by Richard Rive. From *An African Treasury* edited by Langston Hughes. ©1960 by Langston Hughes. Published by Crown Publishers, Inc.

"Must I dirty my hands on scum like you?"

Karlie said nothing. To speak would be to break the spell, the supremacy he felt was slowly gaining.

An uneasy silence, then: "I will call a policeman rather than soil my hands on a Hotnot like you. You can't even open up your black jaw when a white man speaks to you."

Karlie saw the weakness. The white man was afraid to take action himself. He, Karlie, had won the first round of the bench dispute.

A crowd had now collected.

"Afrika!" shouted a joker.

Karlie ignored the remark. People were now milling around him, staring at the unusual sight of a black man sitting on a white man's bench. Karlie merely puffed on.

"Look at the black ape. That's the worst of giving these Kaffirs enough rope."

"I can't understand it. They have their own benches!"

"Don't get up! You have every right to sit there!"

"He'll get up when a policeman comes!"

"After all why shouldn't they sit there?"

"I've said before, I've had a native servant once, and a more impertinent . . ."

Karlie sat and heard nothing. Irresolution had now turned to determination. Under no condition was he going to get up. They could do what they liked.

"So, this is the fellow, eh! Get up there! Can't you read?"

The policeman was towering over him. Karlie could see the crest on his buttons and the wrinkles in his neck.

"Get up, you bloody. . .!" Karlie turned to resist, to cling to the bench, his bench. There was more than one man pulling at him. He hit out wildly and then felt a dull pain as somebody rammed a fist into his face. He was bleeding now and wild-eyed. He would fight for it. The constable clapped a pair of handcuffs on him and tried to clear a way through the crowd. Karlie still struggled. A blow or two landed on him. Suddenly he relaxed and slowly struggled to his feet. It was useless to fight any longer. Now it was his turn to smile. He had challenged and won. Who cared the rest?

"Come on, you swine!" said the policeman forcing Karlie through the crowd.

"Certainly!" said Karlie for the first time. And he stared at the policeman with all the arrogance of one who dared sit on a "European bench."

Starting Time: _____	Finishing Time: _____
Reading Time: _____	Reading Rate: _____
Comprehension: _____	Vocabulary: _____

VOCABULARY: The following words have been taken from the selection you have just read. Put an *X* in the box before the best meaning or synonym for the word as used in the selection.

1. **precarious**, page 150, column 1, paragraph 1
" '...a society that can only retain its precarious social and economic position at the expense of an enormous oppressed mass!' "
☐ a. precautions
☐ b. secure
☐ c. uncertain
☐ d. prejudiced

2. **grounds**, page 150, column 1, paragraph 3
" 'We must challenge the right of any people who see fit to segregate human beings solely on grounds of pigmentation.' "
☐ a. degree
☐ b. basis
☐ c. bounds
☐ d. standards

3. **relegated**, page 150, column 2, paragraph 2
"...people who defied laws which relegated them to a particular class,"
☐ a. transferred
☐ b. assigned
☐ c. released
☐ d. delegated

4. **pernicious**, page 151, column 1, paragraph 3
"He almost had visions of righting this pernicious system,"
☐ a. uncomfortable
☐ b. permissive
☐ c. unbalanced
☐ d. wicked

5. **irresolution**, page 152, column 1, paragraph 14
"Irresolution had now turned to determination."
☐ a. uncertainty
☐ b. constancy
☐ c. irresponsibility
☐ d. fear

SELECTIONS FROM THE BLACK

EXPECTANCY CLUES

The most important aids to word recognition and, therefore, fluency in reading are meaning clues. Good readers use these clues effectively and automatically. Meaning clues permit the reader to anticipate words before he actually reads them.

Expectancy clues are one type of meaning clue. These clues refer to the sorts of words and concepts one might expect to encounter in a given subject. For example, in a story about big city life, the reader should expect to meet words like *subway, traffic congestion, urban renewal, ghetto, high-rise apartments,* and so on. Anticipating or expecting these words enables the reader to move along the printed lines rapidly, with understanding.

Here are two exercises to help you develop your skill in using expectancy clues.

The following words, except two, all appeared in a story about television programs. Think first about the kinds of words you would find in such a story and then examine the words below. Underline the two words you would *not* expect to find in this story.

☐ 1. commercial   ☐ 5. presentation   ☐ 9. monologue

☐ 2. appearance   ☐ 6. applause   ☐10. steamship

☐ 3. gardening   ☐ 7. performer   ☐11. prerecorded

☐ 4. videotape   ☐ 8. cameras   ☐12. preempted

Which of the following phrases would you expect to read in a newspaper story about a political election? Put an *X* in the box before them.

☐ 1. candidate of your choice   ☐ 11. the big-city vote

☐ 2. in the voting booth   ☐ 12. moonlight on the water

☐ 3. honesty in high office   ☐ 13. early returns indicate

☐ 4. at the polls   ☐ 14. heavy turnout expected

☐ 5. driving a city cab   ☐ 15. television debates

☐ 6. campaign for reelection   ☐ 16. at the precinct level

☐ 7. visit to grandma's house   ☐ 17. views on important issues

☐ 8. appealing to minority groups ☐ 18. turkey stuffed with dressing

☐ 9. with impressive lyrics and music   ☐ 19. tantamount to election

☐ 10. lawyers address the jury   ☐ 20. heavily favored in the primary

PARAGRAPHS OF INFORMATION

The next paragraphs we wish to examine are the ones used by the author to pass along information on the subject. For this reason they are called paragraphs of information. These paragraphs contain names, dates, details, facts, explanations, and other factual information.

In a particular chapter or lesson, the reader can expect to find the meat of the matter in paragraphs like these. This is where the author gets down to business and presents the facts. The essential terms have been defined and illustrated and now the reader is ready for the substance of the lesson.

We ask the reader to recognize paragraphs of information because they contain the instructional material he is responsible for. Here is where he finds the data on which he will be examined later.

In presenting his information the author will probably use one of the following methods of development.

1. State an opinion and give his reasons. Look for a clue word used to introduce a series of reasons.

2. Pose a problem and offer a solution. Authors use this method frequently because it incorporates questioning as an aid to learning.

3. Draw a conclusion and then present proof. Actually the proof may come first, preceding the conclusion. Check to be sure that the conclusion logically follows from the proof.

4. Present steps in an argument. Expect here, too, an enumeration. Look for the introductory signal and circle the enumerations.

5. Make a comparison or draw a contrast. Frequently used in paragraphs of illustration, this method may be used to present information, too.

The paragraphs of information are the heart of the lesson. Study them well.

COMPREHENSION: For each of the following statements and questions, select the option containing the most complete or most accurate answer.

1. South Africa's social and economic position is
(c) maintained at the expense of
- ☐ a. the native population.
- ☐ b. the ruling minority.
- ☐ c. an outraged world opinion.
- ☐ d. an inflated economy.

2. Karlie's reaction to the Johannesburg speak-
(g) ers may explain why the South African government
- ☐ a. controls new ideas.
- ☐ b. maintains law and order.
- ☐ c. considers Kaffirs dangerous.
- ☐ d. allows freedom of speech.

3. Karlie's new thinking evolved
(c)
- ☐ a. excitedly.
- ☐ b. dangerously.
- ☐ c. progressively.
- ☐ d. painfully.

4. Insofar as it is a symbol of oppression, the
(g) Johannesburg station bench calls to mind
- ☐ a. Germany's gas chambers.
- ☐ b. taxation without representation.
- ☐ c. the early New England blue laws.
- ☐ d. the Montgomery city buses.

5. Which of the following expresses an impor-
(e) tant idea in the selection?
- ☐ a. I am a free agent; my actions must bear this out.
- ☐ b. There are times when I would like to hang the whole human race, and finish the farce.
- ☐ c. We are all prompted by the same motives, all deceived by the same fallacies.
- ☐ d. By what he calls the better part of his nature, man has been betrayed.

6. Karlie's intellectual processes were
(j)
- ☐ a. honest but immature.
- ☐ b. slow and retarded.
- ☐ c. simple but straightforward.
- ☐ d. dull and plodding.

7. Karlie's form of protest was once advocated by
(g)
- ☐ a. Malcolm X.
- ☐ b. Martin Luther King, Jr.
- ☐ c. George Jackson.
- ☐ d. Kwame Nkrumah.

8. The crowd's vehement protest to Karlie's
(g) mild form of protest is understandable when one considers
- ☐ a. its superiority.
- ☐ b. his background.
- ☐ c. the domino theory.
- ☐ d. the relativity theory.

9. When Karlie returns to his village, Ou Klaas
(f) may consider him
- ☐ a. dangerous.
- ☐ b. harmless.
- ☐ c. liberated.
- ☐ d. superior.

10. Karlie's first blow against man's inhumanity
(h) to man
- ☐ a. made him an extremist.
- ☐ b. made him reconsider.
- ☐ c. lifted his spirit.
- ☐ d. filled him with apprehension.

Comprehension Skills: a—isolating details; b—recalling specific facts; c—retaining concepts; d—organizing facts; e—understanding the main idea; f—drawing a conclusion; g—making a judgment; h—making an inference; i—recognizing tone; j—understanding characters; k—appreciation of literary forms.

SELECTIONS FROM THE BLACK

Unbought and Unbossed

This Society Is As Antiwoman As It Is Antiblack

Shirley Chisholm

Women and Their Liberation

When a young woman graduates from college and starts looking for a job, one question every interviewer is sure to ask her is "Can you type?" There is an entire system of prejudice unspoken behind that question, which is rarely if ever asked of a male applicant. One of my top assistants in my Washington office has always refused to learn to type, although not knowing how has been an inconvenience, because she refused to let herself be forced into a dead-end clerical job.

Why are women herded into jobs as secretaries, librarians, and teachers and discouraged from being managers, lawyers, doctors, and members of Congress? Because it is assumed that they are different from men. Today's new militant campaigners for women's rights have made the point that for a long time society discriminated against blacks on the same basis: they were different and inferior. The cheerful old darky on the plantation and the happy little homemaker are equally stereotypes drawn by prejudice. White America is beginning to be able to admit that it carries racial prejudice in its heart, and that understanding marks the beginning of the end of racism. But prejudice against women is still acceptable because it is invisible. Few men can be persuaded to believe that it exists. Many women, even, are the same way. There is very little understanding yet of the immorality involved in double pay scales and the classification of the better jobs "for men only." More than half the population of the United States is female, but women occupy only 2 per cent of the managerial positions. They have not yet even reached the level of tokenism. No woman has ever sat on the Supreme Court, or the AFL-CIO council. There have been only two women who have held cabinet rank, and at present there are none. Only two women now hold ambassadorial rank in the diplomatic corps. In Congress, there are one woman senator and ten representatives. Considering that there are about 3.5 million more women in the United States than men, this is outrageous.

It is true that women have seldom been aggressive in demanding their rights and so have co-operated in their own enslavement. This was true of the black population for many years. They submitted to oppression, and even condoned it. But women are becoming aware, as blacks did, that they can have equal treatment if they will fight for it, and they are starting to organize. To do it, they have to dare the sanctions that society imposes on anyone who breaks with its traditions. This is hard, and especially hard for women, who are taught not to rebel from infancy, from the time they are first wrapped in pink blankets, the color of their caste. Another disability is that women have been programmed to be dependent on men. They seldom have economic freedom enough to let them be free in more significant ways, at least until they become widows and most of their lives are behind them.

That there are no female Supreme Court justices is important, but not as important as the fact that ordinary working women by the millions are subjected to the most naked and unjustified discrimination, by being confined to the duller and less well-paid jobs or by being paid less than men for doing the same work. Here are a recent year's figures from the Labor Department: white males earned an average of $7179 a year, black males $4508, white women $4142, and black women $2934. Measured in uncontestable dollars and cents, which is worse—race prejudice or antifeminism? White women are at an economic disadvantage even compared to black men, and black women are nowhere on the earnings scale.

Guidance counselors discriminate against girls just as they have long done with young black or Puerto Rican male students. They advise a black boy to prepare for a service-oriented occupation, not a profession. They steer a girl toward her "natural career," of being a wife and mother, and plan an occupational goal for her that will not interfere too much with that aim. The girl responds just as the average young black does, with mute agreement. Even if she feels vaguely rebellious at the limitations being put on her future before it has even begun, she knows how the cards are stacked against her and she gives in.

Young minority-group people do not get this treatment quite as much as they did, because they have been radicalized and the country has become more sensitive to its racist attitudes and the damage they do. Women too must rebel. They should start in school, by rejecting the traditional education society considers suitable to them, and which amounts to educational, social, and economic slavery.

There are relevant laws on the books, just as there are civil rights laws on the books. In the 91st Congress, I am a sponsor of the perennial Equal Rights Amendment, which has been before every Congress for the last forty years but has never passed the House. It would outlaw any discrimination on the basis of sex. Men and women would be completely equal before the law. But laws will not solve deepseated problems overnight. Their use is to provide shelter for those who are most abused, and to begin an evolutionary process by compelling the insensitive majority to reexamine its unconscious attitudes.

The law cannot do the major part of the job of winning equality for women. Women must do it themselves. They must become revolutionaries. Against them is arrayed the weight of centuries of tradition, from St. Paul's "Let women learn in silence" down to the American adage, "A woman's place is in the home." Women have been persuaded of their own inferiority; too many of them believe the male fiction that they are emotional, illogical, unstable, inept with mechanical things, and lack leadership ability.

The best defense against this slander is the same one blacks have found. While they were ashamed of their color, it was an albatross hanging around their necks. They freed themselves from that dead weight by picking up their blackness and holding it out proudly for all the world to see. They found their own beauty and turned their former shame into their badge of honor. Women should perceive that the negative attitudes they hold toward their own femaleness are the creation of an antifeminist society, just as the black shame at being black was the product of racism. Women should start to replace their negative ideas of their femininity with positive ones affirming their nature more and more strongly.

It is not female egotism to say that the future of mankind may very well be ours to determine. It is a fact. The warmth, gentleness, and compassion that are part of the female stereotype are positive human values, values that are becoming more and more important as the values of our world begin to shatter and fall from our grasp. The strength of Christ, Gandhi, and Martin Luther King was a strength of gentleness, understanding, and compassion, with no element of violence in it. It was, in short, a *female* strength, and that is the kind that marks the highest type of man.

If we reject our restricted roles, we do not have to reject these values of femaleness. They are enduring values, and we must develop the capacity to hold them and to dispense them to those around us. We must become revolutionaries in the style of Gandhi and King. Then, working toward our own freedom, we can help the others work free from the traps of their stereotypes. In the end, antiblack, antifemale, and all forms of discrimination are equivalent to the same thing—antihumanism. The values of life must be maintained against the enemies in every guise. We can do it by confronting people with their own humanity and their own inhumanity whenever we meet them, in the streets, in school, in church, in bars, in the halls of legislatures. We must reject not only the stereotypes that others have of us but also those we have of ourselves and others.

In particular, I am certain that more and more American women must become involved in politics. It could be the salvation of our nation. If there were more women in politics, it would be possible to start cleaning it up. Women I have known in government have seemed to me to be much more apt to act for the sake of a principle or moral purpose. They are not as likely as men to engage in deals, manipulations, and sharp tactics. A larger proportion of women in Congress and every other legislative body would serve as a reminder that the real purpose of politicians is to work for the people.

The woman who gets into politics will find that the men who are already there will treat her as the high school counselor treats girls. They see her as someone who is obviously just playing at politics part-time, because, after all, her real place is at home being a wife and mother. I suggested a bright young woman as a candidate in New York City a while ago; she had unlimited potential and with good management and some breaks could become an important person to the city. A political leader rejected her. "Why invest all the time and effort to build up the gal into a household name," he asked me, "when she's pretty sure to drop out of the game to have a couple of kids at just about the time we're ready to run her for mayor?"

Many women have given their lives to political organizations, laboring anonymously in the background while men of far less ability managed and mismanaged the public trust. These women hung

SELECTIONS FROM THE BLACK

back because they knew the men would not give them a chance. They knew their place and stayed in it. The amount of talent that has been lost to our country that way is appalling. I think one of my major uses is as an example to the women of our country, to show them that if a woman has ability, stamina, organizational skill, and a knowledge of the issues she can win public office. And if I can do it, how much more hope should that give to white women, who have only one handicap?

One distressing thing is the way men react to women who assert their equality: their ultimate weapon is to call them unfeminine. They think she is antimale; they even whisper that she's probably a lesbian, a tactic some of the Women's Liberation Front have encountered. I am not antimale any more than I am antiwhite, and I am not antiwhite, because I understand that white people, like black ones, are victims of a racist society. They are products of their time and place. It's the same with men. This society is as antiwoman as it is antiblack. It has forced males to adopt discriminatory attitudes toward females. Getting rid of them will be very hard for most men—too hard, for many of them.

Women are challenged now as never before. Their numbers in public office, in the professions, and in other key fields are declining, not increasing. The decline has been gradual and steady for the last twenty years. It will be difficult to reverse at first. The women who undertake to do it will be stigmatized as "odd" and "unfeminine" and must be prepared to endure such punishment. Eventually the point will be made that women are not different from men in their intelligence and ability and that women who aspire to important jobs— president of the company, member of Congress, and so on—are *not* odd and unfeminine. They aspire for the same reasons as any man—they think they can do the job and they want to try.

VOCABULARY: The following words have been taken from the selection you have just read. Put an X in the box before the best meaning or synonym for the word as used in the selection.

1. **stereotypes**, page 155, column 1, paragraph 2
   "The cheerful old darky on the plantation and the happy little homemaker are equally stereotypes..."
   ☐ a. persons with similar economic potential
   ☐ b. sounds which can be heard with specialized equipment
   ☐ c. documents regarded as having historical significance
   ☐ d. simplified images held in common by members of a group

2. **condoned**, page 155, column 2, paragraph 1
   "They submitted to oppression, and even condoned it."
   ☐ a. allowed
   ☐ b. conducted
   ☐ c. excused
   ☐ d. fought

3. **perennial**, page 156, column 1, paragraph 2
   "...I am a sponsor of the perennial Equal Rights Amendment, which has been before every Congress for the last forty years..."
   ☐ a. persistent
   ☐ b. perishable
   ☐ c. peremptory
   ☐ d. yearly

4. **arrayed**, page 156, column 1, paragraph 3
   "Against them is arrayed the weight of centuries of tradition,"
   ☐ a. arrested
   ☐ b. equipped
   ☐ c. marshalled
   ☐ d. displayed

5. **guise**, page 156, column 2, paragraph 2
   "The values of life must be maintained against the enemies in every guise."
   ☐ a. situation
   ☐ b. form
   ☐ c. dress
   ☐ d. degree

ROOTS

Many English words consist of a base or root word to which prefixes (beginnings) and suffixes (endings) have been added. To the root word **agree** (a verb) we can add both a prefix and a suffix to get **disagreeable** (an adjective) which has an opposite meaning.

Roots are Latin and Greek stems on which our English words are based. For example, **bio** (life) is a Greek root on which our word **biology** (the study of plant and animal life) is built.

Two Roots

1. **dic, dict** are variants of the Latin root for **say**, **speak**, or **word**. We look up words in a **dictionary**.

2. **vers, vert** is also Latin, and it means **turn**. An **inverted** object has been turned upside down.

In the following sentences these two roots have been left out. Space has been left indicating where the roots belong. Add one of these two roots and write your word on the line following the sentence.

1. The secretary copied in shorthand the letter that was —ated.

   _____

2. Their **sub—ive** efforts to overturn the government nearly succeeded.

   _____

3. He **re—ed** to his previous position as soon as we left.

   _____

4. Must you **contra—** everything I say?

   _____

5. A —ator's word is law.

   _____

6. He's quite —atile; he can turn from one activity to another.

   _____

7. He **pre—ed** what would happen in the future.

   _____

8. Put the car in **re—e**; let's go back.

   _____

9. Don't be such an **intro—**; come out of your shell.

   _____

10. You must improve your —ion; your speech is too difficult to understand.

    _____

PARAGRAPHS OF TRANSITION

The recognizable feature of paragraphs of transition is their brevity—they are normally short.

As the name implies, these paragraphs are used by the author to pass logically from one aspect of his subject to another. Through paragraphs of transition authors show a change of thought or introduce a new side to the matter under discussion.

The reader should be alert to an upcoming change when he sees a paragraph of transition. He should know the author is about to switch tracks, to change to a new topic. This knowledge helps the student organize his reading because he knows that the current discussion is ending and that something new is coming.

Transitional paragraphs are valuable in other ways, too. Because they introduce something new, they may function like a paragraph of introduction—they may offer a brief preview of the new concepts the author now plans to discuss; they may state the purpose the author hopes to accomplish by presenting the following information; or they may try to arouse the reader's interest in what is to follow.

In another way, paragraphs of transition may function like a concluding paragraph, summing up for the reader the salient points of the aspect being concluded. Or a restatement of the central thought may be presented to help the reader see where he stands before moving on. Possibly, a conclusion, or partial conclusion, based on the previous information may appear to wind up the discussion before moving on.

It is this combination of functions and its contribution to the reader's organization which makes this brief paragraph so valuable.

Because in any well-written presentation the paragraphs have certain jobs or functions to perform, a knowledge of paragraph roles is valuable to the reader.

SELECTIONS FROM THE BLACK

COMPREHENSION: For each of the following statements and questions, select the option containing the most complete or most accurate answer.

1. The question "Can you type?" reflects
(c)
- ☐ a. an opportunity.
- ☐ b. a compromise.
- ☐ c. an attitude.
- ☐ d. a concession.

2. The argument invoked to justify the absence
(g) of adequate female representation in the more glamorous professions is
- ☐ a. acceptable.
- ☐ b. degrading.
- ☐ c. positive.
- ☐ d. defensible.

3. The cheerful old darky is to the happy little
(g) homemaker as
- ☐ a. sunshine is to happiness.
- ☐ b. captivity is to servitude.
- ☐ c. abuser is to abused.
- ☐ d. problem is to solution.

4. The beginning of the end of racism as well as
(b) sexism will come about through
- ☐ a. understanding.
- ☐ b. surrender.
- ☐ c. victory.
- ☐ d. compromise.

5. Coming from Shirley Chisholm, the state-
(k) ment, "They have not yet reached the level of tokenism," is
- ☐ a. unfortunate.
- ☐ b. exaggerated.
- ☐ c. hilarious.
- ☐ d. ironic.

6. Shirley Chisholm would agree with which of
(c) the following?
- ☐ a. Men should accept total responsibility for female exploitation.
- ☐ b. Women have little control over the servile conditions of their lives.
- ☐ c. Women have contributed to their own exploitation.
- ☐ d. Wives should boycott husbands and families.

7. Statistics indicate that, economically, white
(d) women are almost equal to
- ☐ a. national standards.
- ☐ b. Black women.
- ☐ c. white males.
- ☐ d. Black males.

8. The price women must pay for equality under
(e) the law is
- ☐ a. militancy.
- ☐ b. capitulation.
- ☐ c. extravagant.
- ☐ d. normal.

9. An important factor working counter to
(h) women's liberation is
- ☐ a. family responsibility.
- ☐ b. feminine limitation.
- ☐ c. traditional education.
- ☐ d. constitutional restriction.

10. Which of the following is one of Shirley
(f) Chisholm's important conclusions?
- ☐ a. Equality does not negate femininity.
- ☐ b. Unisex is a desirable aim.
- ☐ c. Blacks deserve special consideration.
- ☐ d. Politics is the rightful domain of men.

Comprehension Skills: a—isolating details; b—recalling specific facts; c—retaining concepts; d—organizing facts; e—understanding the main idea; f—drawing a conclusion; g—making a judgment; h—making an inference; i—recognizing tone; j—understanding characters; k—appreciation of literary forms.

The Autobiography of

"I do not expect to live long enough to read this book in its finished form."

Malcolm X

I have given to this book so much of whatever time I have because I feel, and I hope, that if I honestly and fully tell my life's account, read objectively it might prove to be a testimony of some social value.

I think that an objective reader may see how in the society to which I was exposed as a black youth here in America, for me to wind up in a prison was really just about inevitable. It happens to so many thousands of black youth.

I think that an objective reader may see how when I heard "The white man is the devil," when I played back what had been my own experiences, it was inevitable that I would respond positively; then the next twelve years of my life were devoted and dedicated to propagating that phrase among the black people.

I think, I hope, that the objective reader, in following my life—the life of only one ghetto-created Negro—may gain a better picture and understanding than he has previously had of the black ghettoes which are shaping the lives and the thinking of almost all of the 22 million Negroes who live in America.

Thicker each year in these ghettoes is the kind of teen-ager that I was—with the wrong kinds of heroes, and the wrong kinds of influences. I am not saying that all of them become the kind of parasite that I was. Fortunately, by far most do not. But still, the small fraction who do add up to an annual total of more and more costly, dangerous youthful criminals. The F.B.I. not long ago released a report of a shocking rise in crime each successive year since the end of World War II —ten to twelve percent each year. The report did not say so in so many words, but I am saying that the majority of that crime increase is annually spawned in the black ghettoes which the American racist society permits to exist. In the 1964 "long, hot summer" riots in major cities across the United States, the socially disinherited black ghetto youth were always at the forefront.

In this year, 1965, I am certain that more—and worse—riots are going to erupt, in yet more cities, in spite of the conscience-salving Civil Rights Bill. The reason is that the *cause* of these riots, the racist malignancy in America, has been too long unattended.

I believe that it would be almost impossible to find anywhere in America a black man who has lived further down in the mud of human society than I have; or a black man who has been any more ignorant than I have been; or a black man who has suffered more anguish during his life than I have. But it is only after the deepest darkness that the greatest light can come; it is only after extreme grief that the greatest joy can come; it is only after slavery and prison that the sweetest appreciation of freedom can come.

For the freedom of my 22 million black brothers and sisters here in America, I do believe that I have fought the best that I knew how, and the best that I could, with the shortcomings that I have had. I know that my shortcomings are many.

My greatest lack has been, I believe, that I don't have the kind of academic education I wish I had been able to get—to have been a lawyer, perhaps. I do believe that I might have made a good lawyer. I have always loved verbal battle, and challenge. You can believe me that if I had the time right now, I would not be one bit ashamed to go back into any New York City public school and start where I left off at the ninth grade, and go on through a degree. Because I don't begin to be academically equipped for so many of the interests that I have. For instance, I love languages. I wish I were an accomplished linguist. I don't know anything more frustrating than to be around people talking something you can't understand. Especially when they are people who look just like you. In Africa, I heard original mother tongues, such as Hausa, and Swahili, being spoken, and there I was standing like some little boy, waiting for someone to tell me what had been said; I never will forget how ignorant I felt.

Aside from the basic African dialects, I would try to learn Chinese, because it looks as if Chinese will be the most powerful political language of the future. And already I have begun studying Arabic, which I think is going to be the most powerful spiritual language of the future.

SELECTIONS FROM THE BLACK

Malcolm X articulated the woes and aspirations of the depressed Black mass in a way it was unable to do for itself. When he attacked the white man, he attacked with a violence and anger that spoke for the ages of misery.

Malcolm is revered today for his ruthless honesty in stating the Black's case and for his refusal to compromise.

I would just like to *study*. I mean ranging study, because I have a wide-open mind. I'm interested in almost any subject you can mention. I know this is the reason I have come to really like, as individuals, some of the hosts of radio or television panel programs I have been on, and to respect their minds—because even if they have been almost steadily in disagreement with me on the race issue, they still have kept their minds open and objective about the truths of things happening in this world. Irv Kupcinet in Chicago, and Barry Farber, Barry Gray and Mike Wallace in New York—people like them. They also let me see that they respected my mind—in a way I know they never realized. The way I knew was that often they would invite my opinion on subjects off the race issue. Sometimes, after the programs, we would sit around and talk about all kinds of things, current events and other things, for an hour or more. You see, most whites, even when they credit a Negro with some intelligence, will still feel that all he can talk about is the race issue; most whites never feel that Negroes can contribute anything to other areas of thought, and ideas. You just notice how rarely you will ever hear whites asking any Negroes what they think about the problem of world health, or the space race to land men on the moon.

Every morning when I wake up, now, I regard it as having another borrowed day. In any city, wherever I go, making speeches, holding meetings of my organization, or attending to other business, black men are watching every move I make, awaiting their chance to kill me. I have said publicly many times that I know that they have their orders. Anyone who chooses not to believe what I am saying doesn't know the Muslims in the Nation of Islam.

But I am also blessed with faithful followers who are, I believe, as dedicated to me as I once was to Mr. Elijah Muhammad. Those who would hunt a man need to remember that a jungle also contains those who hunt the hunters.

I know, too, that I could suddenly die at the hands of some white racists. Or I could die at the hands of some Negro hired by the white man. Or it could be some brainwashed Negro acting on his own idea that by eliminating me he would be helping out the white man, because I talk about the white man the way I do.

Anyway, now, each day I live as if I am already dead, and I tell you what I would like for you to do. When I *am* dead—I say it that way because from the things I *know*, I do not expect to live long enough to read this book in its finished form—I want you to just watch and see if I'm not right in what I say: that the white man, in his press, is going to identify me with "hate."

He will make use of me dead, as he has made use of me alive, as a convenient symbol of "hatred"—and that will help him to escape facing the truth that all I have been doing is holding up a mirror to reflect, to show, the history of unspeakable crimes that his race has committed against my race.

You watch. I will be labeled as, at best, an "irresponsible" black man. I have always felt about this accusation that the black "leader" whom white men consider to be "responsible" is invariably the black "leader" who never gets any results. You only get action as a black man if you are regarded by the white man as "irresponsible." In fact, this much I had learned when I was just a little boy. And since I have been some kind of a "leader" of black people here in the racist society of America, I have been more reassured each time the white man resisted me, or attacked me harder—because each time made me more certain that I was on the right track in the American black man's best interests. The racist white man's opposition automatically made me know that I did offer the black man something worthwhile.

Yes, I have cherished my "demagogue" role. I know that societies often have killed the people who have helped to change those societies. And if I can die having brought any light, having exposed any meaningful truth that will help to destroy the racist cancer that is malignant in the body of America—then, all of the credit is due to Allah. Only the mistakes have been mine.

Starting Time: _____   Finishing Time: _____

Reading Time: _____   Reading Rate: _____

Comprehension: _____   Vocabulary: _____

VOCABULARY: The following words have been taken from the selection you have just read. Put an *X* in the box before the best meaning or synonym for the word as used in the selection.

1. **inevitable**, page 160, column 1, paragraph 3
"...it was inevitable that I would respond..."
☐ a. unavoidable
☐ b. indisputable
☐ c. uncertain
☐ d. imaginable

2. **propagating**, page 160, column 1, paragraph 3
"...dedicated to propagating that phrase..."
☐ a. multiplying
☐ b. reproducing
☐ c. disseminating
☐ d. propagandizing

3. **malignancy**, page 160, column 2, line 1
"...the racist malignancy in America,"
☐ a. cancer
☐ b. ill will
☐ c. evil
☐ d. distress

4. **accomplished**, page 160, column 2, paragraph 4
"I wish I were an accomplished linguist."
☐ a. completed
☐ b. expert
☐ c. finished
☐ d. performing

5. **resisted**, page 161, column 2, paragraph 4
"...each time the white man resisted me,"
☐ a. opposed
☐ b. withstood
☐ c. desisted
☐ d. confronted

SYLLABICATION

Knowing how to reduce words to their syllables aids both reading and spelling. Frequently a long word can be recognized and understood if pronounced by syllables. And knowledge of syllabication contributes to accuracy in spelling.

There are rules or generalizations which we can follow when dividing words. One such rule tells us that **ed** added to a word which ends in **d** or **t** becomes a separate syllable, like **wait** and **wait-ed**. When **ed** is added to other words, the words remain one syllable, like **call** and **called**.

The following sentences contain similar words. If, according to the rule above, **ed** is a separate syllable, write the word on the line to the right separating the syllables. If the **ed** word in a sentence remains a one-syllable word, write nothing on the line.

1. The president signed the bill. _____

2. The lookout sighted land. _____

3. She screamed in terror. _____

4. The protestors fasted. _____

5. The release was handed over. _____

6. The clown smirked comically. _____

7. They paired the players. _____

8. Two players were picked. _____

9. They risked everything. _____

10. Millions were touched. _____

11. She minded the children. _____

12. The bills were marked. _____

13. The trespassers were arrested. _____

14. Signs were nailed up. _____

15. Doorways were barred. _____

16. Everyone searched carefully. _____

17. The room was furnished lavishly. _____

18. A stone wall framed the yard. _____

19. The wood was sanded smooth. _____

20. The child smiled sweetly. _____

SELECTION 30

THE HABIT OF READING

The greatest skill you can acquire in life is the habit of reading. If you want to be informed, to achieve on the job, to participate more productively and to enjoy life, you must acquire the desire to read.

As students, you find it hard to read beyond what is required for your courses. But once school has ended and classes are over, either for vacation or for good, you can begin.

You may ask, "How do I begin? Where do I start?" You begin simply— you read books on subjects which most interest you. If you enjoy easy books, begin with them. But by all means, begin.

Most of the selections in this text have been taken from full-length books. There is a bibliography at the back of this text which lists the books from which the selections were taken. If you found one of these selections interesting and easy to read, get the book and read it.

If you enjoy the book, a librarian can find others along the same line which might also interest you. Look through all of the selections in this text again and pick out a book to read.

Another way to begin is with condensed books — these are shortened versions of full-length books. In every *Reader's Digest*, a condensed book is included. Pick up a copy and read one—usually the books are current and interesting. To help build the reading habit, carry your book with you wherever you go. You'll be surprised how opportunities arise when you can read. More than likely you can finish the book in just a few days.

It was Abraham Lincoln who said: "The man who doesn't read a book has nothing on the man who can't." You can find the time to read if you stop and analyze your day.

This then is your goal: carry a book and read it.

COMPREHENSION: For each of the following statements and questions, select the option containing the most complete or most accurate answer.

1. The effectiveness of Malcolm's autobiography
(b) depends largely upon
   - ☐ a. reader objectivity.
   - ☐ b. its ability to convince.
   - ☐ c. its literary value.
   - ☐ d. its wide circulation.

2. The author predicts that riots in America will
(c) increase in frequency and severity because
   - ☐ a. the basic cause of racial dissension has been too long unattended.
   - ☐ b. the Civil Rights Bill will be defeated.
   - ☐ c. the Civil Rights Bill, although ratified, will be too watered down.
   - ☐ d. white backlash will figure increasingly as a negative factor.

3. Which language does the author predict will
(a) be the most powerful politically?
   - ☐ a. Russian
   - ☐ b. Chinese
   - ☐ c. English
   - ☐ d. French

4. The author's probable reason for calling
(h) Arabic the spiritual language of the future is that he
   - ☐ a. identified it with Islam, the religion which embodies the concept of true brotherhood.
   - ☐ b. envisioned a rise to world prominence by Arab-speaking people.
   - ☐ c. envisioned Islam as the religion which would unify America's Black population.
   - ☐ d. foresaw a general revival and appreciation of one of the world's most ancient languages.

5. Which of the following does the author cite
(c) as a subtle form of prejudice inflicted upon Black guests by television hosts?
   - ☐ a. Limiting their questions to racial issues
   - ☐ b. Excluding Black guests from panel discussions
   - ☐ c. Diverting attention from racial issues to general subjects
   - ☐ d. Minimizing Black accusations through humorous interjections

6. "Those who would hunt a man need to re-
(h) member that a jungle also contains those who hunt the hunters." This statement can be considered
   - ☐ a. a promise.
   - ☐ b. a surrender.
   - ☐ c. a challenge.
   - ☐ d. a warning.

7. The author's criteria for judging his effective-
(c) ness on the racial scene was
   - ☐ a. popular white support.
   - ☐ b. sympathetic coverage by the press.
   - ☐ c. resistance and attacks by the press.
   - ☐ d. popular Black support.

8. From the details Malcolm X reveals about his
(j) own background, one is impressed by his
   - ☐ a. lack of personal objectivity.
   - ☐ b. lack of foresight in the face of danger.
   - ☐ c. humble, candid and frank admissions.
   - ☐ d. rise to prominence in spite of his illiteracy.

9. Which of the following views of Malcolm X
(j) appears to be the most accurate?
   - ☐ a. He was unable to understand the complexities of the American social and political scene.
   - ☐ b. He fearlessly courted death knowing that his followers would grow in strength through his martyrdom.
   - ☐ c. He used the racial issues to further his personal aims within the Civil Rights movement.
   - ☐ d. He was a sensitive, perceptive analyst of the racial situation in America.

10. The selection can be considered
(e)
   - ☐ a. a justification of Malcolm's life and convictions.
   - ☐ b. the final document of a man who has fought well but lost.
   - ☐ c. autobiographical and therefore lacking in objectivity.
   - ☐ d. the work of a demagogue.

Comprehension Skills: a—isolating details; b—recalling specific facts; c—retaining concepts; d—organizing facts; e—understanding the main idea; f—drawing a conclusion; g—making a judgment; h—making an inference; i—recognizing tone; j—understanding characters; k—appreciation of literary forms.

SELECTIONS FROM THE BLACK

Selections from the Black

BIBLIOGRAPHY

Abubadika, Mwlina Imiri (Sonny Carson). *The Education of Sonny Carson*. New York: W. W. Norton & Company, 1972.

Angelou, Maya. *I Know Why the Caged Bird Sings*. New York: Random House, 1969.

Baldwin, James. *Go Tell It on the Mountain*. New York: The Dial Press, 1953.

——————. *Going to Meet the Man*. New York: The Dial Press, 1957.

——————. *No Name in the Street*. New York: The Dial Press, 1972.

——————. *Nobody Knows My Name*. New York: The Dial Press, 1961.

Bond, Julian. *A Time to Speak, A Time to Act*. New York: Simon and Schuster, 1972.

Brown, Claude. *Manchild in the Promised Land*. New York: The Macmillan Company, 1965.

Brown, H. Rap. *Die, Nigger, Die*. New York: The Dial Press, 1969.

Carmichael, Stokely. *Stokely Speaks*. New York: Sheed and Ward, 1968.

——————, and Charles V. Hamilton. *Black Power*. New York: Random House, 1967.

Chisholm, Shirley. *Unbought and Unbossed*. Boston: Houghton Mifflin Company, 1970.

Clarke, John Henrik, Editor. *American Negro Short Stories*. New York: Hill & Wang, 1966.

——————, Editor. *Harlem, U. S. A.* New York: Seven Seas Publications, 1964.

Cleage, Albert B., Jr. *The Black Messiah*. New York: Sheed and Ward, 1968.

Davis, Angela Y. *If They Come in the Morning*. New York: The Third Press, 1971.

Davis, Sammy, Jr., and Jane and Burt Boyar. *Yes I Can*. New York: Farrar, Straus & Giroux, 1965.

Douglass, Frederick. *The Narrative of the Life of Frederick Douglass*, 1945.

DuBois, W.E.B. *Dusk of Dawn*. New York: Harcourt, Brace & World, 1968.

Edwards, Harry. *The Revolt of the Black Athlete*. New York: The Macmillan Company, 1969.

Ellison, Ralph. *Invisible Man*. New York: Random House, 1952.

Evers, Myrlie B., and William Peters. *For Us, the Living*. New York: Doubleday & Company, 1967.

Farmer, James. *Freedom—When?* New York: Random House, 1965.

Garvey, Marcus. *Philosophy and Opinions*, 1916.

Greenlee, Sam. *The Spook Who Sat by the Door*. New York: Richard W. Baron, 1969.

Gregory, Dick, and Robert Lipsyte. *nigger*. New York: E. P. Dutton & Company, 1964.

Grier, William H., and Price M. Cobbs. *Black Rage*. New York: Basic Books, 1968.

——————. *The Jesus Bag*. New York: McGraw-Hill, 1971.

Hansberry, Lorraine. *A Raisin in the Sun*. New York: Random House, 1958.

Hayford, Fred Kwesi. *Inside America*. Washington: Acropolis Books, 1972.

Hughes, Langston, Editor. *An African Treasury*. New York: Crown Publishers, 1960.

——————, Editor. *The Book of Negro Humor*. New York: Dodd, Mead & Company, 1966.

——————, Editor. *Stories by Negro Writers*. Boston: Little, Brown and Company, 1967.

Jackson, George. *Soledad Brother: The Prison Letters of George Jackson*. New York: Coward, McCann & Geoghegan, 1970.

Johnson, James Weldon. *Negro Americans, What Now?* New York: The Viking Press, 1962.

Jones, LeRoi. *Blues People: Negro Music in White America*. New York: William Morrow and Company, 1963.

Kelley, William Melvin. *A Drop of Patience*. New York: Doubleday & Company, 1965.

Killens, John Oliver. *Black Man's Burden*. New York: Trident, 1965.

King, Martin Luther, Jr. *The Trumpet of Conscience*. New York: Harper & Row, 1967.

Lester, Julius. *Look Out, Whitey! Black Power's Gon' Get Your Mama*. New York: The Dial Press, 1968.

Malcolm X and Alex Haley. *The Autobiography of Malcolm X*. New York: Grove Press, 1964.

Mann, Eric. *Comrade George*. Cambridge: Hovey Street Press, 1972.

McKissick, Floyd. *Three-Fifths of a Man*. New York: The Macmillan Company, 1969.

Moody, Anne. *Coming of Age in Mississippi*. New York: The Dial Press, 1968.

Owens, Jesse, and Paul Neimark. *I Have Changed*. New York: William Morrow & Company, 1972.

Pantell, Dora, and Edwin Greenidge. *If Not Now, When?* New York: Delacorte Press, 1969.

Rowan, Carl T. *Go South to Sorrow*. New York: Random House, 1967.

Russell, William Felton, and William Francis McSweeny. *Go Up for Glory*. New York: Coward, McCann & Geoghegan, 1966.

Sullivan, Leon. *Alternatives to Despair*. Valley Forge: The Judson Press, 1972.

Teague, Robert L. *Letters to a Black Boy*. New York: Walker & Company, 1968.

Vassa, Gustavus. *The Interesting Narrative of the Life of Oloudah Equiano, or Gustavus Vassa*, 1789.

Walker, Margaret Alexander. *Jubilee*. Boston: Houghton Mifflin Company, 1966.

Washington, Booker T. *Up From Slavery*, 1900.

Wertheim, Bill, Editor. *Talking About Us*. New York: Appleton-Century-Crofts, 1970.

Young, A. S. "Doc". *Negro Firsts in Sports*. Chicago: Johnson Publishing Company, 1963.

Minutes and Seconds Elapsed

Selection	Number of Words	1:20	1:40	2:00	2:20	2:40	3:00	3:20	3:40	4:00	4:20	4:40	5:00	5:20	5:40	6:00	6:20	6:40	7:00	7:20	7:40	8:00	8:20	8:40	9:00	9:20	9:40	10:00	10:20	10:40	11:00	11:20	11:40	12:00	12:20	12:40	13:00	13:20	13:40	14:00	14:20	14:40	15:00
1	1615	1210	970	805	690	605	540	485	440	405	370	345	325	300	285	270	255	240	230	220	210	200	195	185	180	175	165	160	155	150	145	140	140	135	130	130	125	120	120	115	110	110	105
2	2150	1655	1345	1075	935	825	715	650	595	535	500	465	430	405	385	360	340	325	305	295	280	270	260	250	240	230	225	215	210	200	195	190	185	180	175	170	165	160	160	155	150	145	145
3	1800	1385	1125	900	780	690	600	545	500	450	420	390	360	340	320	300	285	270	255	245	235	225	215	210	200	195	185	180	175	170	165	160	155	150	145	140	140	135	130	130	125	125	120
4	2030	1560	1270	1015	880	780	675	615	565	505	470	440	405	385	360	340	320	305	290	280	265	255	245	235	225	220	210	205	195	190	185	180	175	170	165	160	155	150	150	145	140	140	135
5	1425	1095	890	710	620	550	475	430	395	355	330	310	285	270	255	235	225	215	205	195	185	180	170	165	160	155	150	140	140	135	130	125	120	120	115	115	110	110	105	100	100	95	95
6	1925	1480	1205	960	835	740	640	585	535	480	445	420	385	365	345	320	305	290	275	265	255	240	230	225	215	205	200	190	185	180	175	170	165	160	155	150	150	145	140	135	135	130	130
7	1555	1195	970	775	675	600	520	470	430	390	360	340	310	295	275	260	245	235	220	215	205	195	185	180	170	165	160	155	150	145	140	135	140	130	125	125	120	115	115	110	110	105	105
8	1630	1255	1020	815	710	625	545	495	450	405	375	355	330	315	295	280	260	245	230	220	210	205	195	190	180	175	170	165	160	155	150	145	145	140	135	130	130	125	125	120	115	115	110
9	1350	1040	845	675	585	520	450	410	375	335	315	295	270	255	240	225	215	205	190	185	175	170	160	155	150	145	140	135	130	125	120	120	115	110	110	105	105	100	100	100	95	90	90
10	2095	1610	1310	1045	910	805	700	635	580	525	485	455	420	395	375	350	330	315	300	285	275	260	250	245	230	220	215	210	205	195	190	185	180	175	170	165	160	160	155	150	145	145	140
11	1780	1370	1110	890	775	685	595	540	495	445	415	385	355	335	315	295	280	270	255	245	235	225	215	210	200	190	185	180	175	170	165	160	155	150	150	145	140	140	135	130	130	125	120
12	1975	1520	1235	985	860	760	660	600	550	495	460	430	395	370	350	330	315	300	280	270	260	250	240	230	220	210	205	195	190	185	180	175	170	165	160	155	150	150	145	140	140	135	130
13	1910	1470	1195	955	830	735	635	580	530	475	445	415	380	360	340	320	305	290	275	265	250	245	235	225	215	205	200	195	185	180	175	170	165	160	155	150	145	145	140	135	135	130	125
14	1640	1260	1025	820	715	630	545	495	455	410	380	355	330	310	290	275	260	250	235	225	215	205	195	190	180	175	170	165	160	155	145	140	135	135	130	125	120	120	115	115	110	110	110
15	1930	1485	1205	965	840	740	645	585	535	480	450	420	385	365	345	320	305	290	275	265	255	240	230	225	215	210	200	195	185	180	175	170	165	160	155	150	150	145	140	135	135	130	130
16	1500	1155	935	750	650	575	500	455	415	375	350	325	300	285	265	250	240	230	215	205	195	185	180	175	165	160	155	150	145	140	140	135	130	125	120	120	115	110	110	110	105	100	100
17	1750	1345	1095	875	760	675	585	530	485	435	405	380	350	330	310	290	275	265	250	240	230	220	210	205	195	185	180	175	170	160	155	150	145	140	140	135	130	130	125	120	120	115	115
18	1860	1430	1160	930	810	715	620	565	515	465	430	405	370	350	330	310	295	280	265	255	245	230	225	215	205	200	190	185	180	175	165	160	155	150	150	145	140	140	135	130	130	125	125
19	1940	1490	1210	970	845	745	645	585	540	485	450	420	390	370	345	325	305	295	275	265	255	240	230	225	215	205	200	195	185	180	175	170	165	160	160	155	150	145	145	140	135	130	130
20	1265	975	795	630	550	485	420	385	350	315	295	275	255	240	225	210	200	190	180	175	165	160	150	145	140	135	130	125	120	120	115	110	110	105	105	100	100	95	95	90	90	85	85
21	1595	1225	995	795	695	615	565	485	445	400	370	345	320	300	285	265	255	240	230	220	210	200	190	185	175	170	165	160	155	150	145	140	140	135	130	125	125	120	120	115	110	110	105
22	1725	1325	1080	860	750	665	575	520	480	430	400	375	345	325	310	285	275	260	245	235	225	215	205	200	190	185	180	175	165	160	155	150	145	140	140	135	130	130	125	120	120	120	115
23	1500	1155	935	750	650	575	500	455	415	375	350	325	300	285	265	250	240	230	215	205	195	185	180	175	165	160	155	150	145	140	140	135	130	125	125	120	115	110	110	110	105	100	100
24	1795	1380	1120	895	780	690	600	545	500	450	415	390	360	340	320	300	285	270	255	245	235	225	215	210	200	190	185	180	175	170	160	155	150	145	140	140	135	130	130	125	125	120	120
25	1750	1345	1095	875	760	675	585	530	485	435	405	380	350	330	310	290	275	265	250	240	230	220	210	205	195	190	180	175	170	165	160	155	150	145	140	140	135	130	130	125	120	120	115
26	1335	1025	835	665	580	515	445	405	370	335	310	290	265	250	240	220	210	200	190	180	175	165	160	155	145	140	135	130	125	120	120	115	110	105	105	100	100	95	95	90	90	90	85
27	1925	1480	1205	960	835	740	640	585	535	480	445	420	385	365	345	320	305	290	275	265	255	240	230	225	215	205	200	190	185	180	175	170	165	160	155	150	150	145	140	135	135	130	130
28	2075	1595	1295	1035	900	800	690	630	575	520	480	450	415	390	370	345	330	315	295	285	275	260	250	240	230	225	215	210	205	195	190	185	180	175	170	165	160	155	155	150	145	145	140
29	2000	1540	1250	1000	870	770	665	605	555	500	465	435	400	375	355	335	315	305	285	275	265	250	240	230	220	215	210	200	195	190	180	175	170	165	160	155	150	150	145	140	140	135	135
30	1585	1220	990	790	690	610	560	510	440	395	370	345	315	300	285	265	250	240	225	215	210	200	190	185	175	170	165	160	155	150	145	140	135	130	130	125	120	120	115	110	110	110	105

PROGRESS GRAPH

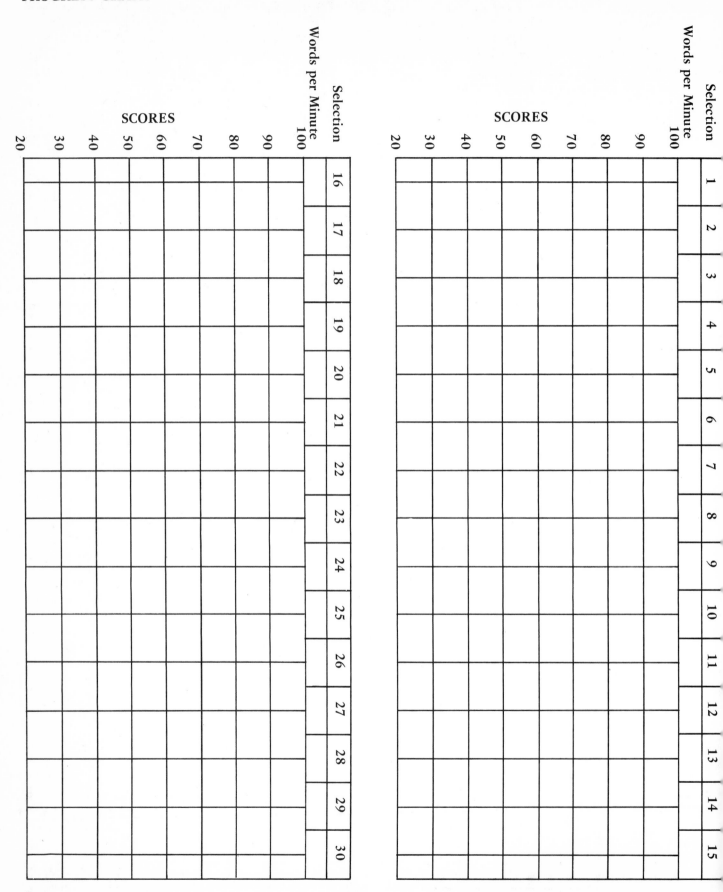

SELECTIONS FROM THE BLACK

COMPREHENSION SKILLS PROFILE

The graph below is designed to help you see your areas of comprehension weakness. Because all the comprehension questions in this text are coded, it is possible for you to determine which kinds of questions give you the most trouble.

On the graph below, keep a record of questions you have failed. Following each selection, fill in one square on the graph for each question missed.

The columns are labeled to correspond with the letter codes accompanying each question.

Before long a pattern will begin to form. A column rising above the others signals an area of reading comprehension weakness. When you discover a particular weakness, give greater attention and time to answering questions of that type.

Further, you might wish to check with your instructor for recommendations of appropriate practice materials.

COMPREHENSION SKILLS

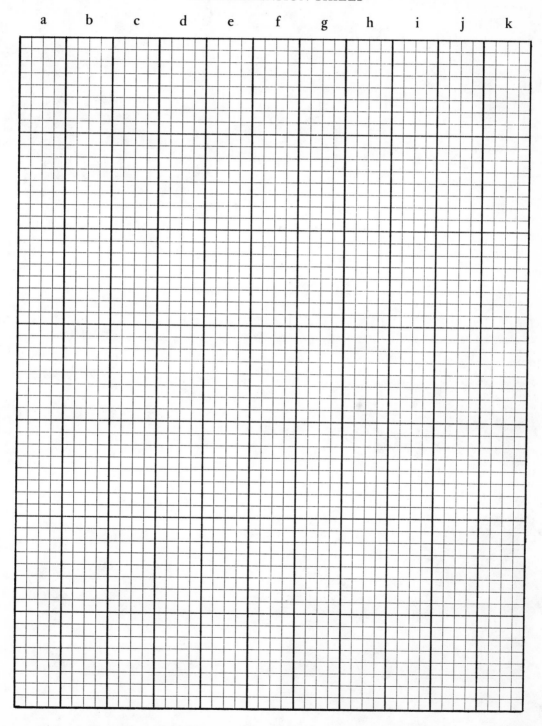